D1602932

THE HANDLESS MAIDEN

JEWS, CHRISTIANS, AND MUSLIMS
FROM THE ANCIENT TO THE MODERN WORLD

SERIES EDITORS
R. STEPHEN HUMPHREYS, WILLIAM CHESTER JORDAN, AND PETER SCHÄFER

Imperialism and Jewish Society, 200 B.C.E. to 600 C.E.,
by Seth Schwartz

A Shared World: Christians and Muslims in the Early Modern Mediterranean,
by Molly Greene

Beautiful Death: Jewish Poetry and Martyrdom in Medieval France,
by Susan L. Einbinder

Power in the Portrayal: Representations of Jews and Muslims in Eleventh- and Twelfth-Century Islamic Spain, by Ross Brann

Mirror of His Beauty: Feminine Images of God from the Bible to the Early Kabbala,
by Peter Schäfer

In the Shadow of the Virgin: Inquisitors, Friars, and Conversos *in Guadalupe, Spain,*
by Gretchen D. Starr-LeBeau

The Curse of Ham: Race and Slavery in the Early Judaism, Christianity, and Islam, by David M. Goldenberg

Resisting History: Historicism and Its Discontents in German-Jewish Thought,
by David N. Myers

Mothers and Children: Jewish Family Life in Medieval Europe,
by Elisheva Baumgarten

A Jewish Renaissance in Fifteenth-Century Spain,
by Mark D. Meyerson

The Handless Maiden: Moriscos and the Politics of Religion in Early Modern Spain,
by Mary Elizabeth Perry

THE HANDLESS MAIDEN

MORISCOS AND THE POLITICS OF RELIGION IN EARLY MODERN SPAIN

Mary Elizabeth Perry

PRINCETON UNIVERSITY PRESS

PRINCETON AND OXFORD

PUBLISHED BY PRINCETON UNIVERSITY PRESS, 41 WILLIAM STREET,
PRINCETON, NEW JERSEY 08540
IN THE UNITED KINGDOM: PRINCETON UNIVERSITY PRESS,
3 MARKET PLACE, WOODSTOCK, OXFORDSHIRE OX20 1SY

LIBRARY OF CONGRESS CATALOGING-IN-PUBLICATION DATA

PERRY, MARY ELIZABETH, 1937–.
THE HANDLESS MAIDEN : MORISCOS AND THE POLITICS OF RELIGION
IN EARLY MODERN SPAIN / MARY ELIZABETH PERRY.
P. CM. — (JEWS, CHRISTIANS, AND MUSLIMS FROM THE ANCIENT
TO THE MODERN WORLD)
INCLUDES BIBLIOGRAPHICAL REFERENCES (P.) AND INDEX.
ISBN 0-691-11358-0 (CL : ALK. PAPER)
1. MORISCOS—SPAIN—HISTORY. 2. MUSLIM WOMEN—SPAIN—HISTORY. I. TITLE. II. SERIES.
DP104.P475 2005
946'.04'088297—dc22 2004044675

BRITISH LIBRARY CATALOGING-IN-PUBLICATION DATA IS AVAILABLE.

THIS BOOK HAS BEEN COMPOSED IN PALATINO

PRINTED ON ACID-FREE PAPER. ∞

PUP.PRINCETON.EDU

PRINTED IN THE UNITED STATES OF AMERICA

1 3 5 7 9 10 8 6 4 2

FOR

Alexander, Ian, Jennifer, Maria, Claire, and Laurel,

WHO REPRESENT HOPE FOR THE FUTURE

CONTENTS

ILLUSTRATIONS

FOREWORD

MADALENA, Lucía de la Cruz, María Jérez, Juana, Beatriz de Robles, Leonor de Morales, Inés Izquierdo, María Taraiona, María Mocandali: what they all had in common was that they were women and they were Moriscas—that is, they were descendants of Muslims who were converted to Christianity in the Spain of the early sixteenth century. Because of these characteristics, they have been twice marginalized: by social sciences researchers in general, and by historians in particular. As Mary Elizabeth Perry tells us, each of them and many of their Morisco companions were actors of the utmost importance, not only in the history of the Hispanic monarchy and the Mediterranean, but also in that of the modern period.

The approach of this work, which the author clearly delineates, deserves careful attention. While historical references to the Morisco minority are numerous, we usually know the destiny of crypto-Muslims only through the discourses and the many mediations of Old Christians (those connected with the monarchy, the Church, and municipalities, and such functionaries as notaries public), with the notable exception of Aljamiado literature (Romance language written in Arabic characters). Perry situates herself within an innovative trend exemplified by the publication in the journal *Sharq al-Andalus* of the proceedings of "La Voz de Mudéjares y Moriscos," a conference organized in 1995 by María Jesús Rubiera in Alicante. Perry, however, is the first to devote a book to Morisco women; moreover, she lets them speak for themselves.

This lively text fully justifies its approach. The author has unearthed essential materials and offers a provocative analysis. Working through bundles of archival documents from the inquisitorial tribunal of Seville and others from royal councils preserved in the archives of Simancas, Perry shows that these traditional materials bring us very useful lessons, provided that we ask good questions of them and vary the angles of attack. She has also made good use of a whole series of previously published documents that have won little notice to date, such as the letter from a Morisco exile in Algiers to an Old Christian friend from Trujillo, his hometown.

Above all, Perry takes into account a great many legends and stories that were extremely popular within Morisco communities. I am particularly struck by the comparison between the concrete personal experiences of the Moriscos of Granada, Seville, or Aragon and the eloquent narrative representations of the battle of the Valley of Yarmuk, Princess

Carcayona's life, or the misfortunes of Job and his wife, Rahma. There is every reason to believe, indeed, that these three tales nourished the crypto-Muslims' imagination. The women who were their heroines served as models to their distant sixteenth-century successors, reinforcing and validating their role. Some fought with the weapons in their power, sticks and rocks; and in that respect the women of Granada of 1569–1570 resembled women at Yarmuk, as they also resembled Rahma and Carcayona, whose simple spoken language Perry effectively quotes from the tales. One heroine, Rahma, is exemplary because of the appalling conditions of her life. She represents the courage and energy needed to ameliorate the most dire situations. Without Rahma's tenacity, Job would have sunk into despair. The other, Carcayona, is focal among Perry's chosen few. She was isolated, betrayed, and mutilated; yet she has a faith that nothing can weaken. We cannot doubt that the message of her story fostered the hope for better days in many Morisco women and encouraged them to play an active role in maintaining the material and, above all, the spiritual inheritance that had been handed down to them. It is no accident that the main fictional work glorifying Moorish combat, *Guerras civiles de Granada* by Ginés Pérez de Hita, assigns a special place to women. Two of them, Luna and Zarçamodonia, embody the qualities and virtues of Moorish women. Luna represents beauty, elegance, refinement. Zarçamodonia, whom Perry discusses at length, embodies determination and perceptiveness. Zarçamodonia manages, thanks to the force of her conviction alone, to reestablish harmony within the world of insurgents of 1568–1570. And yet we should not forget that Pérez de Hita is himself a Morisco who, although well integrated in the society of the Old Christian majority, is particularly sensitive to the misfortunes of his original community. The pages he devotes to Zarçamodonia and Luna are a tribute to all Moorish women.

Rahma, Carcayona, and Zarçamodonia are very different characters, and they represent only a part of the vast range of situations analyzed in *The Handless Maiden*. While most of the women whose cases are examined here are free, Juana and perhaps Madalena exemplify the numerous slaves who had only a first name. Madalena, among the models of religious commitment presented in the book, is accused of secretly practicing ritual ablutions, while Leonor de Morales would be found guilty of overt proselytizing zeal. Leonor is especially interesting, as she is denounced by her own husband. This woman, who proudly faces torture, is the paragon of disorder. She and all her companions are doubly dangerous through acts that both challenge religious orthodoxy and subvert the roles prescribed for men and women.

In a word, Madalena, Juana, Leonor, Beatriz, and their ilk are, despite all their differences, resisters. This seems an appropriate unifying term since it is often used in this book, which is above all a reflection on the essential contribution of women—and the forms of their contribution—to the resistance of minorities whose identity is threatened. Indeed, researchers who have addressed these issues have tended to conclude that by far the most widespread attitude in the Morisco community—in both men and women, but implicitly among more women than men—was that of *taqiyya*, or careful secretiveness, which leads to clandestine practices.

Perry herself, however, is careful not to rely on the term *taqiyya*, which seems to her to imply submission and passivity. The women who inhabit this book are neither submissive nor passive, and through them the author invites us to rethink both our vocabulary and our categories. At the heart of her analysis is resistance in all its forms. Perry first contrasts *conscious active resistance* with *conscious active accommodation*: should we not see in the latter the traditional taqiyya, now viewed through a positive lens? Subsequently, three terms of resistance are defined: overt resistance, covert resistance, and unconscious resistance. If these categorizations do not convince all readers, they serve nonetheless to enrich the debate with a fresh perspective. This book counters the current of works that see in the Morisco community a milieu that not only is seeking complete assimilation, but is also accepted by the vast majority of Old Christian society. While it cannot be denied that in both the Old Christian and the Morisco community a wide range of strategies and opinions were available, it is nonetheless true that those in the minority were always under greater suspicion and constraint in sixteenth-century Spain. That is why the Moriscos resisted, individually and collectively. And it was often women who embodied this resistance.

Bernard Vincent
Paris

ACKNOWLEDGMENTS

SO MANY PEOPLE and organizations have provided invaluable support in the writing of this book that it is not possible to name them all. For financial support, I wish to thank especially the American Council of Learned Societies, the Dean of Faculty for Occidental College, and the Program for Cultural Cooperation Between Spain's Ministry of Education, Culture and Sports and United States Universities. Courteous and unfaltering help from staff and directors of many archives and libraries provided essential support for my research, especially in the Archivo Arzobispal de Sevilla, the Archivo General de Simancas, the Archivo Histórico Nacional, the Archivo Municipal de Sevilla, and the Biblioteca Nacional.

I am grateful to faculty and students at the following universities who invited me to present my work in progress and discussed it with me: the Universidad Complutense de Madrid, the University of California at Davis, the University of California at Los Angeles, the University of Illinois at Chicago, the University of Kansas, the University of Michigan at Kalamazoo, the University of Minnesota, the University of Nevada at Reno, the University of North Carolina at Chapel Hill, Notre Dame University, Ohio State University, and the University of Vienna. Countless conferences and scholarly meetings invited me to present my work, and I very much appreciate the observations and suggestions that scholars from Austria, Finland, France, Italy, Spain, and the United States gave to me. In particular, I wish to acknowledge the continuing support of the study group Dialogica, the Occidental Writing Network, and the Southwest Consortium of Spanish History.

As the notes and bibliography indicate, this study could not have been made without the previous work of hundreds of scholars. Although I cannot name them all, I want to acknowledge especially the helpful suggestions and criticisms of Renato Barahona, Anne Cruz, Teófilo Ruiz, María Helena Sánchez Ortega, Ronald Surtz, and the anonymous readers for Princeton University Press and many other scholarly presses that have published my essays on Moriscos. I deeply appreciate the studies of Moriscos published by Bernard Vincent and his generosity in writing a foreword for this book. Special thanks to Annabelle Rea for translation assistance.

I wish to thank Christopher Brest, who prepared the map of the Morisco expulsion, and Dover Publications for making available the illustrations from the remarkable sixteenth-century book of drawings by Christoph Weiditz.

Brigitta van Rheinberg has provided wise counsel and helpful suggestions in bringing this book to publication, and none of it would have been possible without the able assistance of Alison Kalett and Lauren Lepow. In addition, I am very grateful for the comments of Stephen Humphreys, William Chester Jordan, and Peter Schäfer, editors of the series Jews, Christians, and Muslims from the Ancient to the Modern World.

BRIEF CHRONOLOGY OF THE MORISCOS

1492	Surrender of Granada, last Muslim stronghold in Iberia
1499–1502	Muslim rebellion in Albaicín, Granada
1500	Mass conversions of Muslims in Granada
1501	Burning of Arabic books in Granada
1502	Decree of conversion or expulsion for Muslims in Castile
1503	Aragonese nobility requests protection for Muslim vassals
1510	Beginning of prohibitions imposed on Moriscos
1519	Charles Hapsburg (later Charles V) ascends throne
1520–1521	Forced conversions of Muslims in Germanía Revolt in Aragon
1525	Forced conversions declared to be valid
1525	Charles V extends decree of expulsion or conversion to Muslims in all his kingdoms
1526	Prohibition of all Morisco "particularism"
1556	Philip II ascends the throne
1566	Royal decree against Morisco culture
1568	Morisco rebellion begins in the Alpujarra Mountains
1570	Rebellion defeated; expulsion and dispersion of Granadan Moriscos
1580	Morisco conspiracy for invasion from North Africa is discovered
1582	Morisco intrigue for aid from Muslims in Argel is discovered
1598	Philip III ascends the throne
1608	Council of State decides on expulsion of Moriscos
1609–1614	Royal decrees for expulsion of Moriscos from kingdoms of Spain

ABBREVIATIONS

AAS	Archivo Arzobispal de Sevilla
AGS	Archivo General de Simancas
AHN	Archivo Histórico Nacional (Madrid)
AMS	Archivo Municipal de Sevilla
BN	Biblioteca Nacional (Madrid)

THE HANDLESS MAIDEN

Frontispiece. Morisco Traveling with Wife and Child. *Authentic Everyday Dress of the Renaissance: All 154 Plates from the "Trachtenbuch"* (New York: Dover Publications, 1994), plates 87 and 88.

INTRODUCTION

FROM THE SHADOWS

TWENTY-FOUR SHIPS that crowded into the port of Seville in late November 1570 brought human cargo—some 5,000 women, children, and men.[1] Moriscos, that is, Muslims or their descendants who had been baptized, came as defeated rebels from the Kingdom of Granada. Two years earlier Moriscos had revolted against Christian rule, their rebellion spreading quickly from the Alpujarra Mountains near Granada throughout much of Andalucia. After his armies had finally subdued the rebels, Philip II had ordered the dispersion of some 50,000 Moriscos of Granada throughout the Kingdom of Castile. Now bowing to royal directive, the Count of Priego officially received into the city and lands of Seville 4,300 uprooted Moriscos whom the ships brought into port this November day. The remaining 700 Moriscos traveled on to other regions nearby.

Officials in Seville and in most of the cities and towns ordered to receive Moriscos acquiesced only reluctantly. They would have to find housing for the newcomers and jobs or charitable programs to feed them, tasks that could be of frustrating immensity. Officials had to try to keep the newcomers under some form of surveillance, for they were reputed to be spies of the Turks and had fought for two years against the king's armies. Despite royal attempts to outlaw their religion and culture, Moriscos remained suspect as false converts. Many Catholics believed that these people continued to practice Islam, to speak and pray in Arabic, and to carry out their own rituals of birth, marriage, and death. Rather than fellow subjects of the same king, the Moriscos of Granada seemed to be suspicious foreigners and internal enemies.

Despite this hostility, some officials such as Priego could not help but be moved to pity as he looked upon the Moriscos who had just arrived aboard the twenty-four ships, "so shattered and poor and robbed and ill," in Priego's words, "that there was great compassion."[2]

[1] This and all information about the arrival of the Granadan Moriscos in Seville in 1570 is from a report of December 15, 1570, to Philip II, in Archivo General de Simancas (hereafter AGS), Cámara de Castilla, legajo 2157.

[2] AGS, Cámara de Castilla, legajo 2157. The phrase quoted is "tan destrosados y pobres y robados y enfermos que fue gran compasion." In this and all other quotations from unpublished historical documents, I have preserved the original spelling, punctuation, and diacritical marks.

Apparently attempting to explain to Philip II his reactions to those who had so recently battled against the king's armies, Priego described the passengers as weak and starving. Some appeared to be dying and suffering great need, he reported. Since they were not able to beg alms to sustain themselves, Priego decided to dispose of them as quickly as possible, placing the able-bodied with masters and the ill in hospitals. The count directed the residents of the city who received the Moriscos to treat them well and to keep spouses together as well as children with their parents. He noted the obligation to baptize children of two years and younger, and especially to teach the Christian faith to the newcomers.

It would be easy to move quickly past Priego's report, with its odd mixture of conquest and compassion, to simply conclude that the count was providing yet one more example of the wages of war and rebellion. Yet to dismiss the report panders to traditional views of history as the centuries-long story of victors and vanquished, always written by the victors. Moreover, to ignore this document would be to lose sight of a significant scene in a morality play far more complex than the usual Reconquest drama of Good Christians against Bad Muslims. In fact, Christians held many different attitudes about Moriscos, perhaps because Moriscos varied widely in their responses to Christianization. What follows is a story of Christians wrestling with their consciences while developing political power, and of Moriscos refusing to remain victims, finding impressive strength even in defeat.

From Muslims to Moriscos

The arrival of thousands of Moriscos in the city of Seville in 1570 signaled the beginning of a new chapter in the complex and deeply rooted Christian-Muslim relationships of the Iberian Peninsula.[3] During the previous eight centuries, people of the two faiths had lived through periods of comparative harmony and through times of overt violence as Christians sought to wrest control of the various Iberian kingdoms from Muslim domination. This Reconquest reached a climax in 1492

[3] Moriscos, of course, were technically Christians because they had been baptized. However, many suspected them of being Christian in name only. Throughout this study I use the term "Christian" to refer to Christians without Muslim ancestors, to distinguish them from Moriscos. The religious conflict is more complex than Christian against Muslim, as many Moriscos had become sincere Christians and many Christians were also suspected of not being "true" Christians. Those Christians with either Jewish or Muslim ancestors were frequently called "New Christians," in distinction to "Old Christians," those with neither Jewish nor Muslim ancestors.

with the surrender of the last Muslim ruler in Granada—indeed, the last on Iberian soil. Probably none of the Moriscos who entered the port of Seville in November 1570 was old enough to remember the entry of Ferdinand and Isabel into the city of Granada to accept that surrender. They may have heard a grandparent or great-grandparent tell of this event, however, and of the guarantee that the Catholic Kings made in the document of capitulation that their new Muslim subjects would be free to practice their own faith and live according to its law.[4] Handed down over the generations, Morisco memories also told of the increasing zeal of some Church leaders, such as Francisco Jiménez de Cisneros, to convert Muslims and to reclaim those Christians who had earlier converted to Islam.

To those raised on such memories, it would not seem strange that the Muslims of Granada rose in rebellion against their Christian rulers late in 1499. From the Albaicín quarter of Granada, the rebellion spread into much of Andalucia, and it would not be quelled by Christian forces until 1501. Mass conversions of Moriscos and great fires to burn their Arabic writings on Islam quickly followed. And in 1502 came a royal decree that any Muslim who wanted to remain in the Kingdom of Castile would have to convert to Christianity. Some twenty years later Charles V extended this decree of expulsion to Muslims in all of his Spanish kingdoms, and Church leaders validated the forcible baptism of thousands of Muslims during the Germanía Revolt. A royal pragmatic of 1567 forbade any use of the Arabic language and all Morisco customs.[5] Not surprisingly, then, Moriscos on the ships in the port of Seville in 1570 knew of increasing oppression against not only the faith of Islam but their Hispano-Muslim culture as well.

As his soldiers finally defeated Morisco rebels in 1570, Philip II attempted to shatter the rebellious Morisco community from Granada. Authorities dispersed these people throughout Castile, isolating individual family units in new locations under tighter surveillance by Christian authorities. Yet the relocated Moriscos would develop a variety of strategies for survival and resistance against their rulers. And because of their very success, even when surrounded by Old Christian neighbors—that is, those without Jewish or Muslim forebears—this relocation would be merely the first step of a much more extensive diaspora. Within forty years of their arrival in Seville, these

[4] For the terms of capitulation, see Luis del Mármol Carvajal, *Historia del rebelión y castigo de los moriscos del reino de Granada* (1600), in *Biblioteca de Autores Españoles* (Madrid: Atlas, 1946), 21:146–150.

[5] An excellent chronology of this increasing oppression is in Mercedes García Arenal, *Los moriscos* (Madrid: Editora Nacional, 1975), 15–17.

Moriscos and some 300,000 others would be formally expelled from the Spanish kingdoms.

Politics and religion clearly intertwine in early modern Spain, but not merely in the close collaboration of Crown and Church. It is true that the centralizing monarchy sought the support of the Church, and that this partnership increased the power of the Church. Yet the story of the Moriscos reveals a politics of religion that embraces far more than this collaboration. It demonstrates the significance of religion for a minority group hoping to survive but also to preserve its own identity. It tells of a fledgling state attempting to unify many diverse subject groups against a religious minority that became a convenient common enemy. And it reveals the use of religion to legitimize opposition and the many ways that an apparently powerless minority could use religion to develop its own forms of power.

As religious minorities, Jews and Muslims shared similar experiences of oppression and resistance in this period, but they differed as well.[6] Both groups had faced expulsion from the Spanish kingdoms unless they converted to Christianity, and both Judeo-conversos and Moriscos lived in early modern Spain as minorities suspected of being false converts. Yet Judeo-conversos often enjoyed a higher socioeconomic status than Moriscos. Frequently Judeo-conversos engaged in commerce or professions that brought in some wealth, but Moriscos were more likely to be agricultural laborers, artisans, itinerant merchants, or silk weavers. Judeo-conversos tended to have fluency in more languages and to be more highly educated, although this advantage declined with the passage of purity of blood statutes, which prohibited their entry into some universities.

Armed rebellion was less an option for Judeo-conversos than for Moriscos. From their own history of armed action against Christians beginning in the eighth century, Moriscos knew a Muslim tradition of countless battles during the Reconquest and their rebellions during the sixteenth century. In contrast, Judeo-conversos had a longer tradition of living peacefully within, or even assimilating into, Christian societies. Moreover, Judeo-conversos could not count on groups of their own people from other parts of the world to rally to their side in battle against Hispanic Christian rulers; in contrast, Moriscos were sharply aware of Muslims in nearby North Africa and the Ottoman Empire who held out the promise of armed assistance for them.

[6] For an important discussion of differences between the histories of Moriscos and Jews in Iberia, see Teófilo F. Ruiz, *Spanish Society, 1400–1600* (Harlow, UK, and New York: Longman, 2001), 101–103.

Assumptions and Approaches

To begin to consider the story of the Moriscos, we need to look at some assumptions and approaches that we might use. Although most histories are written from the standpoint of victors who had the power to write and preserve reports of the past, this book will explore the story of the Moriscos from their own viewpoint. This is not to argue that all Moriscos were the same, for these people varied widely by generation, class, place of origin, and length and location of residence in Iberia. Examples of Moriscos in various parts of Spain reveal the diversity of minority strategies for accommodation, resistance, and developing power. Not intended to be a definitive study of Moriscos, this book offers a different perspective to a growing body of scholarship throughout the world.

Much of this study focuses on women's experiences, which I believe deepens our understanding of all Moriscos. We can see these women as representative of all Moriscos who were disempowered and made into "others" in early modern Spain. Marginalized as members of an ethnic minority, Morisco women were still further disempowered by patriarchal assumptions of their own culture.[7] Yet their presence in early modern Spain raises many questions essential to an understanding of the Morisco story. How did Moriscos survive in an increasingly hostile environment, and how did they attempt to preserve their culture? How did traditional gender roles change in the context of oppression? What insights can the lives of these women provide in a study of minority strategies for surviving among hostile and suspicious neighbors? How did women lead and energize resistance against oppression? How did they transform the home into a space of resistance?

As we explore these questions, we see that Moriscas' lives reveal the complexities of cultural accommodation and resistance to oppression that traditional historical interpretations often overlook. Through their experiences, we become aware of the political significance of everyday rituals and the active roles of ordinary people in making history. Overshadowed by armed rebellions and political decrees, Moriscos found strength in their own legends, such as that of the Handless Maiden, Carcayona.[8] Quietly many of these people devised what

[7] Here and throughout, I use the terms "patriarchy" and "patriarchal" to refer to that system in which certain males are privileged to exploit or objectify women, children, and other males.

[8] Francisco Guillén Robles, *Leyendas moriscas sacadas de varios manuscritos existentes en las Bibliotecas Nacional, Real, y de D. P. de Gayangos*, 3 vols. (Madrid: M. Tello, 1885), 1:181–221.

anthropologist James Scott calls "weapons of the weak."[9] Avoiding overt confrontation, Morisco women and men sought to preserve their identities and their culture. Within their homes, they observed Islamic fasts and donned clean clothing on Fridays. Men such as Luis de Berrio of Baeza wrote copies of the Qurʾan in his home and women such as Isabel de Silva of Jaén carried copies of Arabic writings between households, hiding them beneath their skirts.[10]

Yet most historical documents make no mention of the power of such covert resistance and leave many Moriscos voiceless in the shadows. Morisco women do not appear at all in many documents that focus on royal decrees, armed rebellions, and military concerns about Morisco aid to the Turks. In other sources, such as local and Inquisition records, Morisca voices can be heard only indirectly. Such evidence must be read "against the grain," with special attention to questions of power relationships, euphemisms, silences, and formulaic expressions. Most Moriscas neither read nor wrote, yet they had a rich oral tradition, some of which was captured through transcription. During the sixteenth century Morisco women and men hid some of these writings because Christian officials ordered the burning of documents in Arabic and Aljamía, a Castilian dialect written in Arabic script. Although we do not know how many Moriscos owned or read these books and papers, the discovery two and three centuries later of hundreds of the hidden writings provides a valuable source of information about Morisco beliefs and traditions.[11]

[9] James C. Scott, *Weapons of the Weak: Everyday Forms of Peasant Resistance* (New Haven and London: Yale University Press, 1985), develops this theme very thoroughly in his study of a Malaysian village. Such weapons include foot-dragging, minimal compliance, and feigned lack of understanding.

[10] Rafael Gracia Boix, *Autos de fe y causas de la Inquisición de Córdoba* (Cordova: Diputación Provincial, 1983), 210 and 272.

[11] Ottmar Hegyi, *Cinco leyendas y otros relatos moriscos (ms 4953 de la Biblioteca Nacional, Madrid)* (Madrid: Editorial Gregos, 1981), describes the development of Aljamía, 11–16. For more on these concealed writings and their discovery, see A. R. Nykel, *A Compendium of Aljamiado Literature* (New York and Paris: Macon, Protat Frères, 1929), 29–30; Luce López-Baralt, *Islam in Spanish Literature: From the Middle Ages to the Present*, trans. Andrew Hurley (Leiden: E. J. Brill, 1992), 171–174; Julián Ribera and Miguel Asín, *Manuscritos árabes y aljamiados de la biblioteca de la junta* (Madrid: Junta para Amplicación de Estudios é Investigaciones Científicas, 1912), v–xviii, 138, 156–157; Gerard Wiegers, *Islamic Literature in Spanish and Aljamiado* (Leiden and New York: E. J. Brill, 1994). Note that López-Baralt, *Islam in Spanish Literature*, describes an earlier discovery of hidden Aljamiado and Arabic writings in 1728 in Ricla, 172. More information on burning of Arabic writings is in Antonio Domínguez Ortiz and Bernard Vincent, *Historia de los moriscos: Vida y tragedia de una minoría* (Madrid: Revista de Occidente, 1978), 19–21; and in Nykel, *Compendium*, 27–28. An analysis of the range and significance of these writings follows below in chapter 1.

Additional information comes from material culture, such as the veil. By tradition, many Muslim women customarily concealed the face in public, but Christian authorities had banned the veil. Viewing it as a symbol of Muslim culture, they assumed it was further evidence of Moriscos' clinging to their former religion. Yet non-Muslim women had covered themselves, as well, perhaps enjoying the anonymity and allure of the veil. Christian officials had to pass laws many times prohibiting any woman from concealing her face.[12] Figure 1, which presents a German traveler's drawing of a Morisca from Granada in the early sixteenth century, illustrates how these women at that time covered themselves when they went outside their homes.[13]

Most Westerners of the present time assume that prohibitions against the veil would have been an important means of liberating Muslim women from a very male-centered culture, but it is far more likely that for Moriscas in sixteenth-century Spain these prohibitions attacked a culture that they strongly wished to preserve. In many ways, the veil symbolized their identity as women, for their culture used the veil as a major marker that defined gender. Moriscas who accepted this gender prescription, even as a strategy for maintaining their own cultural identity, present one more example of the many ways that women themselves have helped to perpetuate very patriarchal traditions.[14]

And yet the veil could have meant more than the seclusion of women, their objectification, and the wrapping of their bodies to prevent anyone other than the male owner from viewing them. Concealing themselves provided anonymity for women and some protection from unwanted attention. Behind their veils, they were able to withdraw and assume a mask that let the masked one see without becoming open to

[12] For example, in 1639 the city council of Seville approved for the fourth time in only a few years the prohibition against women's covering their faces; see Archivo Municipal de Sevilla (hereafter AMS), Sección 4, siglo XVII, Escribanías de Cabildo, tomo 29, número 18.

[13] Christoph Weiditz, *Das Trachtenbuch des Christoph Weiditz* (The Netherlands, 1531–1532) (Berlin and Leipzig: Von Walter de Gruyter and Company, 1927). I want to thank Ida Altman, who first told me of this source. The drawings have been reproduced in Christoph Weiditz, *Authentic Everyday Dress of the Renaissance: All 154 Plates from the "Trachtenbuch"* (New York: Dover Publications, 1994).

[14] Leila Ahmed, *Women and Gender in Islam: Historical Roots of a Modern Debate* (New Haven: Yale University Press, 1992); cf. Lila Abu-Lughod, *Veiled Sentiments: Honor and Poetry in a Bedouin Society* (Berkeley and Los Angeles: University of California Press, 1986), who concludes that veiling speaks of sexuality and chastity and is best understood as "the covering of sexual shame," 162. But also see Trinh Minh-ha, *When the Moon Waxes Red: Representation, Gender and Cultural Politics* (New York and London: Routledge, 1991), 151.

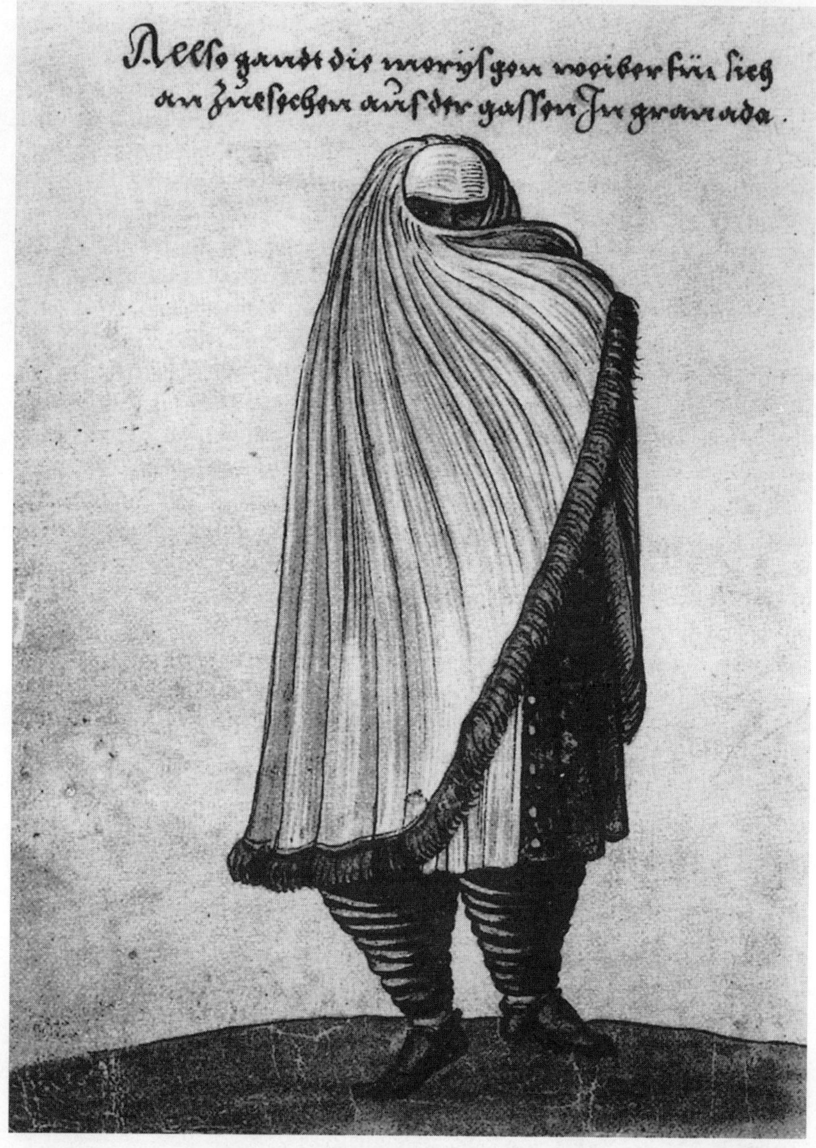

Fig. 1. Morisca in Street Dress. *Authentic Everyday Dress of the Renaissance: All 154 Plates from the "Trachtenbuch"* (New York: Dover Publications, 1994), plate 84.

the other's gaze. Paradoxically, women who covered their faces accepted the female identity of Muslim culture; but at the same time, they could construct their own identity, subverting their oppression and transforming it into a strategy for protection and a base for liberation. A convention that symbolized their conformity to their own male-dominated culture, the veil also became a symbol of resistance against those who would attack their cultural identity.

Tradition has veiled Moriscas—not only through Muslim costume, but also through histories that discount or completely overlook the lives of these women. In fact, a veil of phallocentric assumptions has covered most women of the past with unquestioned assertions that they have been mere pawns or passive victims, exotic ornaments perhaps, but in the background far behind the "real" actors in history—men with military might and political power. It is true that some historians have noted the existence of a very few women, but usually because they acted either as treacherous Jezebels or as "manly women."[15]

History has obscured Moriscas not only with sexist attitudes, but also with racist assumptions that the lives of minority people have little effect on the drama of the past.[16] At most, this history has assumed, minority people play a few supporting roles or, occasionally, a role as victims or rebels. Their struggles and triumphs are so marginalized by many historians that we may not even be aware of their presence in an

[15] Manly women did not have to dress like men in order to behave with the courage, daring, and strength attributed to men in the early modern period; but they often did. For more on this subject, see Carmen Bravo Villasante, *La mujer vestida de hombre en el teatro español: Siglos XVI–XVII* (Madrid: Sociedad General Española de Librería, 1976); Vern and Bonnie Bullough, *Cross-Dressing, Sex, and Gender* (Philadelphia: University of Pennsylvania Press, 1993); Rudolf M. Dekker and Lotte C. van de Pol, *The Tradition of Female Tranvestism in Early Modern Europe* (New York: St. Martin's Press, 1989); Marjorie Garber, *Vested Interests: Cross-dressing and Cultural Anxiety* (New York and London: Routledge, 1992); Melveena McKendrick, *Women and Society in the Spanish Drama of the Golden Age: A Study of the Mujer Varonil* (London: Cambridge University Press, 1974); Simon Shepherd, *Amazons and Warrior Women: Varieties of Feminism in Seventeenth-Century Drama* (Brighton, UK: Harvester, 1981); Julie Wheelwright, *Amazons and Military Maids: Women Who Cross-dressed in the Pursuit of Life, Liberty and Happiness* (London: Pandora Press, 1989); and Annie Woodhouse, *Fantastic Women: Sex, Gender and Transvestism* (New Brunswick: Rutgers University Press, 1989).

[16] I use the term "racist" here because people of Muslim ancestry were commonly believed to have genetically inherited certain characteristics and limitations. See Miguel Angel de Bunes Ibarra, *La imagen de los musulmanes y del norte de Africa en la España de los siglos XVI y XVII: Los charácteres de una hostilidad* (Madrid: Consejo Superior de Investigaciones Científicas, 1989); and Thomas F. Glick, "On Converso and Marrano Ethnicity," in *Crisis and Creativity in the Sephardic World, 1391–1648*, ed. Bernard R. Gampel (New York: Columbia University Press, 1997), 59–60.

"invisible invisibility."[17] As minority women, then, Moriscas are twice veiled—once for their gender and again for their ethnicity. And, paradoxically, these women who had been veiled by their male-dominated culture serve as a metaphor for Morisco men who became increasingly disempowered in the sixteenth century and turned all the more often to hiding themselves behind a veil of apparent assimilation.

With conscious effort, we can allow these people to reveal themselves and counter their obscurity in history. Through attention to subtext and silences, we enable them to emerge from behind the veil of indirect historical records filled with omissions and unspoken assumptions. Acknowledging a veil of protective silence, we listen for quietly clandestine conversations at the neighborhood fountain or within the churches that Moriscos had to attend. We look to find more layers of meaning hidden below the surface of official documents, such as lists of Moriscos relocated in the Great Dispersion of 1570, the records of those penanced by inquisitors, the numbers of those enslaved or slain.

Our focus on Morisco women challenges superficial conclusions about all Moriscos. Far from being powerless, Moriscas direct us to consider more encompassing definitions of power. Although they held no political offices, directed no armies, and rarely held power *over* others, they clearly developed power *with* others and assumed leading roles in guiding their people and preserving their culture or assimilating to Christian culture. By prescription, most Moriscas were expected to live in domestic seclusion; in actuality, however, many of them transformed their homes into sites of assimilation—or into cells of resistance, as they taught Arabic prayers to their children and observed the holy fast of Ramadan. Morisco women and men used bonds of family and kinship and adapted the structures of their community to survive waves of increasing oppression throughout the sixteenth century.

To study Moriscos actively seeking to resist and survive oppression precludes the traditional paradigm of center and margins. Assuming that the real agents of history are at the center of power and all others simply provide context, this paradigm easily regards Morisco women as members of a culture dominated both by its own men and by victorious Christians. Such a definition overlooks any historical agency exercised by these women and reduces them to victims who acted only in obedience to orders or to resist only out of desperation. Likewise, if we regard Morisco women and men as marginal, we see them only from the perspective of those at the center of official power. We accept

[17] Ada María Díaz, "Toward an Understanding of Feminismo Hispánico in the USA," in *Women's Consciousness, Women's Conscience*, ed. Barbara Hilkert Andolsen, Christine E. Gudorf, and Mary D. Pellauer (San Francisco: Harper and Row, 1987), 51–61.

a set of hegemonic assumptions decreed by those in power which serve to preserve the whole notion of hegemony—that is, that one elite group dominates through controlling institutions and ideas to which others are expected to conform. To subject Moriscos to a paradigm that strengthens and validates the very hegemony that oppressed them betrays their lives and denies their role as agents in history.

Equally serious, this paradigm overlooks differences within both center and margins. Christians who defeated Muslims in Granada in 1492 and subsequently worked to consolidate a monarchy and empire included a great diversity of people within their centers of power, ranging from religious zealots who hated Muslims to landed nobles sympathetic to the Muslims who would become their vassals and extract with their labor the wealth of the land. Muslims also varied considerably, for they came from different lands outside Iberia, lived for different periods of time within the Spanish kingdoms, enjoyed varying amounts of wealth, and experienced widely ranging degrees of assimilation. Those who lived in mountainous and rural regions had far fewer contacts with Christians than did urban Muslims, who even intermarried with Christians and learned their language. Moreover, Moriscos who were forcibly baptized during such violent events as the Germanía Revolt differed from those whose families had converted voluntarily centuries before.

The assumption that Moriscas can be studied as a single homogeneous group of minority women overlooks their many differences from one another and subjects them to further oppression. Women of color have insisted that race plays a very significant role, not only in marginalizing them from an Anglo-male-dominated center, but also in the ways they define themselves and resist domination. These women do not want others to define them, as cultural critic bell hooks points out, nor do they want others to interpret their experiences.[18] They resist domination not only from a patriarchal center, but from other marginalized peoples as well, because allowing other people to describe them erases or transforms their differences, reinscribing "patterns of colonial domination, where the 'Other' is always made object, appropriated, interpreted, taken over by those in power, by those who dominate."[19] In my judgment, this argument applies to both women and men of any race, class, or ethnicity.

[18] bell hooks, *Yearning: Race, Gender, and Cultural Politics* (Boston: South End Press, 1990), 55.

[19] hooks, *Yearning*, 125, and 151–152. See the thoughtful discussion of problems with using "marginality" and "other" in discussions of the past, in Mark D. Meyerson, introduction to *Christians, Muslims, and Jews in Medieval and Early Modern Spain: Interaction and Cultural Change*, ed. Mark D. Meyerson and Edward D. English (Notre Dame, IN: University of Notre Dame Press, 1999), esp. xii–xiii.

Although it would be easy to become lost among several layers of difference as we consider the Morisco community in early modern Spain, it is possible to recognize these people as having multiple identities that include sameness as well as difference.[20] Yet to reduce difference to binary oppositions, such as same/different or center/margins, completely overlooks the intermingling of categories and limits the study of Moriscos.[21] Instead, we can move beyond categories of race, ethnicity, class, and gender to examine intersections of differences where more than two polarized categories exist and where categories may bleed together and intermingle. For example, we can see Moriscos as a group identified as both racial and ethnic: racial, because many believed they inherited cultural distinctions through their blood; and ethnic, since many also believed that education and "Christianization" could erase their differences.[22]

The issue of difference becomes so complex that it seems to defy any theoretical analysis, forcing us to beat a hasty retreat to the comfortable old center/margins paradigm where differences exist but remain well concealed by a simple opposition. Unwilling to simply reduce differences to a center/margins opposition, however, we can ask questions about these differences. And we can consider not only those questions that distinguish our subjects, but also those that make us subjects in our interactions with and responses to our subjects.[23]

[20] Mae Gwendolyn Henderson, "Speaking in Tongues: Dialogics, Dialectics, and the Black Woman Writer's Literary Tradition," in *Feminists Theorize the Political*, ed. Judith Butler and Joan W. Scott (New York and London: Routledge, 1992), found in studying black women writers that these women "speak from a multiple and complex social, historical and cultural personality" that produces "a multiple *dialogic of differences*," but at the same time they carry out "a *dialectic of identity* with those aspects of self shared with others," 147, author's emphasis.

[21] Françoise Lionnet, *Autobiographical Voices*, quoted in Sidonie Smith, "Who's Talking / Who's Talking Back? The Subject of Personal Narrative," *Signs* 18:2 (Winter 1993),asks us to look at "intermediary spaces where boundaries become effaced and Manichean categories collapse into each other," 406.

[22] Biological determinism is evident in assumptions of purity of blood laws, discussed in Albert A. Sicroff, *Los estatutos de limpieza de sangre. Controversias entre los siglos XV y XVII*, trans. Mauro Armiño (Madrid: Taurus, 1985). For assumptions of cultural transmission of difference, see Francisco Borja de Medina, S.I., "La Compañía de Jesús y la minoría morisca (1545–1614)," *Archivum Historicum Societatis Iesu* 57 (1998): 3–136.

[23] To approach difference "objectively" precludes any recognition of our own subjectivity, which is the product not only of our position but of our historical context. Subjectivity asks us to look at the construction of meaning and to be aware of our participation in this construction. It includes pluralities of identification as well as interaction as subjects with our historical subjects. Trinh T. Minh-ha, *Woman, Native, Other: Writing Postcoloniality and Feminism* (Bloomington: Indiana University Press, 1989), refers to this interaction as endless, a "to-and-fro movement between the written woman and the writing woman," 30.

Difference provided identity for Moriscos, and it was through their difference from a dominant norm that their Christian rulers most often identified them. Here it is important to acknowledge that norms and differences are constructed, not innate.[24] Violent and hierarchical rather than neutral, difference is postulated through opposition in which one term is marked as deviating from the unmarked term assumed to be the norm. In early modern Spain, many who tried to explain Morisco difference fell back on three fallacious explanations: those of biology (that difference results from the innate essence of a subject), objectivity (that difference can be observed neutrally), and naturalization (that difference occurs within a universal category of nature unaffected by a particular context).[25]

The study of Morisco difference can reduce them to a colonized group, which raises significant methodological problems. We want to avoid colonizing our subjects and making these people into "objects," but our sources seem to work against us. A major problem in writing history is that so many historical documents reflect an elite male viewpoint from the center, an "imperialist gaze," which construes the other as a mere object and exercises an exclusive subject-defining status for itself.[26] Gayatri Chakravorty Spivak has noted that historians' knowledge of subaltern or insurgent subjects is so dependent on elite or counterinsurgent documentation that they can see subalterns only in contradistinction to the elites.[27] Even the language we use to describe them imposes hierarchical assumptions on them. As we seek actors in history other than elite males, we try to respect them—and this raises the issue of positionality. Where can we stand when we speak of others in a culture so permeated by a dominant viewpoint? Is there, in fact,

[24] Feminist scholars argue that the differences of Moriscas and other minority people are social constructions that should be critically analyzed. Discussing the problem of writing "the history of difference," Joan W. Scott has noted that historians often present "experience" as "evidence for the fact of difference, rather than as a way to explore how difference is established, how it operates, how and in what ways it constitutes subjects who see and act in the world." See her essay "Experience," in *Feminists Theorize the Political*, ed. Judith Butler and Joan W. Scott (New York and London: Routledge, 1992), 22 and 25.

[25] Toril Moi, *Sexual/Textual Politics: Feminist Literary Theory* (London and New York: Methuen, 1985), passim; for more on Moi's theory, see Paul Julian Smith, *Representing the Other: 'Race,' Text, and Gender in Spanish and Spanish American Narrative* (Oxford: Clarendon Press, 1992), 28. Sidonie Smith, "Who's Talking/Who's Talking Back?"esp. 402, suggests that one way to avoid these fallacies is to read the sources to hear "the polyphony of voices, to sort through various truth claims and interpretations."

[26] Lee Edelman, *Homographesis: Essays in Gay Literary and Cultural Theory* (New York and London: Routledge, 1994), 47.

[27] Gayatri Chakravorty Spivak, *In Other Worlds* (London and New York: Methuen, 1987), esp. 197–211; and P. J. Smith, *Representing the Other*, 18.

any position " 'outside' that dominance which is uncompromised by it"?[28] Must we become outsiders in order to write about women and disempowered men as active agents of the past, or to escape the "otherness" imposed by the dominant center?[29]

Two cultural critics suggest ways to solve these problems, but each warns us against making Moriscos into objects of study and "objective" discussion. "A conversation of 'us' with 'us' about 'them,' " observes Trinh Minh-ha, "is a conversation in which 'them' is silenced. 'Them' always stands on the other side of the hill, naked and speechless, barely present in its absence."[30] Certainly Morisco women and men stand speechless in most historical records; but to fill their silences with my own voice and speak for them is to reduce them to objects, as bell hooks observes, and to transform myself to colonizer.[31] Warning of mistakes to avoid, hooks and Trinh urge us to recognize differences among and within minority people, within ourselves. We who seek to know more about Moriscos begin by recognizing our differences from them—differences not only in geography and time period, but also in culture and ethnicity. At the same time, we try to avoid romanticizing them into exotic unreal creatures, as Westerners have done so often when describing people from Africa, Asia, and the Middle East.[32]

All of this raises the methodological question of how historians can possibly avoid colonizing the people they describe. After all, we historians decide which sources we will use and how we will interpret them. We select examples and organize ideas, attempting all the while to impose meaning on the past. Some historians have restored dignity and agency to ordinary people in the past, and women historians have demonstrated the politics of gender-specific experience.[33] In critiquing

[28] P. J. Smith, *Representing the Other*, 29.

[29] Vinay Bahl, "Cultural Imperialism and Women's Movements," *Gender and History* 9:1 (April 1997): 5.

[30] Trinh, *Woman, Native, Other*, 67.

[31] hooks, *Yearning*, 151–152.

[32] Edward W. Said, *Orientalism* (New York: Pantheon, 1978).

[33] See, for example, the thoughtful introduction to *Becoming Visible: Women in European History*, ed. Renate Bridenthal and Claudia Koonz (Boston: Houghton Mifflin, 1977), esp. 2–5; E. P. Thompson, "The Moral Economy of the English Crowd in the Eighteenth Century," *Past and Present* 50 (1971): 76–136; Natalie Zemon Davis, *Society and Culture in Early Modern France* (Stanford: Stanford University Press, 1975); Joan Wallach Scott and Louise Tilly, *Women, Work and Family* (New York: Holt, Rinehart and Winston, 1978). Most notably for Spain, see Luis R. Corteguera, *For the Common Good: Popular Politics in Barcelona, 1580–1640* (Ithaca: Cornell University Press, 2002); and Ruiz, *Spanish Society*. For Moriscas in particular, see E. William Monter, *Frontiers of Heresy: The Spanish Inquisition from the Basque Lands to Sicily* (Cambridge: Cambridge University Press, 1990), esp. 226–227; and Bernard Vincent, "Las mujeres moriscas," in *Historia de las mujeres en occidente*, ed.

traditional history, these historians have made us more aware of the politics of representing people from the past, yet we continue to struggle with the question of how to develop a healthy collegial relationship between our subjects and ourselves.[34]

One way to acknowledge the variations of Moriscos and their diverse identities separate from our own is to recognize persons and call them by name. Throughout this book I will use names whenever possible, to superimpose on numbers and general categories individuals such as Lucía de la Cruz, Joan Valenciano, and Juana the slave. Although many Moriscos had Muslim names and may have continued to use them privately, these have been lost to us because Christians prohibited them and imposed Christian names in baptism. With regret for their lost Muslim names, we can nevertheless deliberately state their only available names as a political act—just as bell hooks named her mother and grandmother "in resistance" to the erasure of minority women from a "history recorded without specificity, as though it's not important to know who—which one of us—the particulars."[35]

Listening to hooks and Trinh, I have tried to develop a methodology for studying Moriscos that looks for the particulars and values the differences. Consciously I have adopted three specific approaches: recognizing subtexts, contextualizing Moriscos' lives, and questioning assumptions of the paradigms we use. With this methodology, I believe that we can challenge traditional interpretations which place powerful men or impersonal forces at center stage. Moreover, we can replace that old center/margins model for history with a tapestry paradigm of many weavers—the Moriscos of early modern Spain, the many people with whom they lived, the historian who knits together a variety of sources, we who live in the present time, and those who come after us.

Telling the Morisco Story

In telling the story of the Moriscos, the seven chapters that follow will examine a small part of this tapestry. Chapter 1 considers memories and legends that Moriscos brought with them during the relocation of

---

Georges Duby and Michelle Perrot, trans. Marco Aurelio Galmari (Madrid: Taurus, 1992), 3:585–595.

[34] A discussion of the significance of "the politics of representation" for colonized groups is in hooks, *Yearning*, 72. For feminist concerns with the political consequences of theoretical positions in history, see Judith Bennett, "Feminism and History," *Gender and History* 1:3 (1989): 251–272; and Joan Wallach Scott, *Gender and the Politics of History* (New York: Columbia University Press, 1988), esp. 15–17.

[35] hooks, *Yearning*, 116.

1570. In Spain they lived with buildings and monuments, fountains and gardens that served as reminders of times past when Muslims ruled. Memories of actual events from the medieval past intertwine with imaginative metaphors carved in stones and written in stories, such as that of Carcayona, the Handless Maiden. The epitome of the idealized Muslim woman, Carcayona also represented the hopes of an increasingly oppressed people in the sixteenth century. Her story shows how legends could empower Moriscos to resist the prohibition of their religious beliefs and culture.

Christians clearly acknowledged Muslim difference, and the terms of the surrender of Granada in 1492 declared that Muslims would be free to continue their own religion. Heavy-handed attempts to convert them, however, led to an armed rebellion of Muslims that began late in 1499 and ended in 1502 with the royal decree that Muslims who wanted to remain would have to convert to Christianity. Chapter 2, "Madalena's Bath," analyzes the process by which Muslim difference became transformed into Morisco deviance. Not satisfied with prohibiting Islam, Christian officials went on to forbid all expressions of Muslim culture. They sexually stigmatized Moriscos, portraying the women as promiscuous and lewd, the men as perverted and effeminate. Assuming that Moriscos threatened the purity of their society, Christian authorities punished them and prohibited expressions of Muslim culture and the embodied knowledge by which they identified themselves.

In the face of increasing prohibitions on their culture, Moriscos withdrew into their homes, where they hoped to continue some of their traditional practices. Chapter 3, "Dangerous Domesticity," shows how the home became a primary forum for resistance against Christian regulations. Here women in particular taught their children the Arabic language and prayers of Islam. They observed Islamic dietary restrictions and Muslim customs of eating and bathing. Gathering in their homes, Moriscos circumcised their sons and observed the fast of Ramadan. As Christian officials expelled male religious leaders, Morisco women took on the primary responsibility for preserving Muslim identity. Their homes became increasingly dangerous, with Christian officials entering them unexpectedly to look for signs of resistance. Not surprisingly, Inquisition records show the active roles that Moriscas played in this resistance and, in addition, the rituals of punishment imposed on them.

After years of increasing oppression, an armed rebellion erupted in 1568 among Moriscos in the Alpujarras, a mountainous region near Granada. Chapter 4, "With Stones and Roasting Spits," describes Moriscas' experiences in the almost two-years-long war. A Christian eyewitness reported that his forces had killed some women among the enemy "because they fought as men although they had no weapons but stones and roasting spits."[36] In contrast, another account tells of Zarçamodonia, who donned helmet and armor to slay with her sword the Christian enemy.[37] Other reports describe Moriscas seeking to protect their families, moving into caves higher in the mountains as Christian forces slowly gained control over the rebels. Victorious soldiers captured and enslaved many of these women and children. A smaller number escaped to what they hoped was safer ground, only to be ensnared by Philip II's order to uproot some 50,000 Moriscos from the Kingdom of Granada and disperse them throughout Castile.

Chapter 5, "Patience and Perseverance," analyzes the tremendous project of relocating Moriscos of Granada throughout Castile—both as punishment for their rebellion and as a strategy to neutralize their power. Reports and census documents on Moriscos in Seville after 1570 indicate the many ways that Moriscos struggled to keep their families alive and intact. Women's work made a major difference in the survival of their families, especially in the many female-headed households and households of enslaved Moriscos. Local records show how Morisco slaves lived and worked. The Inquisition case of Juana, slave of Francisco de Piña in Gibraltar, details the example of a Morisca slave prosecuted for attempting to leave Christian Spain in the boat of other fugitives who had set sail for Muslim North Africa. Rahma, the wife of Job in the Morisco version of the Old Testament story, personifies the hopes and struggles of these people.

The debate among Christians about how to solve "the Morisco problem" ended abruptly in 1609 when Philip III issued the first of several decrees expelling Moriscos from his kingdoms. Chapter 6, "The Castigation of Carcayona," considers several other proposals for dealing with Moriscos as well as the poignant discussion over whether expelled Moriscos should be required to leave their young children behind to be raised as Christians in Spain. An analysis of external and internal issues facing the central monarchy reveals the political imperatives that played a major role in the decision to expel some 300,000 Moriscos. Some reports of the expulsion emphasized the great sorrow of those who had to leave their homes for distant lands, but others

[36] Biblioteca Nacional (Madrid), hereafter BN, ms R 31.736, *Relación muy verdadera sacada de una carta que vino al Illustre Cabildo y regimiento desta ciudad* (Seville: Alonso de la Barrera, 1569): "y entre ellos algunas mugeres porque peleavan como los hombres con que ellas no tenían mas armas q piedras y assadores."

[37] Ginés Pérez de Hita, *Guerras civiles de Granada* (1595–1597) , ed. Paula Blanchard-Demouge (Madrid: E. Bailly-Bailliére, 1913–1915), 2:252–253.

described the Moriscos singing and dancing as they left, the women dressed in their jewels and best clothing.

Chapter 7, "Warehouse Children, Mixed Legacies, and Contested Identities," asks what happened to the Moriscos after the expulsion. Authorities took hundreds of young children from their Morisco parents so they could be raised as Christians in Spain. To placate nobles whose wealth depended on Morisco vassals, Philip III allowed about 6 percent of the Morisco population to remain in his kingdoms. He also exempted from the expulsion Moriscos who had taken religious orders and Moriscas who had married Old Christian men. The case of Beatriz de Robles provides an example of a Morisca married to an Old Christian who did not have to leave during the expulsion. Later, however, inquisitors prosecuted her, not for following Islam, but for fashioning her own assimilated identity—one that seemed to them too close to the heresy of illuminism. Appearing especially in the sixteenth century in Spain, this heresy emphasized individual experience of God without any need for priest or Church. For the most part, Morisco slaves remained in Spain under the control of Christian owners. Some Moriscos left Spain but returned later, attempting to escape detection. Whether they departed or stayed in Spain, Moriscos left mixed legacies, contested identities, and the timeless legend of the Handless Maiden.

In the following pages this book will attempt to hear the voiceless, see those who have been veiled, and illuminate some of the spaces of history still in the shadows. By focusing on the experiences of women of this persecuted minority group, I hope to make some contribution to providing a broader definition of power, a better understanding of the dynamics of difference and deviance, a closer examination of the politics of religion, and a deeper appreciation for how ordinary people—both women and men—became active players in the drama of human history. For us in the twenty-first century, the stories of these people present important lessons in faith, culture, and power.

1

MEMORIES, MYTHS, AND THE HANDLESS MAIDEN

MORISCOS RELOCATED from Granada in 1570 could take few material possessions with them, but they all brought memories of the past that directly shaped their sense of identity and the strategies they would use to survive in their new homes. Such memories, of course, varied widely according to generation, place of origin, class, and gender. Moreover, they differed from written history and do not necessarily indicate a historical consciousness. Muslims and Moriscos living under the rule of Christians in Iberia, in fact, may have found it wiser to have no history that others could view as a challenge.[1] Yet their memories could serve not only to preserve information about the past, but also to motivate and justify efforts to change the present and create a future.[2]

Most Morisco memories included some awareness that they lived in a very different world from the Muslims who had earlier ruled much of the Iberian Peninsula. No longer holding dominant political power, Moriscos had to abandon or hide traditional costumes and bathing vessels, writings and musical instruments. Nevertheless, they saw all around them buildings and monuments that reminded them of past glories, a golden past when Muslim rulers lived in sumptuous palaces and muezzins called the faithful to prayer from high minarets.[3] Deeply carved in stone and wood, these memories not only preserved the past

[1] L. P. Harvey, *Islamic Spain 1250 to 1500* (Chicago: University of Chicago Press, 1990), notes that subject Muslims living in Christian kingdoms found it wiser to "have no history, to live discreetly and unperceived," 68.

[2] Karen Fields, "What One Cannot Remember Mistakenly," in *History and Memory in African-American Culture*, ed. Genevieve Fabre and Robert O'Meally (New York: Oxford University Press, 1994), 161.

[3] Moriscos may well have idealized this past when Muslims ruled Iberia, but they may also have recognized that in that past Christians and Muslims had lived together, sometimes committed violence against one another, and even combined certain cultural patterns; for more on the ways that Christians and Muslims had lived together in the late medieval period, see Molly Greene, *A Shared World: Christians and Muslims in the Early Modern Mediterranean* (Princeton: Princeton University Press, 2002); Mark D. Meyerson, *The Muslims of Valencia in the Age of Fernando and Isabel: Between Coexistence and Crusade* (Berkeley and Los Angeles: University of California Press, 1991); and David Nirenberg, *Communities of Violence: Persecution of Minorities in the Middle Ages* (Princeton: Princeton University Press, 1996).

but also mythologized it, so that memory and myth intertwined to play an active role in shaping Morisco attitudes and decisions in the sixteenth century.

Moriscos had oral and written myths, as well as those constructed in stone and bricks and wood. Over centuries these myths had passed down informally from generation to generation in stories, poems, dances, and songs. Scholars believe that in the fifteenth and sixteenth centuries Muslims and Moriscos wrote down some of these myths in the Arabic script of Aljamía.[4] Many of the Morisco myths remained hidden until the eighteenth and nineteenth centuries, when workmen demolishing ancient buildings in Ricla and the village of Almonacid de la Sierra (province of Zaragoza) found hundreds of writings that had been hidden beneath false floors.[5] Undoubtedly placed there by Moriscos during the sixteenth century when official prohibitions sentenced most Arabic writings to the bonfire, the cache represents an attempt to preserve Muslim culture, the Arabic language, and Aljamía. The hidden writings discovered some three centuries later range from amulets and cabalistic notations through treatises on magic and popular beliefs, legends, laws, prescriptive literature, medicine, Arabic grammars and vocabularies, polemics against Christians, sermons, liturgies, prophecies, and the Qur'an itself.

Although most of the legends in the hidden writings focus on male heroes, such as Muhammad, Alexander the Great, and Joseph, the son of Jacob, a heroic female protagonist appears in "The Story of the Maiden Carcayona, Daughter of King Nachrab, with the Dove."[6] A

[4] Guillén Robles, *Leyendas moriscas*, 1:14–17. Most scholars believe that these legends were originally told in Arabic, but they were translated into Aljamía because fewer Mudejares and Moriscos understood Arabic as they continued to live under Christian rule. *La historia de la doncella Carcayona, hija del rey Nachrab con la paloma* is available as BN ms 5313. Pino Valero Cuadra presents an interesting analysis of the story in "La leyenda de la doncella Carcayona," *Sharq al-Andalus* 12 (1995): 349–366.

[5] Nykel, *Compendium*, 29–30; Guillén Robles, *Leyendas moriscas*; López-Baralt, *Islam in Spanish Literature*, 171–174; Ribera and Asín, *Manuscritos árabes y aljamiados*, v–xviii, 138, 156–157; Wiegers, *Islamic Literature in Spanish and Aljamiado*, passim. For the discovery of Aljamiado and Arabic writings in 1728 in Ricla, see López-Baralt, *Islam in Spanish Literature*, 172. Information on burning of Arabic and Aljamiado writings is in Domínguez Ortiz and Vincent, *Historia de los moriscos*, 19–21; and in Nykel, *Compendium*, 27–28.

[6] The legend of Carcayona is reprinted in Guillén Robles, *Leyendas moriscas*, 1:42–53 for the Castilian version, and 181–221 for the Aljamiado version. Although Guillén Robles includes two versions of the legend, I will refer primarily to the Aljamiado. For another version of the Aljamiado tale, see Alvaro Galmés de Fuentes, "Lle-yeísmo y otras cuestiones lingüisticas en un relato morisco del siglo XVII," in *Estudios dedicados a don Ramón Menéndez Pidal* (Madrid: Consejo Superior de Investigaciones Científicas, 1957), 273–307. I am very grateful to Ronald Surtz, who pointed out to me this alternative version of the tale.

beautiful young woman victimized first by her father and then by her mother-in-law, Carcayona shines as a heroine attractive to both women and men. For women, Carcayona proves that loyalty, virtue, and piety overcome all evils. For men, Carcayona represents the prize for faithful and chivalric rescue. For everyone, this legend provides an image of the ideal woman in Morisco culture of Golden Age Spain. She was beautiful, virtuous, steadfast in her faith, and closely connected with nature.

But Carcayona was handless. In the tale, when she insists to her father that an angel disguised as a dove has told her about the true God, Allah, and the worthlessness of her father's idols, he orders her hands cut off. Then he cruelly banishes her to the wilderness; there a white doe brings a handsome prince who falls in love with her. The story has a much happier ending than do the Moriscos, who were finally expelled from Spain beginning in 1609, victimized and seemingly as helpless as the handless Carcayona. No friendly animals or handsome prince could rescue them from the tragic consequences of their expulsion. Nevertheless, the legend of Carcayona can be read as a metaphor for a people who suffered a major reversal in fortune and cruel punishment imposed by an unjust ruler. Together with memories of a golden past inscribed in buildings and monuments, this legend shows how stories of the past became not only powerful myths that provided a context for Morisco lives in sixteenth-century Spain, but also "wandering ghosts" that directly affected the strategies they chose for survival.[7]

Memories Carved in Stone

People living in sixteenth-century Spain learned their history not so much from books as from the very stones on which they walked, the buildings and monuments that surrounded them. Women and children who went to fill water containers for their families or their employers used fountains that had been constructed long before by Muslims in countless towns throughout the Iberian Peninsula. In Seville, the water came from springs several kilometers away, passing through conduits supported by stone arches and through underground pipes that distributed it to many sectors of the city.[8] Fountains constructed from

[7] For more on the power of the past, see Simon R. Doubleday, *The Wandering Ghosts of Spanish History* (Cambridge: Harvard University Press, forthcoming).

[8] Antonio Collantes de Terán Sánchez, *Sevilla en la baja edad media: La ciudad y sus hombres* (Seville: Ayuntamiento, 1977), 84; and Jacinto Bosch Vilá, *La Sevilla islámica, 712–1248*, no. 92 of *Historia de Sevilla*, ed. Francisco Morales Padrón (Seville: Universidad de Sevilla, 1984), 228–233.

stone or bricks, some decorated with *azulejos*, or glazed and painted tiles, revealed the artistry of Muslim craftsmen.

By the sixteenth century many of the buildings and monuments memorialized Christian monarchs who had carried out the Reconquest against Muslim rulers, but other buildings predating them gave mute testimony to the glory and grandeur of al-Andalus, or Muslim-ruled Spain. In Cordova, for example, the Great Mosque, which Muslims had begun to construct in the eighth century and subsequently enlarged and refined, still stood, renamed and sanctified as a Christian cathedral, but commonly called "La mezquita." In an apparent effort to appropriate the grandeur of this building, Charles V ordered the construction of a large ornate cathedral within it. Yet not even the excessive ornament and gilt of this cathedral could rival the splendor of the bold marble columns and arches of the mosque, nor could they erase the memory of a Muslim past.

Moriscos in Granada found an everyday reminder of the once formidable majesty of Muslim rulers as they looked upward to the Alhambra, the "red fortress" that dominates the city below. In the fourteenth century Nasrid kings had outdone one another in building exquisite palaces and courtyards within the walls of this mighty fortress, softening its original military purpose with gardens and fountains. Clearly they had felt some pride, as evident in the Arabic inscription around the basin of the Fountain of Lions. God gave to Muhammad V "abodes which grace by their perfection all abodes," the inscription asserts, and which contain "wonders like unto which God did not allow beauty to find an equal."[9] After Granada, the last Muslim stronghold on the Iberian Peninsula, fell to Ferdinand and Isabel in 1492, Christians began to build a Franciscan monastery in the Alhambra gardens. But neither this intrusion nor the subsequent construction of a palace for Charles V within the Alhambra walls could eclipse the grandeur and beauty of a monument that still evoked a time of Muslim glory.

Christians, too, recognized the beauty of Muslim buildings. In Seville, Pedro the Cruel so admired the decor and workmanship of buildings in the old Moorish Alcázar that he hired Muslim artisans to build his palace within the fortress. Unable to read Arabic, Pedro does not seem to have noticed that his Muslim workers had installed at the entrance to his palace blue tiles bearing an Arabic inscription which declared that there is no conqueror but God. Inside the palace the carved and coffered ceilings, spectacular tile work, and graceful arches

[9] Oleg Grabar, *The Alhambra* (Cambridge: Harvard University Press, 1978), 124. Grabar believes that the author of the poem in which the lines appear is Ibn Zamrak, and gives the translation of the entire poem, 124–127.

speak far more of a Muslim past than of the glory of a Christian ruler. Just outside and to the rear of the Alcázar, the specter of a Muslim past still moves through a lush garden of exotic trees and ornamental waterways.

Moriscos brought by ship to relocate in Seville in 1570 must have seen the Torre de Oro, which appears in figure 2. This tower had stood as a sentinel along the Guadalquivir River and its port since the thirteenth century, when the caliph Abu Yaʿqub Yusuf had ordered its construction and that of its twin across the river. A chain between the two towers could be raised to control river traffic.[10] By the sixteenth century the twin tower had long since disappeared, but the Torre de Oro still stood as a symbol of a Moorish past, its golden-hued tiles reflecting the light of both the present and the past.

Muslims in the medieval city of Seville built their Great Mosque at about the same time as the Torre de Oro. Although Christians decided to raze this mosque soon after they had taken the city in 1248, they spared its minaret and patio of orange trees to incorporate them into the huge Gothic cathedral that they built in its place. With the confidence of conquerors, they transformed the patio of orange trees into a cathedral cloister and the minaret into a bell tower. They added a Renaissance top with a figure of Faith as a weathervane and renamed the minaret the Giralda, but none of these transformations could disguise the tower's Moorish design. Any Morisco in sixteenth-century Spain could have looked to it not simply as the bell tower of the cathedral, but as a Muslim construction where a muezzin once called the faithful to prayer. And Moriscos could see it as an encouraging symbol of survival despite attempts to co-opt it as part of a huge Christian cathedral.

Even during their lifetimes, Moriscos of sixteenth-century Spain participated in carving history into stone, for their labor directly supported the construction of many more buildings and monuments. Both men and women of this community carried out the heavy work of building as well as the finely detailed craft of ornamentation.[11] While

[10] Bosch Vilá, *La Sevilla islámica*, 160.

[11] Collantes de Terán Sánchez, *Sevilla en la baja edad media*, found evidence in the *padrones* that women as well as men worked in construction, 335. The padrones for this area show that the most common occupations for Muslim men were construction, masonry, water systems, carpentry, and tile making, 336. See also Klaus Wagner, *Regesto de documentos del Archivo de Protocolos de Sevilla referentes a judíos y moros* (Seville: Universidad, 1978), who found a large number of Muslims listed as masons and potters, 8–9. Ramón Carande, *Sevilla, tortaleza y mercado: Las tierras, las gentes y la administración de la ciudad en el siglo XIV*, 3rd ed. (Seville: Diputación Provincial de Sevilla, 1982), points out that the numerical superiority of women over men in the fourteenth century may account for the fact that many women worked as peons for masons and tilemakers, 50–51.

Fig. 2. Torre de Oro, Seville. Photograph by Ruiz Vernacci, in Marqués de Lozoya, *Historia del arte hispánico* (Barcelona: Salvat Editores, 1931), plate 25.

men were more likely to be masons and plasterers, women worked as peons in construction and carried out the silk spinning and weaving essential for the sumptuous hangings in countless palaces and the lovely costumes of wealthy Christians. Workshops producing azulejos employed women and men to form, paint, and glaze the distinctive Moorish ceramic tiles.

Architecture and decoration of buildings constructed in sixteenth-century Spain clearly reflected Muslim motifs and uses of space, even when combined with Italian classicism. In constructing the university founded by Cardinal Jiménez de Cisneros at Alcalá de Hénares, architect Pedro de Gumiel used the painted wooden ceilings and segmental-arched windows so commonly seen in the "Mudéjar style" that Muslims had developed earlier under Christian rule.[12] In the classically designed El Escorial, azulejos decorated the royal apartments of Philip II and his daughter, the Infanta Isabel Clara Eugenia. The severe classical facades of Philip II's Escorial and the Lonja (businessmen's exchange) of Seville, both the work of Juan de Herrera, concealed inner courtyards and beautiful fountains, important legacies of Muslim architecture.[13]

Instead of simply following the Italian style and returning to "classics," the architects and artists of sixteenth-century Spain created a unique style, the plateresque, which features wood and stone carved as a goldsmith works precious metal.[14] Closely related to the Mudéjar style, plateresque ornament uses low relief with recurrent patterns indifferent to balance and accent.[15] Muslim arabesque and botanical motifs abound in the plateresque ornamentation of many public buildings constructed in the sixteenth century, such as the Ayuntamiento (city hall) of Seville. The palace of Charles V constructed in the Alhambra followed an Italianate style but also used the plateresque in garlanded window frames and on the capitals of the south doorway.[16]

Muslim influence persisted in the proud architecture of the sixteenth century. Some buildings and monuments commemorated imperial events, while others exalted the nobles who constructed palaces and places of burial that would honor themselves and their families. For example, Diego Siloe came to Granada in 1528 to build the Church of

[12] George Kubler and Martin Soria, *Art and Architecture in Spain and Portugal and Their American Dominions 1500 to 1800* (Middlesex, UK: Penguin Books, 1959), 4–5.

[13] For more on the buildings and monuments constructed in sixteenth-century Seville, see José Gestoso y Pérez, *Sevilla monumental y artística*, 3 vols. (Seville: Andalucia Moderna, 1892).

[14] J. A. Gaya Nuño, *Historia del arte español* (Madrid: Editorial Plus Ultra, n.d.), 218, 225.

[15] Kubler and Soria, *Art and Architecture*, 4.

[16] Kubler and Soria, *Art and Architecture*, 10.

San Jerónimo as a mausoleum for Fernández de Córdoba. He covered the transept with a cupola, which combines the Gothic, Mudéjar, and Italian styles.[17] Siloe united the Mudéjar with the plateresque here and in numerous palaces of Andalucia. In Seville the Enríquez de Ribera family built its famous town palace, the Casa de Pilatos, noted for its inner courtyard and garden, fountains, and glazed tile work. Greek and Roman gods held places of honor in this palace beneath a Mudéjar ceiling that featured polychromatic wood carved in motifs of ornamental borders, flowers, and fruits.[18]

A Muslim legacy continued in Spanish Renaissance buildings because countless Moriscos carried out the actual construction and decoration of many sixteenth-century buildings. These artisans and workers used particular techniques that earlier Muslims under Christian rule had refined into the Mudéjar style. Although this style varied across Castile, Aragon, and Andalucia, it usually called upon the elemental forms of arches, inner courtyards, and fountains, ornamenting them with materials such as wood, plaster, and glazed tiles.[19] During the sixteenth century, the Mudéjar use of the dome or vault evolved into cupolas decorated with plaster or wood carved into intertwining knots, constituting "an absolutely national art, that of the *carpintería de lo blanco*."[20]

Such monuments and buildings preserved Muslim memories in many towns and cities of the Spanish kingdoms. Repeatedly, Christians found skilled artisans to be Moriscos. The cathedral of Toledo may have the vaulted ceilings and breathtaking height of the Gothic style, but much of its interior decor is Mudéjar. The Casa de Pilatos, the town palace in Seville that the Enríquez de Ribera family constructed in the sixteenth century, glorifies Mudéjar art more than it does the feats of this powerful family. One story about this palace describes Morisco workers carving the interior arches with the arabesques of Arabic script unreadable to most Christians. Some years later the elaborate carvings on one gallery arch of this noble home caught the eye of a visitor who could read Arabic. To his great amazement, the visitor saw that they duplicated the curves and lines of Arabic letters to spell out a bold message of defiance from the Morisco workers: "Eternal happiness," the carvings proclaimed, "for Allah."[21]

[17] Gaya Nuño, *Historia del arte español*, 233.

[18] Joaquín González Moreno, *Aportación a la historia de Sevilla* (Seville: Editorial Castillejo, 1991), 187–197.

[19] Gaya Nuño, *Historia del arte español*, 76.

[20] Gaya Nuño, *Historia del arte español*, 82.

[21] González Moreno, *Aportación a la historia de Sevilla*, 197.

The Handless Maiden

Legends, stories, and myths also preserved memories meaningful to Moriscos and particularly important in shaping their resistance to Christian attempts to obliterate their traditions and identity.[22] Many of the stories have been lost, swallowed up in an oral tradition that became more and more silent. Others, among those that had been written down, fell victim to Christian authorities who ordered the burning of all writings in Arabic or Aljamía. The few that survived centuries of hiding present protagonists who had to survive injustice, hardships, defeats, and exile—themes that must have appealed to Moriscos living under increasing oppression in the sixteenth century.

Using Aljamiado writings as a source of evidence for Moriscos raises important methodological problems. We do not know who told these stories, nor where, nor with what variations. Because Moriscos of Granada and Valencia were more likely to know Arabic than Aljamía, they undoubtedly knew Arabic versions that may have varied from the Aljamiado writings that have survived. Furthermore, Aljamiado stories such as the tale of Carcayona cannot be considered a clear and defining statement of the thinking of all Moriscos. Nevertheless, the fact that this story was recorded in Aljamía suggests that at least some Moriscos believed it was important to preserve it as the use of Arabic declined in the sixteenth century. I present Carcayona and other Aljamiado stories not as complete worldviews for all Moriscos of early modern Spain, but as one way to illuminate their complex culture and its impact on their responses to issues of faith, identity, accommodation, and resistance.

The story of Carcayona reads as a Muslim version of the Handless Maiden tale, a story that has been known in many variations around the world.[23] As a metaphor for both the power and the powerlessness of Moriscos, the story presents an idealized view of a gendered order

[22] Corteguera, *For the Common Good,* discusses the political significance of myths at 20–22.

[23] Handless Maiden tales have been classified as type 706 in Antti Aarne, *The Types of the Folktale: A Classification and Bibliography,* trans. and enl. Stith Thompson, Folklore Fellows Communications, vol. 75, no. 184 (Helsinki: Helsingin Liikekirjapaino Oy, 1961), 240–241; I wish to thank Anne Cruz for suggesting this and other helpful sources. Some other versions of this tale are titled "The Handless Bride," "The Orchard," and "Silver Hands." Clarissa Pinkola Estés, *Women Who Run with the Wolves* (New York: Ballantine, 1995), discusses the tale in chapter 14, 387–455. For more on analysis of fairy tales, see Marie-Louise von Franz, *The Feminine in Fairy Tales* (Dallas: Spring Publications, 1972); and Vladimir Propp, *Morphology of the Folktale,* trans. Laurence Scott (Austin and London: University of Texas Press, 1979).

in which men must be strong, active, and protective, while women must be obedient, enclosed, and nurturing. Specifically, the story of Carcayona provides insights into the lives of the women of this community before Philip III ordered the Moriscos' expulsion from his kingdoms in the early seventeenth century. A study of the documentary evidence of the lives of these women, juxtaposed with a close reading of their version of the Handless Maiden tale, challenges assumptions about female power and powerlessness. How, for example, does passive victimization camouflage active female agency in history? How does feminine dependency become a strategy for survival—for accommodation, but also for resistance? As we consider these questions, the story of the Handless Maiden can deepen our understanding of the paradoxes and complexities of archival evidence to show how Moriscas, far more than mere passive victims, played active roles in resisting Christian dominance.

The Aljamiado tale of Carcayona presents her as the beautiful daughter of a king of the "rromanos" in ancient India.[24] Her mother died in childbirth; as she grew into puberty, her father made incestuous advances toward her. When he "demanded her body," the young girl asked, "Well, O father, why do you want to begin something that could shame you all the days of your life and then of your death? Have you heard of any king who did this with his daughter?"[25] Without replying, her father left in shame.

One day as Carcayona is praying to a bejeweled and golden idol that her father has given her, an angel in the form of a golden dove flies in and alights first on her head and then on that of the idol. She marvels at the sight "because the dove was of yellow gold, and its tail of vermillion pearls, and its feet of silver, and its beak of white pearls, enameled with seed pearls."[26] Declaring the idol worthless, the dove tells her of the true God, Allah. In a long dialogue as the maiden asks to learn more "of those words so good that their sweetness has entered my heart," the dove summarizes all the basic beliefs of Islam.[27] Describing all of creation as the work of Allah, the dove tells the maiden of a paradise of seven beautiful castles that awaits the faithful and, for those

[24] Guillén Robles, *Leyendas moriscas*, 1:182.

[25] Guillén Robles, *Leyendas moriscas*, 1:186: "Y demandóle su cuerpo. 'Pues, oh padre! por qué quieres tu innovar cosa que te avergüenzen por ello los días de tu vida y empués de tu muerte? has oído dezir de algún rrey que hiziese eso con su hiya?"

[26] Guillén Robles, *Leyendas moriscas*, 1:187: "porque la paloma era de oro amarillo, y su cola de perlas bermeias, y sus piedes de plata, y su pico de perlas blancas, esmaltado con aljófar."

[27] Guillén Robles, *Leyendas moriscas*, 1:189: "Díme más de esas palabras tan buenas, que sus dulzuras han entrado en mi corazón."

who disobey Allah, a hell where "they neither die nor live, and each day for them pain upon pain grows in the fire."[28]

After the dove leaves, Carcayona repeats its message to her father, who tries to convince her that she is mistaken and that she must continue to worship the idol. She replies that he is the one who is wrong. As she persists in worshiping only Allah, her father fears that her disobedience will cause him to lose his kingdom. "O daughter!" he says, "Return to who you are, or I will do what I have to."[29] Yet Carcayona does not flinch: "O father! although you cut off my hands and burn me with fire, I will not stop serving Allah, my lord."[30] Finally her father orders that her hands be cut off and that she be abandoned on a mountain. She cries aloud to Allah, "and the angels wept for her and prayed to Allah for her."[31] Wounded and afraid in the wilderness, Carcayona prays to Allah, who leads her to a sheltering cave. Here she finds many fierce wild beasts, but they do not attack her. "Rejoice that the piety of Allah is on you," they tell her, bringing her food, and playing with her "as the dog with its master."[32]

At the same time, the king of Antioch comes hunting in the area. He follows a doe who leads him to the cave where he finds the beautiful maiden, Carcayona. Falling in love with her, he converts to her religion and takes her home as his wife. They also take the doe with them. Soon the new wife is pregnant, but her husband is called away to battle in a distant place. Once he has gone and a baby boy is born to Carcayona, a letter comes to her mother-in-law supposedly from her son, the king. "Dear mother," the letter begins, "when this letter arrives, throw the witch out of my castle and my kingdom, for she has bewitched everyone, and has made us abandon our law, for that son that she gave birth to is not mine; and if you do not do what I command, you will never see me again."[33] Sorrowfully, the queen mother sends off to the

[28] Guillén Robles, *Leyendas moriscas*, 1:201: "que ni mueren, ni viven; y cada día les crece pena sobre pena en el fuego."

[29] Guillén Robles, *Leyendas moriscas*, 1:210: "Oh hiya! tórnate de lo qu'estás, sino yo haré lo que dicho tengo."

[30] Guillén Robles, *Leyendas moriscas*, 1:211: "Oh padre! aunque me cortases las manos, y me quemes con fuego, no cesaré sino en servir á Allah, mi señor."

[31] Guillén Robles, *Leyendas moriscas*, 1:211–212: "Y los ángeles lloraban por ella y rrogaban á Allah por ella."

[32] Guillén Robles, *Leyendas moriscas*, 1:213–214: " 'Alégrate, que la piedad de Allah es sobre tí.' Y jugaban con ella, como el perro con su amo, y traíanle las frutas y comía de ellas." Note that in the Castilian version, the dove does not give as much instruction in Islam, and a white doe appears to lead her to a sheltering cave, licks her wounded arms to heal them, and brings her food, 46.

[33] Guillén Robles, *Leyendas moriscas*, 1:216: "Señora madre, cuando llegaré esta carta sacarás á la hechizera de mi alcázar y de mi reyno, que ella nos ha hechizado á todos, y

wilderness her daughter-in-law, her grandchild, and the doe that had first led the king to rescue Carcayona.

Once more in the wilderness, Carcayona cries out to Allah. The golden dove appears and tells Carcayona that Allah is with her and will have pity on her. It directs her to pray to Allah for the restoration of her hands, urging her to ask this favor so that Allah will not be denied his power of goodness. As Carcayona prays, she falls asleep and later awakens to find her hands miraculously restored. Delighted, she gathers up branches to construct a shelter where she and the child and the doe can live.

Meanwhile, the king of Antioch has returned home to find that his wife, his son, and the doe have been banished. Realizing that some women of "great envy" have forged the letter to his mother, he sets out to find Carcayona again.[34] Allah guides him to the shelter she has built. The king calls "with his loudest voice," but Carcayona "did not want to respond, because he had betrayed her and ordered her thrown out of his house."[35] He convinces her that he did not write the letter ordering her banishment, and he rejoices in the miracle of her restored hands. "O my love," he says to her, "let us go to our kingdom." But she replies, "I will not return to the place of such evil people." As the storyteller recounts, "the king did not stop from entreating her, and telling her that there would be a new city, where the religion of Allah could be taught."[36] They agree that together they will build a new city on the banks of the Euphrates. "And it was populated then in a short time and they called it *the city Carcayona*, and they taught in it the religion of Allah, may he be glorified."[37] The story then concludes with Arabic words and the affirmation "There is no force or power, but in God, the high, the great."[38]

In its simplest form, the story conforms to Vladimir Propp's morphology for the fairy tale with two "moves," or major events, of "vil-

---

nos ha hecho dexar nuestra ley, que aquel hiyo que ha parido no es mío; y si no hazes lo que yo mando, nunca más me verás."

[34] Guillén Robles, *Leyendas moriscas*, 1:216: "Y así como el rey fué partido, Carcayona parió un hiyo, y las otras uyeres tuvieron grande envidia, y ordenaron una carta, como que el rey la enviaba á su madre."

[35] Guillén Robles, *Leyendas moriscas*, 1:219: "con lo más alto de su voz, y no quería responderle, porque le había hecho trayción y mandarla echar de su casa."

[36] Guillén Robles, *Leyendas moriscas*, 1:220: " 'Oh mi amada! vámanos á nuestro reino.'—'Yo no tornaré al lugar de tan mala yente.' Y no cesó el rey de rogarla, y dezirle que la haría una cibdad de nuevo, para que enseñasen en ella la religión de Allah."

[37] Guillén Robles, *Leyendas moriscas*, 1:220–221: "Y fué luego poblada en poco tiempo, y llamáronla *la cibdad Carcayona*, y enseñaron en ella la religión de Allah, ensalzado sea."

[38] Guillén Robles, *Leyendas moriscas*, 1:221: "No hay fuerza ni poder sino en Dios, el alto, el grande."

lainy."[39] In the first act of villainy, Carcayona's father orders her hands cut off and exiles her to the wilderness, clearly a sentence of death. Then, after she has survived and married the king of Antioch, a forged letter tricks his mother, who carries out the second act of villainy. She banishes not only the handless Carcayona to the distant mountain, but her infant son and the doe, as well. Unlike the Grimm version that blames a Devil for victimizing the Maiden, the Morisco tale clearly identifies the cruel perpetrators as human actors—her own father, and her mother-in-law who is tricked by envious women. The villainy, then, constitutes not merely abuse but betrayal by the very adults who should have protected her.

The tale of Carcayona shows what happens when men and women violate the gender order. King Nachrab instigates the drama by incestuous advances that pervert his protective fatherly role. Carcayona questions him, asking how she can be both wife and daughter to him. After the visit of the dove, Carcayona breaks more gender prescriptions by speaking out against her father's religion and disobeying his orders. The king further betrays the masculine role of protective father by ordering the amputation of his daughter's hands and her abandonment in a distant wilderness. The king of Antioch's mother conforms to the feminine role of carrying out what she believes are her son's orders to banish her daughter-in-law and grandchild. But in doing so, she betrays the feminine role of nurturing love.

Yet Carcayona's disobedience of her father and refusal to follow her husband home do not result in evil. Refusing to observe the rule of passive obedience for females, Carcayona brings what she believes is a better religion to her world and builds a shelter for herself and her child in the wilderness. Her story implies that she has remained obedient to a higher imperative—that of the "true word" of Allah. Rather than merely allowing the king to rescue her and take her back to his home, she does not agree to go with him until he urges her to come with him to build "a new city" where the religion of Allah can be taught.[40] Carcayona thus refines the ideal of woman; more than a creature of passive docility, the perfect woman must obey Allah above all,

[39] Propp, *Morphology of the Folktale*, 92.

[40] Note that the ending of this Aljamiado version of the story differs from that of the Castilian version, in which Carcayona obediently returns to his palace with her husband, and there everyone rejoices in the restoration of her hands: "Benido el día el prinzepe subió á su mujer en su caballo con su yjo en brazos, y el prinzepe á pié tomaron el camino de la ziudad, y llegando . . . sus dueñas y donzellas de la prinzesa binieron luego á darle de comer y bestir, como lo tenían de costumbre, y qüando bieron un milagro tan grande, y verla con ermosas manos, almiradas y contentas y con grande alegría daban grazias á Dios," Guillén Robles, *Leyendas moriscas*, 1:52.

and this obedience justifies her disobedience to men. Rather than depending on men's protection, she must make decisions and take action to ensure the survival of herself and her children.

Myth, Memories, and Power

Whether written as stories or carved in stone and wood, myths and memories played a powerful role in early modern Spain, for they served to justify oppression by a dominant order as well as to encourage resistance against it. At first glance, the story of Carcayona and the memories inscribed in buildings and monuments might seem mere fantasy, far removed from the reality of the lives of sixteenth-century Moriscos. Yet they could remind Moriscos of the power of their faith and the glory of a past when Muslims had ruled Iberia. And they symbolized to Christians what they yet needed to dominate if they were to maintain their hard-won political control. Not surprisingly, Christians attempted to destroy or transform these memories by burning Moriscos' writings and reconfiguring their buildings and monuments as symbols of Christian power.

Moriscos' memories of their past persisted even more strongly as the bonfires of their writings and the co-opting or razing of their buildings converted them into myths. No longer simple memories of actual people who had lived in the past, they evolved into symbols of powerful beings whose dilemmas and actions helped them understand their own problems. Moreover, they became a form of the social consciousness so essential to the shared interpretive frameworks that people construct.[41] Struggling to make sense of a world that must have sometimes seemed chaotic and overwhelming, Moriscos could look to their myths for reassurance and inspiration. They also found in them possible strategies that they could follow in sixteenth-century Spain. Myths of both story and monument grew especially powerful as they became a source of shared identity, and the power of these myths must have increased as those in authority attempted to proscribe them.

Although the myths of Carcayona and the Ibero-Muslim monuments may seem unrelated, they both raise questions about power. It is true that the story of the handless princess appears to be more about powerlessness, while the myths of those marble arches, carved ceilings, and thick-walled fortresses exalt the power of Muslims in a glori-

[41] Jonathan D. Hill, introduction to *Rethinking History and Myth: Indigenous South American Perspectives on the Past*, ed. Jonathan D. Hill (Urbana and Chicago: University of Illinois Press, 1988), 5.

ous past when they had ruled much of the Iberian Peninsula. However, just as Carcayona becomes powerless when cruel authorities treat her unjustly, Muslim buildings and monuments lose their power as symbols of Muslim grandeur when Christian conquerors take them over to represent their own glory. The construction of a Christian cathedral within the Great Mosque of Cordova, for example, represents not only an arrogant intrusion but indeed a rape that defiled and degraded the glory of former Muslim rulers.

In a sense, Muslim buildings and monuments suffer a mutilation as grave as that of Carcayona. The fate of the Great Mosque of Seville, recounted above, exemplifies this. After Ferdinand III and his forces took the city in the thirteenth century, the victorious Christians razed the mosque, leaving only its minaret and patio of orange trees, which were incorporated into the construction of a huge Gothic cathedral. More than merely the destruction of a sacred Muslim site, the construction of this cathedral mutilated it, leaving only a few parts of it intact, but even then disfiguring and reducing them to conform to the needs of a hostile and victorious enemy.

As the victim of mutilation, Carcayona represents powerlessness, but her story is also about power: that of Allah, who acts as a source of empowerment, but also the perverted power of abusive humans. Allah exercises power not only in sending the dove and the doe to the young maiden; he also emboldens her to speak out against her father's religious beliefs. Although Allah does not or cannot prevent the evil carried out by Carcayona's father and her mother-in-law, he nevertheless has the power to resolve her ordeals miraculously. At the story's end she is no longer the powerless maiden without hands; she has regained her hands and has built a shelter for her child, the doe, and herself. She has become a testimony to the "true word," a sign of Allah's loving power to work through humans and animals. She proves that Allah empowers the faithful to survive, even to overcome great suffering and build a new city dedicated to the worship of the true God.

Undoubtedly, the story of Carcayona appealed to Moriscos of sixteenth-century Spain, for they could identify with this victim of cruel injustice. All around them they could see evidence of the mutilation of the buildings and monuments that represented a glorious past. In a very real sense, the regulations forbidding the practice of their religion and culture left them wounded like the Handless Maiden. Forced to convert to Christianity if they wished to remain in the Spanish kingdoms, these people lost their religious leaders and mosques. The Christian icons that they had to worship must have seemed idolatrous to them. They had to replace their Muslim names with Christian ones and their clear monotheistic faith with a doctrine of the Trinity that they saw as polytheism. After purchasing a few years of grace, they could no longer speak Arabic nor have any writings in Arabic or Aljamía. Officials forbade their dances and songs, their baths and rituals marking life passages such as birth, marriage, and death. As inquisitors increased their persecution of Moriscos, even their cooking and eating practices became suspect as evidence of apostasy, that is, backsliding into a previous religion. Unable to define themselves through their culture and religion, Moriscos must have felt like the Handless Maiden—betrayed and wounded in this case by Christian officials who had promised Muslims, in the terms of the surrender of Granada in 1492, that they could freely practice their own religion.

Just as Carcayona suffered for her loyalty to the true religion, Moriscos also suffered. Inquisitors who prosecuted them must have seemed as cruel and unjust as Carcayona's father and mother-in-law. And just as Carcayona found that her religion was not only a cause of her suffering but, even more important, a source of empowerment, Moriscos also found in their religious beliefs a source of hope and a powerful motivation for preserving their identity and resisting oppression.

Paradoxically, the story of Carcayona provides inspiration for accommodation as well as resistance.[42] She survives in the wilderness because she befriends the animals and then obediently marries the young king who falls in love with her. She follows him to his homeland and lives with him in his palace with his mother. In many ways, Carcayona shows that she can maintain her own integrity while accommodating others, that she can keep the true faith while living with those who do not share it. Her story validates the experiences of many Moriscos in sixteenth-century Spain who externally conformed to the dominant Christian culture while maintaining internal loyalty to Islam. This longtime Muslim tradition of *taqiyya*, or "precaution," had developed earlier as Muslims sought to preserve Islam even when living under oppression.[43]

[42] Irene Silverblatt points out the Gramscian basis for this "contradictory consciousness" and the dual notions of "accommodation in resistance" and "resistance in accommodation," which she attributes to Eugene D. Genovese, *Roll Jordan Roll: The World the Slaves Made* (New York: Vintage, 1974). See her article, "Political Memories and Colonizing Symbols: Santiago and the Mountain Gods of Colonial Peru," in Hill *Rethinking History and Myth*, 174–194 nn. 12 and 14, 193.

[43] Most scholars believe that taqiyya originated with Muslim Shiʿas living under Sunni domination, particularly those dissenters who joined the secret societies of Ismaʿilis, Nusayris, and Druses. See, for example, H. Lammens, *Islam: Beliefs and Institutions*, trans. Sir E. Denison Ross (London: Methuen & Co., 1968), 168; *The Shorter Encyclopaedia of*

Accommodation had long been practiced by Muslims who had lived and intermingled with Christians for centuries on the Iberian Peninsula. Intermarriage had occurred in the medieval period, although Christian rulers had forbidden it and officials of both Islam and Christianity strongly advised against it, concerned with preserving the purity of their respective religions and the loyalty of their members. Moriscos who married Old Christians were more likely to become "Christianized," it was believed, and to permit their children to be educated as Christians. Not surprisingly, some Muslim leaders warned their people not to remain in places where they would be subject to Christian rulers, for taqiyya could not protect Muslims from contamination by contact with these people.[44]

Although we do not know precisely how much impact Aljamiado literature had on Moriscos of Golden Age Spain, the story of Carcayona—especially in oral form—could have played an important role in supporting Morisco resistance as well as accommodation. With a female protagonist, the legend could have been especially helpful for Moriscas as they sought to understand and justify their resistance to assimilation attempts. Like Carcayona, these women had entered the political realm by resisting unjust authorities in their own homes. Moreover, the Handless Maiden offered encouragement, for she had been rewarded for her steadfast loyalty to the true faith; her hands had been restored. To Moriscas, the white doe that was so crucial to Carcayona's survival in the mountain wilderness signified a steadfast Allah who would not forsake those believers victimized for their faith.

Carcayona's supportive role was not limited to the women of the Morisco communities, for she held out to all Moriscos the hope for rescue if only they remained loyal to the true faith. During the sixteenth century countless Morisco prophecies of rescue circulated, along with rumors that the Turks were poised to land and bring them military victory, or that the French Huguenots were ready to send them arms, or that unnamed people in North Africa would invade to

Islam, ed.. H.A.R. Gibb and J. H. Kramers (Ithaca: Cornell University Press, 1961), 561–562; Alvaro Galmés de Fuentes, *Los moriscos (desde su misma orilla)* (Madrid: Instituto Egipcio de Estudios Islámicos, 1993), 108–113; Louis Cardaillac, "Un aspecto de las relaciones entre moriscos y cristianos: polémica y taqiyya," in *Actas del coloquio internacional sobre literatura aljamiada y morisca* (Madrid: CLEAM, 1978), 3:107–122; and sura 16:106 of *The Holy Qur'an: Text, Translation and Commentary*, trans. and comm. Abdullah Yusuf Ali, 2 vols. (Cambridge, MA: Hafner Publishing Co., 1946), 1:685. Note that not all Muslims accepted taqiyya, and some leaders believed that living under the rule of non-Muslims would dilute their faith because they could not express it outwardly; see Domínguez Ortiz and Vincent, *Historia de los moriscos*, 134–135.

[44] Domínguez Ortiz and Vincent, *Historia de los moriscos*, 134–135.

vanquish their Christian oppressors.[45] Remembering the rescue and reward of Carcayona could encourage Moriscos to hold firm in their faith and to trust in Allah's divine providence.

In contrast, Christians developed their own myths about Moriscos that justified their harsh insistence on absolute loyalty and assimilation. Moriscas may have seen their resistance to assimilation as a sacred duty to preserve the true faith, but Christian authorities saw it as treacherous obstinacy—treacherous because it meant disloyalty to both Crown and Church. In fact, some Moriscos did communicate with enemies of Spain in North Africa and in Turkey, and a small number of Turks had come to help the Moriscos during the Alpujarras rebellion of 1568–1570.[46] These reports reinforced the stereotypical view that vilified all Moriscos as spies for the Turks. As one contemporary Christian, Pedro de Valencia, warned, "There are not ten, nor a hundred, nor a thousand, nor a hundred thousand, but many more spies and soldiers that the [Ottoman] Empire and Sect of the Ismaelists have in Spain."[47]

Even as they attempted to conform to the dominant Christian culture (at least externally), Moriscos (and also conversos, and crypto-Jews who had ostensibly chosen to convert to Christianity) became counteridentities against which Christians could unify and define themselves.[48] Furthermore, they expressed their difference through religion, which provided both metaphor and a language of resistance.[49] It is no accident that Christians increasingly oppressed Moriscos during the sixteenth century, for this was a critical time for a developing Spanish state in search of a unifying identity. Not all Christians, of course, saw Moriscos as counteridentities to be opposed, and many Moriscos believed that they had become good Christians. Moreover, most residents of sixteenth-century Iberia identified themselves as residents of a region rather than as members of a unified state or empire.

[45] For examples, see García Arenal, *Los moriscos*, 55–62; López-Baralt, *Islam in Spanish Literature*, 198. For prophecies that the end of a sinful era was approaching, see Wiegers, *Islamic Literature in Spanish and Aljamiado*, 240–242.

[46] For reports that Moriscos were aiding the Turks against Spain, see Domínguez Ortiz and Vincent, *Historia de los Moriscos*, 28–30; Luis Cabrera de Córdoba, *Relaciones de las cosas sucedidas en la corte de España, desde 1599 hasta 1614* (Madrid: J. Martín Alegria, 1857), 367; and BN ms 8888, Pedro de Valencia, *Obras varias* (Zafra, 1606). Both Diego Hurtado de Mendoza, *La guerra de Granada*, in *Biblioteca de Autores Españoles* (1797) (Madrid: Atlas, 1946), 21:64–122, and Mármol Carvajal, *Historia del rebelión*, report that Turks helped Moriscos to fight in this rebellion.

[47] Pedro de Valencia, *Obras varias*, 12.

[48] Peter Sahlins, *Boundaries: The Making of France and Spain in the Pyrenees* (Berkeley and Los Angeles: University of California Press, 1989), 107.

[49] Sahlins, *Boundaries*, 9 and 123.

Nevertheless, demonizing Moriscos as biologically and culturally Other provided a myth for the infant state that veiled its divisive regionalism and sacralized its origin in the Crusades of the Reconquest. This myth claimed continuity with a holy war against the infidel, culminating in the defeat of the Muslims in 1492. Many Christians perceived Moriscos as direct descendants of those Muslims whom their ancestors had defeated in a seven-centuries-long series of wars and skirmishes. Christian authorities claimed the glory and legitimacy of Reconquest heroes who had defeated the Muslims. Out of medieval Reconquest experiences a "Spanish consciousness" began to develop, deeply marked by "the profound infiltration of the concepts and mentalities of the Crusades."[50]

Yet Muslims also claimed their own myths of the past, and they found in both stories and monuments a paradoxical lesson. On the one hand, these myths urged the Moriscos of early modern Spain to resist oppression and reclaim their position of honor and power. On the other hand, they suggested that accommodation might function as a subversive form of resistance and provide an even more powerful strategy for survival.

[50] Ron Barkai, *Cristianos y musulmanes en la España medieval (El enemigo en el espejo)* (Madrid: Ediciones Rialp, 1984), 213. Simon R. Doubleday develops the hegemonic rationale for creating a common enemy in his unpublished paper, "On the Age of Spanish Ghosts," presented to the Society for Spanish and Portuguese Historical Studies, Madrid, July 2003.

2

MADALENA'S BATH

MORISCOS IDENTIFIED themselves not only through their myths and memories, but also through their bodies, which became the primary means that some Christians used to transform Morisco difference into deviance. Consider the case of Madalena Morisca, who stood before inquisitors of the tribunal of the Holy Office of Seville in 1609, accused of washing herself as a Muslim.[1] Rather than including a family name or the name of a husband or owner, as most Inquisition records listed women, the clerk who recorded testimony in this case added to Madalena's Christian name the term "Morisca." His choice of this term indicates the social and political significance of religious status in this period. It also reveals a politics of difference in which people in power attempted to transform into a badge of shame those identifications that less powerful people held for themselves and sought to preserve as honor.

Inquisitors had called Madalena to appear before them to answer the accusations of two witnesses. Both people had testified that they had seen her very early one morning when she came into their common courtyard, in the town of Medina Sidonia, to bathe herself. They watched as she washed her legs and thighs, face and head. One witness swore that she had washed her "shameful parts," but the other said that he had arrived too late to see that particular part of her bathing. Inquisitors took these accusations very seriously, for they treated bathing as evidence of an attempt to preserve Islamic ritual ablutions even after baptism. Madalena had to take this accusation seriously, too. For her, the washing of her body represented not only a dangerous act that identified her as a deviant who must be punished, but also a form of self-identity. Her body thus became the focus for both self-knowledge and oppression.[2]

[1] All information for this case is from Archivo Histórico Nacional (Madrid), hereafter AHN, Inquisición, legajo 2068, pt. 3, no. 14; and legajo 2075, no. 19. Note that the person recording this report may have mispelled her name for "Magdalena," which is the more common form in Spain.

[2] In many ways, Madalena's case can be read like that of Eleno de Céspedes, which Israel Burshatin has analyzed as a "narrative of a frontier culture whose boundaries were being displaced from the political map to the bodies of those subordinated by Castilian and 'old' Christian rule." See his important essay, "Written on the Body: Slave or

Madalena's story is not simply that of one isolated woman sneaking an early morning bath in what she thought was a deserted courtyard. In early modern Spain, tens of thousands of other Moriscas literally embodied their own identities in dress and bathing, dances and songs, prayers and fasts, remedies and love magic, food and family, and in celebrations of birth, marriage, and death. Morisco men also embodied their identities, but historical records often subsume this into accounts of their rebellions and military actions. Moreover, women played a major role in preserving Hispano-Muslim culture as their male religious leaders had to retreat into exile and many Morisco men disappeared into captivity or hiding.[3] Yet both men and women preserved and passed on to the younger generation certain habits and knowledge of the body that sustained their culture. In contrast, most Christian authorities regarded embodied Morisco knowledge not as a valuable heritage, but as evidence of difference that they found increasingly intolerable.

A variety of historical sources shows that embodied knowledge demonstrates the power of oppression and the strength of resistance, as well as significant evidence of "muted groups" in history, those people for whom historical records provide little direct voice.[4] Moriscos left few written records of their thoughts and ideas, but historical documents describe their bodies, how they used them and identified themselves through their bodies. Inquisition records tell of charges against accused Moriscos, testimony against them, and how they responded. Ecclesiastical records discuss the problems with Moriscos and proposals for how these should be solved. Local and royal documents include several debates about "the Morisco problem" and proposals for its solution. Literature of the time in both Castilian and Aljamía reveals

---

Hermaphrodite in Sixteenth-Century Spain," in *Queer Iberia: Sexualities, Cultures, and Crossings from the Middle Ages to the Renaissance*, ed. Josiah Blackmore and Gregory S. Hutcheson (Durham: Duke University Press, 1999), 420–456.

[3] For an example of the expulsion of Muslim religious leaders, see the case of Yuce de la Vaçia, an alfaquí expelled by order of the Inquisition in Cuenca in 1495, in app. 1 of Mercedes García Arenal, *Inquisición y moriscos. Los procesos del Tribunal de Cuenca* (Madrid: Siglo Veintiuno, 1983), 119–120. In countless cases, Morisco men were captured and enslaved during the rebellion of the Alpujarra, 1568–1570. In many other cases, men penanced by the Inquisition were sentenced to "perpetual prison," which was commuted to service as a galley slave; see, for example, the case of Baltasar Junila, a Morisco arrested by the Tribunal of the Inquisition in Cordova in 1573, in Gracia Boix, *Autos de fe*, 142–143. Many of the Morisco households listed for the city of Seville in 1581 were headed by females; see AGS, Cámara de Castilla, legajo 2183. See chapters 3, 4, and 5, below, for more on the disappearance of men from Morisco households.

[4] The phrase is from David Sibley, *Outsiders in Urban Societies* (New York: St. Martin's Press, 1981), 16.

Moriscos' cultural practices, attitudes, and concerns that both Christians and Moriscos used to identify Moriscos through their bodies.

Madalena's bath, then, discloses more than the body of a single woman. It demonstrates the bodily nature of Moriscos' strong sense of identity, which becomes the basis for long-lasting and, occasionally, unconscious resistance against acculturation. At the same time, it reveals the process by which Christians transformed Morisco difference into deviance and inscribed it on the Morisco body. Finally, it shows how the punishment of Moriscos demonstrates the political significance of embodied knowledge in religious conflicts and in the writing of history.

Moriscos' Embodied Self-Knowledge

Not all Moriscos learned an embodied self-knowledge in the same way. Males and females clearly learned different things from and about their bodies, beginning with rituals to welcome and name the newborn baby and ending with rituals to bury the dead. Moreover, differences in class, region, pre-Iberian origin, and length of time in Iberia also affected the ways that Moriscos learned about themselves through their bodies. After 1570, when Philip II decreed that some 50,000 Moriscos of Granada should be relocated throughout Castile, local variations of Moriscos' knowledge bled together and spread to places that had little previous knowledge of Muslims or Moriscos. Historical evidence cannot tell us about all the variations in the ways that Moriscos developed self-knowledge, but it does show very clearly that much of this self-knowledge was learned through the body and became an important basis for self-identity.

Consider, for example, the *fadas*, or rituals of Hispanic Muslims to welcome newborn babies. These celebrations continued in modified forms following the royal edicts that required Muslims to convert to Christianity or leave the kingdoms of Spain in the early sixteenth century.[5] A ceremony in which the infant was welcomed to the community and consecrated to Allah on the seventh day following birth, the fadas included readings from the Qur'an and often animal sacrifice. Traditionally, the baby's father played a major role as he professed his faith and named the child, taking it in his arms and introducing it as a Muslim.

[5] Michelle Ann Fuerch, "Tratado jurídico: Edición crítica del manuscrito Aljamiado-Morisco inédito 4987 de la Biblioteca Nacional de Madrid" (Ph.D. diss., Wayne State University, Detroit, MI, 1982), 171–176. Ribera and Asín, *Manuscritos árabes y aljamiados,*

After Christians required conversion by Muslims and prohibited their fadas, women gradually took over the ceremonies, which became less overtly Islamic and more private. They no longer included a reading of the Qurʾan or the ritual sacrifice of an animal. Instead, they became occasions to welcome the infant and to neutralize Christian baptism by washing away the baptismal chrism. The women gathered together in one of their homes and undressed the infant, revealing its body. They placed it on a cloth with grains of wheat and barley and gold and silver items. After reciting prayers, they washed the child and dressed it in clean clothing. As all the women present took hold of the edges of the cloth beneath the child, one group of them asked its name and another group responded. Then they lifted the cloth holding the child and raised their voices together in an ululation described in historical records as "li li li li."[6]

Traditionally, circumcision followed for male babies on the eighth day after birth, although this was increasingly delayed to the eighth year because Christian authorities sought to prevent circumcision through control of Morisco birth practices.[7] Some Christian travelers to Africa had reported on circumcision of girls, but historical records contain no evidence of female circumcision in Spain.[8] A common Spanish term for circumcision at this time, *retajar*, was derived from an Arabic word that denoted circumcision as a practice of purification.[9] Instructions from Charles V to the archbishop of Granada in 1526 included the directive to watch Morisco midwives very strictly because they were believed to circumcise newborn infants.[10] Later in the century, the Crown would issue specific prohibitions against Morisco midwives,

---

present ms 32, "Miscelánica" (sixteenth century), which includes a description of the ceremony "para las criaturax de las fadax," 129–130.

[6] Fadas are described in Dolors Bramon, "El rito de las fadas, pervivencia de la ceremonia preislámica de la 'Aqiqa," in *Las prácticas musulmanas de los moriscos andaluces (1492–1609)*, ed. Abdejelil Temini (Zaghouan: Centre d'Etudes et de Recherches Ottomanes, Morisques, de Documentation et d'Information, 1989), 33–35; García Arenal, *Los moriscos*, 96; and Pedro Longás, *Vida religiosa de los moriscos* (Madrid: Ibérica, 1915), 256–261.

[7] Domínguez Ortiz and Vincent, *Historia de los moriscos*, 92; for more on male circumcision, see Bernard Vincent, "The Moriscos and Circumcision," in *Culture and Control in Counter-Reformation Spain*, ed. Anne J. Cruz and Mary Elizabeth Perry(Minneapolis: University of Minnesota Press, 1992), 78–92. Christian authorities regarded the circumcision of both Judeo-conversos and Moriscos as physical evidence of apostasy, and they attempted to prohibit both Judeo-converso and Morisco midwives. See Renée Levine Melammed, *Heretics or Daughters of Israel: The Crypto-Jewish Women of Castile* (Oxford and New York: Oxford University Press, 1999), esp. 140–149; and n. 11 below.

[8] Bunes Ibarra, *La imagen de los musulmanes*, 250.

[9] Vincent, "The Moriscos and Circumcision," 79.

[10] Domínguez Ortiz and Vincent, *Historia de los moriscos*, 122.

who were said to prevent baptism of newborn infants and to carry out circumcision of baby boys.[11]

The Inquisition considered circumcision a very serious indication of apostasy, or false conversion, and inquisitorial records show that many Moriscos were accused of being circumcised and of carrying out circumcision on others. María Hernández de Zorzala, for example, was accused of telling a young Morisca that if she had a son, she should call María to be the *comadre* (midwife or godmother) so that she could circumcise him, "which they do to all the boys in Berbery so that they are Moors."[12] In another case, a Morisco couple who feared they would be accused of having already circumcised their son took the child to the parish priest to be baptized in Cordova in 1588, carrying with them a written notice that the child had been "born circumcised."[13] Many adult males who had spent some time in Berbery or North Africa were accused of having become Muslims and having allowed themselves to be circumcised. In Murcia Hernando Alonso told inquisitors that he had been captured in the war of Portugal and taken to Fez, where he had allowed himself to be circumcised so that Muslims would not kill him.[14] Clearly, circumcision had become a very significant and dangerous marker of religious identity.

As Morisco children grew older, they heard and learned to imitate the Arabic language that Moriscos in Valencia, Granada, and some isolated mountain hamlets continued to use. They sang and danced as they saw other Moriscos celebrate traditional musical festivals called *zambras* and *leilas*.[15] Some of them learned to play the drums, flutes, trumpets, lutes, mandolins, and zithers so important to Morisco music. A drawing that depicts a Morisco dance and musical instruments in sixteenth-century Granada appears in figure 3.

The children quickly became familiar with traditional Muslim foods and with the Muslim practice of eating while seated on the ground.

[11] "Instrucción de los moriscos valencianos," of 1561, reprinted in García Arenal, *Los moriscos*, 110, calls for expelling Morisco midwives and all religious leaders of the Moriscos. Domínguez Ortiz and Vincent, *Historia de los moriscos*, point out that Morisco midwives were suspected of performing abortions as well as circumcisions, and of avoiding baptism, 122.

[12] AHN, Inquisición, legajo 1856, expediente 11, quoted in Juan Aranda Doncel, *Los moriscos en tierras de Córdoba* (Cordova: Monte de Piedad y Caja de Ahorros de Córdoba, 1984), 338: "si pariese un hijo había de ser su comadre y le había cortar el ollejo de su natura, que en algaravía se decía taharon, y que en Berbería se hacía a todos los niños para que fuesen moros."

[13] Quoted in Aranda Doncel, *Los moriscos*, 302; the phrase is "nació circuncidado."

[14] AHN, Inquisición, legajo 2022, no. 13 (1583).

[15] Julián Ribera, *Historia de la música árabe medieval y su influencia en la española* (Madrid: Editorial Voluntad, 1927), 236–237.

Fig. 3. The Morisco Dance. *Authentic Everyday Dress of the Renaissance: All 154 Plates from the "Trachtenbuch"* (New York: Dover Publications, 1994), plates 89 and 90.

Both boys and girls learned Muslim taboos against consuming pork and, in some regions, wine. They observed the ritual slaughter of animals, but girls were more likely than boys to learn Muslim food-preparation methods, such as cooking meat in oil rather than fat.[16] Girls were taught more, also, about domestic remedies and how to heal the body in their homes. From their mothers and other older women, they learned the secrets of love magic, using amulets and potions and special recipes to control the body and its desires.[17]

[16] More information on these Morisco practices is in García Arenal, *Los moriscos*, 87–95.

[17] Aljamiado writings are especially rich sources for Morisco practices of domestic healing and love magic, most notably the following examples in Ribera and Asín, *Manuscritos árabes y aljamiados*: *Libro de dichox marabilloxox*, 99–101; *Libro de las suertes*, 103–105; and the last section of ms 59, *Miscelánea*, which contains cabalistic formulas, amulets, magic recipes, and conjurations. María Helena Sánchez Ortega discusses important aspects of love magic in "Sorcery and Eroticism in Love Magic," in *Cultural Encounters: The Impact of the Inquisition in Spain and the New World*, ed. Mary Elizabeth Perry and Anne J. Cruz (Berkeley and Los Angeles: University of California Press, 1991), 58–92. Also see the interesting essay by Yvette Cardaillac-Hermosilla, "Quand les morisques se mariaint," *Sharq al-Andalus* 12 (1995): esp. 483–486.

In their homes many Morisco children learned Arabic prayers and the rituals of Islam, including daily ablutions and the fast of Ramadan. To purify their bodies before prayer, they washed their faces and heads, their hands up to the elbows, their feet up to the calves.[18] Following the example of their elders, they rinsed their mouths and nostrils and ears three times, and cleaned between their toes as they washed their feet. They cleaned their bodies after eliminating waste, and later they would recognize that they must wash themselves following sexual activity. After menarche, girls carried out the ablutions to purify their bodies following menstruation and giving birth.[19]

Marriage brought more experience of sex and the body, especially to Moriscas. Women took over the preparation of the bride, and some even specialized in leading these preparations as *maestra de bodas*, or wedding director. The women bathed the bride and, before dressing her, applied henna to her face, hair, hands, and feet.[20] Then they formed a procession to take the bride to her new residence. Through the streets they danced and sang, some playing flutes, stringed instruments, drums, and even trumpets.[21] Traditionally, the bride was to keep her eyes closed during the procession, and she could not speak when she reached the groom's house until after the wedding night—in some cases, for the next seven days.[22] The next morning the wedding mistresses would wish the couple well and cut the bride's hair to the level of her throat.[23] Once pregnant, these young women learned more about their bodies and the life they nurtured within them.

The birth of children brought to both men and women opportunities for learning and teaching embodied knowledge. As parents, Moriscos played a central role in socializing their children. Figure 4, for example, shows how mothers dressed their daughters in clothing similar to their own. Teaching ritual ablutions and the raising and lowering of their bodies for praying the *zala* five times a day as they faced East, Morisco parents replicated for their children their own childhood initiation into

[18] This and all information on ablutions and prayers is from BN ms 4987, *Tratado jurídico;* also see the critical edition: Fuerch, "Tratado jurídico," 76–177.

[19] BN ms 4987, *Tratado jurídico*; Fuerch, "Tratado jurídico," 120–121.

[20] Vincent, "Las mujeres moriscas," 3:592. Additional information on marriage is in Cardaillac-Hermosilla, "Quand les morisques," 477–505.

[21] Ribera, *Historia de la música*, 236. Note that ritual ablutions were prescribed for both bride and groom.

[22] The 1587 case of Isabel, Morisco widow of Cebrián and slave of Doña Teresa Mesia, before the Inquisition in Cordova indicates that at least in some Morisco marriages, brides were not to speak to their husbands for the first seven days ("Y al tiempo que se casó, guardó una ceremonia de moros, que fué los primeros siete días de su casamiento no hablar con su marido, aunque estaban juntos"), Gracia Boix, *Autos de fe*, 223.

[23] Longás, *Vida religiosa*, 277–283.

Fig. 4. Morisca and Child. *Authentic Everyday Dress of the Renaissance: All 154 Plates from the "Trachtenbuch"* (New York: Dover Publications, 1994), plate 80.

embodied knowledge. María de Hocayaz, for example, was said "to have taught her children many prayers and ceremonies of the sect of Muhammad and to have said and done them."[24] For many Moriscos, the lessons that they learned as children would persist, sometimes even unconsciously, because they had apprehended them with movements and the senses of their bodies.

Morisco women and men became more aware of the knowledge that they sought to preserve in their families, even as they acted to prepare for burial the bodies of family members who had died. By tradition, family members and friends washed the body and then dressed it in a clean shirt or chemise and head covering. Sometimes the garments were decorated with silk embroidery and gold and silver.[25] Attempting to avoid the presence of a Christian priest, they shrouded the body in clean linen and gathered around it in one of their homes to say Muslim prayers together. If they could, they would bury the body on its side in virgin soil with its head facing the direction of Mecca.[26] As was pointed out by Jaime Bacaria, a Morisco from Elche, Christian and Morisco burial practices differed distinctly. Moriscos buried their dead each in its own grave away from the church, he said, while Christians were "in error and deceived" as they buried their dead together in or near the church.[27]

Throughout their lives, Moriscos acquired self-knowledge through body experiences that gave them an identity so deeply inscribed that they resisted Christian pressure to assimilate. In many cases, they had to hide this resistance behind a passive conformity to the laws of their Christian rulers. They accepted Christian names at baptism, for example, although they might continue to use Muslim names in their homes. In addition, some Moriscos carried out overt resistance against Christian pressure to abandon their embodied self-knowledge and forsake their self-identities so well learned through their bodies. During the 1568–1570 Morisco rebellion in southern Spain, women even joined in the physical fighting against Christian forces.[28]

[24] Gracia Boix, *Autos de fe*, 166, for her case before the Inquisition of Cordova in 1577; the phrase is "haber enseñado a sus hijos muchas oraciones y ceremonias de la secta de Mahoma y haberlas hecho y dicho."

[25] AHN, Inquisición, libro 991, contains information on burial practices in testimony against several Moriscos in Zaragoza.

[26] Morisco burial practices are discussed in Longás, *Vida religiosa*, 285–290; and in García Arenal, *Inquisición y moriscos*, 62–63.

[27] AHN, Inquisición, legajo 2022, no. 9: "los dichos christianos ivan herrados o engañados." He was sentenced to appear in an auto de fe, to abjure de vehementi, a public humiliation, but no more stringent penalties because he appeared to be of "little understanding" ("hombre de poco entendimiento").

[28] *Relación muy verdadera sacada de una carta*, n.p.

From Difference to Deviance

Morisco difference became transformed into deviance as Christians used strategies that they had already developed against Judeo-conversos. Even before the Christian-Morisco hostilities of the sixteenth century, many cities and guilds in Iberia had passed regulations called "purity of blood laws," which assumed that impurity is inherited through the blood. Originally aimed against Judeo-conversos, these regulations increasingly proscribed Moriscos, as well, from enjoying certain privileges, such as holding particular offices or titles, engaging in specified occupations, or attending universities.[29]

Christians and Muslims had known about their cultural and religious differences from centuries of living together, but the subjugation of all Hispanic Muslims to Christian rule by 1492 led to a sexualization of those differences.[30] Perhaps in response to their own fears of Muslim military might, victorious Christian warriors "feminized" the defeated Muslims, stripping them of their masculine markers by prohibiting them from carrying knives and by denigrating their culture. Although the terms of the Muslims' capitulation in 1492 granted them the right to observe their own religion, this right disappeared in less than a decade. During the sixteenth century Muslim differences became Morisco deviance as Christians focused on Morisco bodies as the site of their cultural practices.

Bathing and ritual washing, for example, had long been recognized as a difference. Christians often conflated into a single category of Islamic ritual the practices of bathing the entire body, washing the hands, and ritual ablution. One chronicler attributed Christian military victories to Muslim baths, which, he declared, "were the cause of a certain softness in their bodies, and of excessive pleasure, from which there proceeded idleness and other deceits and evil dealings which they inflicted on one another in order to sustain their customary ease."[31] In the sixteenth century, this sexualized rhetoric took on the

[29] Sicroff, *Los estatutos de limpieza*; Henry Kamen, *Inquisition and Society in Spain in the Sixteenth and Seventeenth Centuries* (Bloomington: Indiana University Press, 1985), discusses these statutes, esp. 115–133. Also see Linda Martz, "Pure Blood Statutes in Sixteenth-Century Toledo: Implementation as Opposed to Adoption," *Sefarad* 54 (1994): 83–107.

[30] Louise Mirrer, *Women, Jews, and Muslims in the Texts of Reconquest Castile* (Ann Arbor: University of Michigan Press, 1996), 54–56.

[31] Pulgar, quoted in Harvey, *Islamic Spain*, 271. See also José Jiménez Lozano, *Judíos, moriscos y conversos* (Valladolid: Ambito, 1982), 100, for the assertion that Castilian contempt for "effeminate" bathing had led to the destruction of most Muslim bath buildings by the end of the fifteenth century.

legal form of directives from the Crown, which told local authorities that among those tasks they must perform to "instruct" and Christianize Moriscos, they were required to enter their homes and remove any baths or bathing vessels.[32]

As the Inquisition began to prosecute Moriscos who continued their Muslim traditions, it aimed its institutional power against such bathing practices. It issued edicts of faith that publicly called on the faithful to denounce themselves and others for engaging in forbidden acts, including baths and washing, as evidence of Morisco apostasy. In their edicts inquisitors transformed such customs into a deviance of the flesh as they condemned "bathing the arms, the hands, elbows, face, mouth, nose, ears, legs, and shameful parts."[33] And witnesses used the same language as they denounced Moriscos for bathing "the legs, thighs, face . . . and head," including their "shameful parts."[34] A witness in Murcia had noticed that her roomer, Beatriz de Mendoça, frequently had her daughter carry water to her room; one night she had looked into the room and found Beatriz "stark naked, although she did not see her wash."[35] In another case, Juan Carazón, under questioning by inquisitors of Cuenca, confessed that he had stripped naked to carry out the ritual bathing that he believed would free him from the "fires of Chiana, which is hell."[36]

Christians sexualized Muslim differences in marriage rituals and practices. They imputed to Moriscos a lack of sexual restraint because they married cousins within forbidden degrees of relatedness, thus breaking the Christian taboo. Many Christians regarded such marriages as incest.[37] To friar Jaime Bleda, preacher-general of the Dominican Order, Moriscos were "male goats" or "cuckolds."[38] Damián Fon-

[32] See the informe from Madrid to Valencia printed in García Arenal, *Los moriscos*, 116–125.

[33] AHN, Inquisición, libro 1244, 107: "bañándose los brazos, de las manos, los cobdos, cara, boca, narices, oydos, y piernes y partes vergonzosas."

[34] AHN, Inquisición, legajo 2068, no. 17: "labarse las piernas, muslos, rostro . . . y caveça . . . las partes vergonçosas."

[35] AHN, Inquisición, legajo 2022, no. 21: "avia visto a la dicha Beatriz desnuda en cueros aunque no la bio labar."

[36] García Arenal, *Inquisición y moriscos*, app. 4, 137: "se desnudava en carnes y se lavaba . . . por que dios me las libre de los fuegos de Chiana que era el infierno."

[37] BN ms R11918, Damián Fonseca, *Justa expulsión de los moriscos de España: con la instrvccion, apostasia, y traycion dellos y respuesta á las dudas que se ofrecieron acerca desta materia* (Rome: Iacomo Mascardo, 1612), 110–111. See also Bernard Vincent, "50,000 moriscos almerienses," in *Almería entre culturas siglos XIII al XVI*, Coloquio Almería Entre Culturas (Amería: Instituto de Estudios Almerienses, 1990), 507.

[38] BN ms R 15.119, Jaime Bleda, *Corónica de los moros de España* (Valencia: Felipe Mey, 1618), 897; the term he used is "cabrón."

seca, Dominican chaplain to the Conde de Castro and ambassador in Rome, asserted that Moriscos asked for the rites of holy matrimony in the Christian church only after carrying out the Muslim wedding—a complex rite of Qurʾanic readings, dowry agreements, dyeing red with henna parts of the bride's body, and singing and dancing the leilas and zambras that secular instructions and inquisitorial prosecution repeatedly forbade.[39]

In fact, some Moriscos did continue to marry in the Muslim manner and wrote marriage contracts in Arabic that followed traditional formulas. A betrothal contract written in Arabic and found by agents of the Inquisition in the home of Gaspar Febrer, a Morisco in the Kingdom of Valencia, began with these words: "Praise be to God, unique in perfection, glorious and exalted, perfect in acts and words, who harmonizes the hearts of women and of men."[40] Listing the property that both bride and groom would bring to the marriage, the contract also noted that the groom married her "in virtue of the word of God—may it be glorified and magnified—in accordance with the *Sunna* of the one sent from God—may God bless him—and accordingly it is written that he must treat the wife kindly while maintaining her at his side or must dismiss her gently and give her good company and treat her well and with privilege."[41] Her father gave the bride in marriage, assuring that "she is virgin, subject to his paternal authority, healthy in body and mind, free from compromise and legal restrictions."[42]

Polygamy appeared to be even more depraved to Christians, who believed that this Muslim practice could overturn an entire social order based on monogamy. Multiple wives, after all, threatened the careful distribution of women as property of triumphant or privileged men in monogamous unions. In practice, few Moriscos took more than one wife except in times of crisis when men were killed or went into exile.

[39] Ana Labarta, "Contratos matrimoniales entre moriscos valencianos," *Al-Qantara* 4 (1983): 57–87; Fonseca, *Justa expulsión*, 110–111; and Bernard Vincent, *Minorías y marginados en la España del siglo XVI* (Granada: Diputación Provincial de Granada, 1987), 55–70.

[40] Labarta discusses and excerpts this contract and others in "Contratos matrimoniales," 57–87. She translated this passage as "Alabado sea Dios, único en la perfección, glorioso y excelso, perfecto de actas y palabras, el que armoniza los corazones de las mujeres y de los hombres," 64.

[41] Labarta, "Contratos matrimoniales," 65: "La desposa en virtud de la palabra de Dios—glorificada y ensalzada sea—de acuerdo con la *Sunna* del enviado de Dios—Dios le bendiga—y según está escrito que se ha de tratar amablemente y la esposa mientras se la conserve al lado o se la ha de despedir bondadosamente y darle buena compañía y tratarla bien y [con] privilegio."

[42] Labarta, "Contratos matrimoniales," 65: "ella es virgen, está bajo su patria potestad, sana de cuerpo y mente, libre de compromiso y plazo legal."

Nevertheless, Christians declared that the Qur'an provided for polygamy and, according to Franciscan Arabist Ricoldo de Montecrucio, "gives a very great license so that a man can have many women, young ones and as many as he can take in battle and can maintain, and not only single women," he added significantly, "but even those belonging to others."[43] To people critical of Moriscos, polygamy could destroy a social order in which women belonged to dominant men. These critics suspected that Moriscos hid their polygamy behind the more commonly accepted practice of concubinage.[44]

Critics such as Don Alonso Gutiérrez and Pedro Aznar Cardona condemned polygamy and other Morisco marriage traditions that increased their birthrate, comparing their "very great multiplication" to that of "bad weeds."[45] Moriscos "marry their children at a very young age, apparently at eleven years for girls and twelve for boys," complained Aznar Cardona, and "[t]heir intent is to grow and multiply."[46] In fact, the implication that Moriscos engaged in more and earlier sexual activity has been contradicted by recent research, which found that in sixteenth-century Granada the average age for marriage for all men was 24–25 years and for women 18–19 years, with Moriscas marrying approximately 12 to 14 months earlier than Old Christian women.[47] But even the one year's difference in age of marriage for women could produce more children, as Serafín de Tapia Sánchez found among the Moriscos of Avila.[48] Repeatedly many Christians expressed fears about Morisco fertility, their anxieties not only fueled by genuine evidence of population increase among Moriscos, but also confirmed by the fact

[43] BN, ms R 4.037, Ricoldo de Montecrucio, *Reprobación del Alcoran*, n.p., chapter 1: "Da lice[n]cia muy larga para q vn ombre pueda tener muchas mugeres, ma[n]cebas y moças ta[n]tas qua[n]tas pudiere algu[n]o tomar en la guerra y pudiere ma[n]tener, y no solame[n]te las solteras mas avn las mugeres ajenas."

[44] Vincent, "50,000 moriscos almerienses," 507.

[45] Informe of Don Alonso Gutiérrez, reprinted in Pascual Boronat y Barrachina, *Los moriscos españoles y su expulsión: Estudio histórico-crítico*, 2 vols. (Valencia: Francisco Vives y Mora, 1901), 1:635; Pedro Aznar Cardona, quoted in García Arenal, *Los moriscos*, 233.

[46] Aznar Cardona, quoted in García Arenal, *Los moriscos*, 233.

[47] Vincent, *Minorías y marginados*, 49. See also James Casey and Bernard Vincent, "Casa y familia en Granada," in *La familia en la España mediterránea (siglos XV–XIX)*, ed. Francisco Chacón (Barcelona: Crítica, 1987), 172–211; Margarita María Birriel Salcedo, "Mujeres y familia, fuentes y metodología," in *Conceptos y metodología en los estudios sobre la mujer*, ed. Barbara Ozieblo (Málaga: Universidad de Málaga, 1993), 43–69; and Margarita María Birriel Salcedo, "La experiencia silenciada, las mujeres en la historia de Andalucía. Andalucía moderna," in *Las mujeres en la historia de Andalucía*, Actas del II Congreso de Historia de Andalucía (Cordova: Junta de Andalucía, 1994), 44.

[48] Serafín de Tapia Sánchez, *La comunidad morisca de Avila* (Salamanca: Gráficas Varona, 1990), esp. 400.

that most Moriscos married, undeterred by a Christian veneration of virginity and celibacy.[49]

Slaveowners expected sexual services from their slaves, and their relations with Morisca slaves resulted in numerous offspring. Children born to slave women inherited the mother's slave status if the father was a slave or free commoner, but they inherited their father's status if he was of the nobility and acknowledged his paternity.[50] Some slaveowners freed the children they had sired when they were baptized, or granted them freedom in their wills. In some cases, slaves were able to earn enough money to buy freedom for themselves and for their offspring.[51] Whether slave or free, however, these children of Moriscas would face the restrictions imposed by purity of blood laws. Moreover, authorities took steps to ensure the inscription of slave status on their bodies, branding many on the face or arms and minutely recording their visible and distinctive features such as moles, eye color, and bodily defects.[52]

With the growth of the Morisco population, Morisco differences came to be perceived as increasingly dangerous deviance, and the body was identified as the site of deviance. Not surprisingly, proposals for solutions to the "Morisco problem" frequently included enslavement or high marriage taxes as a way to discourage marriage. Some proposals even called for castration.[53] Francisco de Sarria argued that Moriscos should be forbidden to marry among themselves and should marry only Old Christians, that is, Christians with no Jewish or Muslim ancestors. To enforce this prohibition, he proposed that any children born of a union between Moriscos should be enslaved as "servants of the Church." His concern with punishing those who would defile the purity of faith is also evident in a section of this same manuscript on the case of Lucrecia de León, penanced by the Inquisition in Toledo, and alludes to false visions, demons, and the "amazon of heaven."[54]

[49] Domínguez Ortiz and Vincent, *Historia de los moriscos*, 83–84.

[50] Antonio Domínguez Ortiz, "La esclavitud en Castilla durante la edad moderna," *Estudios de Historia Social de España* 2 (1952): 369–428, esp. 413; Abdelwahab Bouhdiba, *Sexuality in Islam*, trans. Alan Sheridan (London: Routledge & Kegan Paul, 1985), 105; Aurelia Martín Casares, *La esclavitud en la Granada del Siglo XVI* (Granada: Universidad de Granada and Diputación Provincial de Granada, 2000), 255–256 and 341–347.

[51] Vincent, "50,000 moriscos almerienses," 502–503.

[52] Domínguez Ortiz, "La esclavitud," discusses descriptions of slaves' identifying features, 424; for branding of slaves, see BN ms VE 26-1, *Pragmática y declaración sobre los moriscos del Reyno de Granada* (Madrid: Alonso Gómez, 1572), n.p.

[53] See the informe of D. Alonso Gutiérrez reprinted in Boronat y Barrachina, *Los moriscos españoles*, 1:637; see also Domínguez Ortiz and Vincent, *Historia de los moriscos*, 71.

[54] BN ms 721, Francisco de Sarria, *Alegación porque se justifica el cautiverio de los hijos de los Moriscos, no siendo de legítimo matrimonio travada, y contrahido con Christianos Viejos,*

Even as they disapproved of Moriscos for their "excessive" sexual activity that resulted in high fertility, Christians accused Moriscos of sodomy and other nonreproductive sexual behavior that they strongly condemned. To Christians such as theologian Pedro Aznar Cardona, who wrote a justification for the expulsion of Moriscos, Muhammad had "injured" marriage by approving polygamy, marriage within prohibited degrees, and sodomy.[55] Asserting that the Qur᾿an invited both men and women to engage in sodomy, Christian moralists used secular laws and the Inquisition to prosecute what they called "the nefarious sin."[56] In this offense, almost exclusively prosecuted against males, some of the accused purportedly took the passive role prescribed for women in heterosexual relations, thus perverting the gender order and subverting the order of "nature."[57]

Inquisitors issued edicts of grace to publicize those acts and beliefs that the faithful must denounce in themselves and in others. As evidence of "the sect of Muhammad," faithful Christians must look for those who said Jesus was a prophet rather than the son of God, that Mary was not a virgin before, during, and after giving birth.[58] They must tell inquisitors about people who observed Friday as a holy day and changed into clean clothing on this day, who ate meat on Fridays and other days prohibited by the Church, and who ceremonially slaughtered the animals they ate. The Christian faithful must denounce

1–12. Note that most Christian clerics cautioned against Christian women's marrying Morisco men because they assumed that the husband dominated the family and determined its religion. For an important study of sexual relations and taboos between Christians and Jews in an earlier period, see David Nirenberg, "Conversion, Sex, and Segregation: Jews and Christians in Medieval Spain," *American Historical Review* 107:4 (2002): 1065–1093; and Nirenberg, *Communities of Violence*.

[55] BN ms R 2856, Pedro Aznar Cardona, *Expulsión justificada de los moriscos españoles* (Huesca: Pedro Cabarte, 1612), 96–114.

[56] Often called "pecado nefando," sodomy cases were prosecuted by the Inquisition in Aragon and by secular justice in Castile. Authorities prosecuted many Moriscos for sodomy, but they prosecuted many Christian clerics, as well. For Inquisition prosecution of sodomy, see Rafael Carrasco, *Historia de los sodomitas. Inquisición y represión sexual en Valencia* (Barcelona: Laertes Editorial, 1986); Ricardo García Cárcel, *Herejía y sociedad en el siglo XVI: La inquisición en Valencia 1530–1609* (Barcelona: Ediciones Península, 1980), 288; and Monter, *Frontiers of Heresy*, 276–302. For the secular prosecution of sodomy in Castile, see Mary Elizabeth Perry, " 'The 'Nefarious Sin' in Early Modern Seville," *Journal of Homosexuality* 15:3–4 (Spring 1988): 63–84, reprinted in *The Pursuit of Sodomy: Male Homosexuality in Renaissance and Enlightenment Europe*, ed. Kent Gerard and Gert Hekma (New York and London: Harrington Park Press, 1989). An example of Christian rhetoric pointing to the Qur᾿an as the basis for Muslim and Morisco sodomy is in Ricoldo de Montecrucio, *Reprobación*, n.p., chapter 1.

[57] Vincent, *Minorías y marginados*, 66.

[58] This and the following information on evidence of apostasizing from Islam are in AHN, Inquisición, libro 1244, Edicto de la fe, fols. 105–109.

people who observed the fast of Ramadan or raised and lowered their bodies in prayer, and—as we have seen—those who bathed their arms, hands, face, mouth, nose, ears, legs, and "shameful parts." Furthermore, they must name those who blasphemed the Holy Sacrament or behaved rudely during Mass, as had Gómez Enrejmeda, a Morisco who was said "to pass his hand over his face and place his nose between his fingers so that it appeared that he made a derisive gesture" when the priest elevated the Holy Sacrament.[59]

In case after case, inquisitors condemned Moriscos who had been denounced by witnesses for praying or bathing "as a Muslim," for keeping the fast of Ramadan or Islamic food taboos, for singing or dancing or dressing "in the Muslim manner," for observing Muslim rituals at birth, marriage, and death.[60] Inquisitors seem to have been especially concerned about Moriscos who were accused of teaching Islam to others. Defendants in most of these cases were women who were said to have taught their language and customs to children. Leonor Hernández, for example, was accused of teaching Islam to her two sons, and witnesses said that Lucía de la Cruz taught the religion to those outside her family.[61] The Inquisition prosecuted both Morisco men and women for attempting to leave Spain for North Africa where, inquisitors believed, they would return to their original religion of Islam.[62]

To justify their opposition to Moriscos, Christian writers cited biblical passages such as Saint John's vision of the beautiful woman in heaven, shod in the moon and dressed in the sun, crowned by the stars, and threatened by a seven-headed dragon.[63] To Damián Fonseca, an outspo-

[59] AHN, Inquisición, legajo 2022, no. 8: "pasar la mano por la cara y poner las narizes entre los dedos de modo que les paresia dava higas." Inquisitors gave him a comparatively lenient sentence "porque era hombre grueso y çerrado las narizes" (because he was a heavy man and his nostrils were closed).

[60] For many of these cases against Moriscos in the tribunal of the Inquisition in Seville, see AHN, Inquisición, legajo 2075; in Murcia, see AHN, Inquisición, legajo 2022; in Zaragoza, see AHN, Inquisición, libro 991; in Cordova, see Gracia Boix, *Autos de fe*.

[61] For examples in the Inquisition records for Seville, see AHN, Inquisición, legajo 2075, no. 8 for Leonor Hernanez; no. 11 for Lucía de la Cruz; and no. 19 for Hieronymo Rodriguez de Giomar, who confessed that María Hernández had taught him Islam. In "Las mujeres moriscas," 593, Vincent reports that Inquisition records show "the fundamental role of their mothers or their grandmothers in the matter of education."

[62] AHN, Inquisición, legajo 2075, no. 4 for the case of Ysabel de Herrera, who was accused of attempting to go to Berbery "to convert to being a Moor"; no. 9 for Pedro, Berber slave, who "wanted to go to Berbery to be a Moor"; and no. 14 for Juana, a slave who attempted to sail from Spain for Berbery with other slaves, Moors, and Christians of Berbery.

[63] Rev. 12:1–4. Note that the vision here reported is that of a woman about to give birth and threatened by a dragon that wants to devour her child.

ken critic of Moriscos, the lovely woman represented the pure Church; and the leering dragon that menaced her was none other than Muhammad.[64] This curious marriage of biblical citations and sexual imagery characterized much of the rhetoric in which Christians described Moriscos. It contrasts starkly with the myths and memories that provided Moriscos with images of hope and glory. While the tale of Carcayona depicted difference positively in portraying the strength needed to preserve goodness against great opposition, Saint John's vision represents difference as a dangerous menace that must be opposed.

Sexual-religious imagery was limited neither to potential rape scenes nor to rhetoric. Spanish Christians sexualized Moriscos through laws and institutions in a process that transformed difference from Christians into deviance of the body so dangerous that it could not be tolerated. More important, this construction of a sexualized Other engendered an enemy against which Christians from all the diverse parts of Iberia could unite. Fonseca's maiden, in my judgment, represented not only the pure Church but a nascent central state that was developing hand in hand with a Church very much embroiled in the politics of early modern Spain. As sexualization transformed Moriscos into a dangerous deviant group, it provided imagery to justify and explain Christian oppression.[65] In their rhetoric, laws, and institutions, Christians seized the power to say who Moriscos were and what they represented, and their message was clear: Moriscos represented the impure, the lewd, and the nefarious—in a word, pollution. Christians had not only a right but a duty to defend themselves against this pollution.

Yet pollution is not a simple matter. Anthropologist Mary Douglas has reminded us to look for deeper meanings of pollution, which "is never an isolated event."[66] To her, this notion makes sense only "in reference to a total structure of thought" that provides a gendered view of the world and the basic conceptualization necessary to any society. It legitimizes hierarchy and authority, establishes rules for inclusion, and justifies exclusion—qualities also essential for a political state. In early modern Spain, the Christian ruling class used religion to legitimize its authority, and it used pollution to justify exclusion. Purity of blood statutes, for example, excluded people of Muslim or Jewish descent from certain offices, from many professions, and from attending

[64] Fonseca, *Justa expulsión;* this apocalyptic vision for Christians contrasts starkly with Morisco apocalyptic visions, discussed below in chapters 3 and 6.

[65] hooks, *Yearning*, points out that sexuality "has always provided gendered metaphors for colonization," and this "political power of representations cannot be ignored," 57 and 72.

[66] Mary Douglas, *Purity and Danger: An Analysis of Concepts of Pollution and Taboo* (New York and Washington: Frederick A. Praeger, 1966), 41.

university. Never completely effective, these statutes were circumvented by false genealogies that new converts purchased and also by local communities that saw little reason to enforce them. Nevertheless, purity of blood statutes implied that "tainted" people would pollute "pure" Christians through marriage, and their offspring would clearly be tainted. These laws assumed that converted Jews and Muslims, often called "New Christians," could never attain the purity of "Old Christians." As historian Ricardo García Cárcel has noted, purity of blood statutes transformed an old religious problem of difference into a new social problem of biology.[67]

In many ways, oppression of Moriscos involved "rituals of separation" that Douglas noted would hold in relationship the "key-stone, boundaries, margins and internal lines" of the "total structure of thought."[68] Through solemn public announcements and ceremonies, Christian sheriffs and clerics separated Moriscos from their mosques and bathhouses, their religious leaders and language, their music and dance, their traditions of food preparation and consumption. Forbidding such aspects of their culture, authorities believed, provided the best defense against Moriscos' powers of pollution. Old Christians also separated themselves from Moriscos through rituals of genealogical accounting required by purity of blood statutes that strongly discouraged intermarriage, through inquisitorial rites that prosecuted and punished Moriscos for apostasy, and through slavery that literally branded Morisco arms and faces.

Golden Age literature justified such rituals by emphasizing the deceit of these people and their proclivity for witchcraft. Traditions of witchcraft, which historical records describe among Christians as well as Moriscos, included love magic, through which women in particular sought to control the object of their affection.[69] Note here the sexual

[67] Ricardo García Cárcel, "Las mujeres conversas en el siglo XVI," in *Historia de las mujeres de Occidente*, 3:603–604.

[68] Douglas, *Purity and Danger*, 41.

[69] Julio Caro Baroja, *Los moriscos del Reino de Granada (Ensayo de Historia Social)* (Madrid: Artes Gráficas, 1957), 113, makes this point and says there was not much difference in the love magic of Christians and Moriscos. For more on women and love magic, see María Helena Sánchez Ortega, *La mujer y la sexualidad en el antiguo régimen: La perspectiva inquisitorial* (Madrid: Ediciones Akal, 1992), 138–153; Sánchez Ortega, "Sorcery and Eroticism in Love Magic," 58–92; and Cardaillac-Hermosilla, "Quand les morisques," 477–505. For literary references, see Caro Baroja, *Los moriscos del Reino de Granada*, 229–230, where he discusses the old Morisca witch in *La pícara Justina* and the fame of Moriscas as witches in *Guzmán de Alfarache*; and also José María Delgado Gallego, "Maurofilia y maurofobia, dos caras de la misma moneda?" in *Narraciones moriscas* (Seville: Editoriales Andaluzas Unidas, 1986), esp. 22–30 for discussion of Cervantes's exemplary story, "El coloquio de los perros."

basis for Christian fears of Morisco pollution. The practice of witchcraft not only gave women power over men and thus inverted gender power positions; it also threatened to rob men of control over their own sexuality. Morisco beliefs appear in Aljamiado literature, such as the *Libro de dichox marabilloxox,* which includes charms for capturing the person one loves and cabalistic signs for love affairs, as well as one recipe for the man who hates his wife and another to make a man love a particular woman.[70] Several cases before the Inquisition demonstrate the persistence of love magic traditions; for example, a Morisca of Aragon asked another Morisca for a piece of paper containing a written formula that would restore peace between her husband and herself.[71] Such formulas not only used the forbidden writing of Aljamía but also assumed the power of women to know and to use supernatural forces.

Christians saw sexual menace in Moriscos' inversion of gender prescriptions by which Christians attempted to order their world. Morisco women performed heavy physical work and agricultural labor that Christians usually left to men.[72] And Morisco men dressed as women to entice Christian soldiers into deadly ambush.[73] As Christian oppression increased during the sixteenth century, Morisco women assumed roles that men usually carried out in their community, particularly as religious teachers and leaders of an opposition to Christian attempts to obliterate their culture.[74] Reports from the battlefields of the rebellion of 1568–1570 described a Morisca amazon armed with sword and helmet, as well as Moriscas fighting alongside the men.[75]

In their very appearance, Moriscos presented themselves as dangerous deviants from Christian gender prescriptions. Traditional Morisco costumes in Granada, for example, featured *calzas,* or loose trousers,

[70] Ribera and Asín, *Manuscritos árabes y aljamiados,* 99–101.

[71] Jacqueline Fournel-Guérin, "La femme morisque en Aragon," in *Les Morisques et leur temps* (Paris: Centre National de la Recherche Scientifique, 1983), 536.

[72] For example, see the response of the town of San Clemente, quoted in Domínguez Ortiz and Vincent, *Historia de los moriscos,* 40; and Collantes de Terán Sánchez, *Sevilla en la baja edad media,* 335.

[73] Hurtado de Mendoza, *La guerra de Granada,* 109.

[74] Inquisition cases abound with evidence of women's roles as religious leaders, teachers, and opposition leaders. In addition to AHN, Inquisición, legajo 2075, for the tribunal of Seville, see Juan Aranda Doncel, "Las prácticas musulmanas de los moriscos andaluces a través de las relaciones de causas del tribunal de la inquisición de Córdoba," in *Las prácticas musulmanas de los moriscos andaluces (1492–1609),* ed. Abdejelil Temini, Actas del III Simposio Internacional de Estudios Moriscos (Zaghouan: Centre d'Etudes et de Recherches Ottomanes, Morisques, de Docmentation et d'Information, 1989), 20–21; García Cárcel, *Herejía y sociedad,* 229; and Monter, *Frontiers of Heresy,* 226–227.

[75] *Relación muy verdadera sacada de una carta,* n.p. Bunes Ibarra, *La imagen de los musulmanes,* notes that in certain Berber tribes women traditionally went to war with the men, 240.

for women and sometimes the *marlota*, a long robe, or "skirts" for men.[76] Christoph Weiditz, who traveled in Iberia during the early sixteenth century, drew women in their traditional costumes in Castile, Aragon, and Portugal. None of the costumes appears more exotic than that of the Moriscas with calzas gathered close to the lower leg. When they went out on the street, these women added a pleated garment that covered most of the body and face, as we saw earlier in figure 1. The drawings of Weiditz suggest the contrast between dress for Christian women and that for Moriscas. Although Morisca costumes actually covered the body more completely than did the clothing Christian women usually wore, Moriscas may have appeared to Christians as more seductive in their enticing difference and mystery.

Despite the evidence of communities in which Moriscos lived peacefully with Christians, many Christian authorities perceived Moriscos as a foreign group—not only as potential spies for the Turks, but also because their very presence symbolized disorder. In gendered form their presence became a sexual menace that seemed especially dangerous.[77] It unleashed a gender inversion in which some women sought to control the sexuality of men, assumed many male roles, and also wore trousers. At the same time, the men were believed to encourage juvenile sexual activity in both early marriages and liaisons with boys, engaging in nonreproductive heterosexual behavior and "unnatural" homosexual acts of sodomy. Not surprisingly, both sexual and ethnic purity acted as pillars to support political legitimacy in early modern Spain.[78]

Nevertheless, not all Christians feared Moriscos as a threat to the purity of their society, nor did they all withdraw behind the membranes of their social body, hoping that this would protect them from the menace of difference. For centuries Christians and Muslims had negotiated the boundaries between their cultures, intermingling often as neighbors and foes, less often but more intimately through marriage and other sexual relationships. In using the body as a metaphor for society, in fact, we see not only the fear of polluting intrusions but also

[76] Vincent, "50,000 moriscos almerienses," 508.

[77] R. I. Moore makes this point very clearly as he discusses the political applications of Douglas's theory of pollution in his book, *The Formation of a Persecuting Society: Power and Deviance in Western Europe, 950–1250* (Oxford: Basil Blackwell, 1987), 100. Mirrer, *Women, Jews, and Muslims*, 47–80, shows that Christians effeminized Jewish and Muslim men in late medieval Castilian literature.

[78] See Elizabeth Lehfeldt's important essay, "Ruling Sexuality: The Political Legitimacy of Isabel of Castile," *Renaissance Quarterly* 53 (2000): 31–56, esp. 48–49 for the political significance of both ethnic and sexual purity for establishing the political legitimacy of Isabel.

the permeability of social boundaries. Because certain membranes, such as the tympanum and the hymen, can be penetrated, they permit what may be problematic transitions between inside and outside the body.[79] Christians violated Morisco hymens through sexual behavior, and they outraged Morisco tympani by prohibiting their language and music, insisting that all aural communication must be through the Castilian tongue and musical traditions.

Yet even as they perceived Moriscos and Muslims as sources of pollution, many Christians paradoxically transformed Morisco difference into an eroticism that could lead to a mingling of their bodies.[80] Christian men demonstrated their subjugation of Muslim men by taking their women as slaves and concubines, and they also sought Moriscas and foreign Muslim women in the countless brothels of early modern Spain.[81] While the numbers of these women is not known, their sexual availability was assumed—not only because they were in a brothel, but also because they were female "others."[82] Brothel patrons sought them out for the very eroticisms forbidden in Christian culture; and they valued them for their knowledge of love magic and spells.

Some Moriscos and Christians intermarried, and in 1526 Charles V even encouraged intermarriage as a way to promote assimilation. Later in the sixteenth century, Ignacio de las Casas, a Morisco Jesuit, wrote in support of intermarriage between Christians and Moriscos.[83] However, religious leaders on both sides opposed it, fearing that marriage to a person outside their religion would dilute their faith. Records show that in reality few Christians and Moriscos intermarried.[84] Perhaps the disadvantages enacted in purity of blood statutes discouraged such marriages, and a mutual suspicion dampened the eroticism of difference. Christian views of Morisco men as effeminate and passive may have further restrained Christian women from taking an interest in them, although these men were also seen as embodying a dangerous masculinity powerful in both procreation and military action. Morisco women, whom many Christians believed were lewd and wanton, might have been exotic sexual objects; but they seemed to be appro-

[79] P. J. Smith, *Representing the Other*, 88–90.

[80] See Pedro Calderón de la Barca, "Amar después de la muerte," in *Teatro Selecto* (Madrid: Librería de Pderlado, Páez y Compañía, 1910), 2:451–569, for some genuine love relationships between Christian and Morisco men and women.

[81] Vincent, *Minorías y marginados*, 65; the phrase in Spanish is "moras de allende."

[82] Mirrer, *Women, Jews, and Muslims*, esp. 2 and 31. See also Vincent, *Minorías y marginados*, 65.

[83] Borja de Medina, "La Compañía de Jesús," 21.

[84] Vincent, *Minorías y marginadas*, 25–27.

priate marriage partners for a Christian man only if they brought with them a substantial dowry.

Morisco differences, in fact, became distorted and exaggerated into stereotypes that further marginalized them. Ironically, however, the more that Christians marginalized their enemy, the more menacing and resisting and polluting this enemy became.[85] Using their imagistic power, Christian writers portrayed Morisco men as flabby and effeminate sodomites and pedophiles—perhaps in an effort to discredit their masculine reproductive and military powers. Christian critics described Morisco women as obstinate, lewd, and treacherous, slyly hiding behind veils. For many, such an alien and polluting presence required active opposition to protect the purity of the social body.

Frustrated in their efforts to enforce assimilation, Christian authorities complained about Morisco "obstinacy" and "perversity."[86] Emphasizing such Muslim practices as circumcision and polygamy, writers such as Pedro Aznar Cardona portrayed Morisco women and men through gender-specific sexual stereotypes, describing the women as wanton, the men as lascivious, and both as multiplying like rabbits or weeds.[87] Moreover, Christians proposed sexual solutions for the "Morisco problem," whether forced assimilation through intermarriage, or castration and slavery as a means to limit and finally to terminate their reproduction.[88]

Foreign Bodies in the Body Politic

In their difference, Moriscos appeared to be foreign bodies that had invaded the body politic and required a defense against the pollution they caused. Viewing the body as a social construct that acts as a metaphor for society, we see it not only as the site of difference, deviance, and resistance, but also as the site of prohibition, condemnation, and punishment.[89] Christian authorities attempted to weaken the Moriscos'

[85] Sibley, *Outsiders*, describes the process of polarization that increases and confirms stereotypes, at 29.

[86] Memorial of Fray Nicolás del Río to Philip III, from Valencia, June 13, 1606, reprinted in García Arenal, *Los moriscos*, 125–133.

[87] Aznar Cardona, *Expulsión justificadas*, quoted in García Arenal, *Los moriscos*, 233.

[88] For solutions suggested for the "Morisco problem," see the informe of Don Alonso Gutiérrez, reprinted in Boronat y Barrachina, *Los moriscos españoles*, 1:637; and Domínguez Ortiz and Vincent, *Historia de los moriscos*, 71.

[89] Trinh speaks of the body of ethnic women as "site of differences," in *Woman, Native, Other*, 44.

determination to preserve their strongly embodied self-identity through a variety of strategies, each of which targeted the Morisco body. They pathologized their difference as illness or wound that had to be contained, neutralized, purged, bled, or burned. Their responses inscribed deviance on the Morisco body even as they punished it.

Once the Inquisition arrested a person who had been denounced, it imprisoned and examined the suspect. The bodies of these prisoners were now caught in a web of confinement and made to appear before inquisitors and respond to their questions. Usually those who voluntarily confessed to accusations against them did not have to endure examination under torture. The prisoners who did not confess to the satisfaction of inquisitors were "put to the question with torture."[90] Drawing upon methods already used by other ecclesiastical and secular tribunals, the Inquisition usually chose to use the pulley, the rack, or water torture. Examiners stripped both men and women prisoners of their clothing before they began the torture.[91]

Because inquisitors believed that women would be more likely than men to break when stripped and subjected to torture, they often tried to arrest women along with men, hoping the former would give evidence against the latter. Ana Calabera, however, declared to the officer who took her into custody in Zaragoza that she would not denounce her brother or cousins even if the torture tore her into pieces.[92] Ana Serrano confessed to inquisitors in the same tribunal that she had prepared the body of her two-year-old son for burial in the Muslim manner, but she insisted that she had done these things "for love," and not to carry out a Moorish ceremony. Obviously dissatisfied with her explanation, inquisitors ordered that she be examined under torture "for intention and accomplices."[93] When prisoners such as Ana Serrano finally made a satisfactory confession while being tortured, they had to ratify their confessions the next day so that they could not later rescind them as statements made under duress.

To better control their prisoners, inquisitors sought to isolate them not only from outsiders but also from other prisoners. Lack of space, however, meant that many Moriscos found ways to communicate with one another and even to perform Islamic ceremonies while they were confined in prison. A Morisca imprisoned with Gerónima de Alquerini in Zaragoza told inquisitors that she had seen Gerónima perform ritual

[90] See the case of Isabel, widow of Bachiller Pedro de Molina, in Gracia Boix, *Autos de fe*, 55.

[91] Kamen, *Inquisition and Society*, 175.

[92] AHN, Inquisición, libro 991, 131v–132.

[93] AHN, Inquisición, libro 991, 130–130v; the phrases are "por amor" and "por la intención y complices."

bathing and Muslim prayers in prison many times. Inquisitors added one hundred lashes to their punishment for Gerónima "because she had made [Muslim] ceremonies" in the prison.[94] Angela de Ambroz also received one hundred lashes when she was sentenced "for having communicated her confessions with fellow prisoners, violating the oath of secrecy that she had given."[95]

In cases where the wrongdoing seemed especially serious, the Holy Office could add "perpetual prison," but lack of prison space and supervision meant that inquisitors could rarely enforce lifetime imprisonment. Sometimes it was commuted for men to galley service for a certain number of years or, for women, to service in a hospital or convent. Baltasar Junila, for example, confessed to the Inquisition in Cordova that he had lived as a Moor from the time he had joined Morisco rebels in the mountains. He was sentenced to "perpetual prison, and that five years of that detention be at the oars in the galleys of his majesty without pay, and after complying to return to this Holy Office so that it might order what he must do."[96] Although five years of galley service may sound much more lenient than a life term in prison, rowing the galleys could be so harsh that it would become a life sentence ending with early death.

Inquisitors had the power to increase or decrease punishments, depending on the offense and the prisoner's status. They added whippings to punishments for slaves and for prisoners who had committed especially serious offenses. We have already seen that Gerónima de Alquerini received the additional punishment of one hundred lashes "for having made [Muslim] ceremonies in the prison," after another prisoner testified against her.[97] Inquisitors in Cordova not only added one hundred lashes to the punishment of Isabel, slave of Juana González, but also required her to appear at the auto de fe with a rope around her neck and carrying the candle of a penitent. Her status as slave compounded the offense she had committed: spitting after receiving the Holy Sacrament.[98] Inquisitors added the rope and candle in the punishment of another slave, Diego el Aulé, because he had disputed and blasphemed Christian teachings; however, they also sentenced him to two hundred lashes and required his owner to instruct him in the

[94] AHN, Inquisición, libro 991, 128v–129: "por aver hecho ceremonias."

[95] AHN, Inquisición, libro 991, 167v–168: "por hacer comunicado sus confessiones con las compañeras de carcel contraviniendo al juramiento de secreto que avia prestado."

[96] Gracia Boix, *Autos de fe*, 142–143: "cárcel perpetua; y que tenga la carcelería por cinco años en las galeras de su majestad al remo y sin sueldo y complidos vuleva a este Santo Oficio para que se le ordene lo que deba hacer."

[97] AHN, Inquisición, libro 991, 128v–129: "por aver hecho ceremonios en la carcel."

[98] Gracia Boix, *Autos de fe*, 55.

faith.[99] To the punishment of Gaspar Gasto, found guilty of living as a Moor and teaching others to do so, inquisitors in Zaragoza added one hundred lashes because he had met with other Moriscos in prison and encouraged them to profess Islam even when they were tortured.[100]

Those found to be unrepentant or relapsed heretics faced the punishment of being burned alive. They were "relaxed" to the secular arm of justice because law prohibited the Inquisition from actually carrying out a death sentence. Frequently prisoners facing the sentence to burn at the stake would choose to "repent" at the last minute in an auto de fe so that strangulation before burning would make their deaths less painful. When inquisitors in Cuenca told Francisco de Espinosa that they would have to excommunicate him for his "crimes of heresy" and "could relax his person to the justice and secular arm," they added that they wanted "to use with him equity and mercy and not to follow the rigor of justice." He made the confession they wished and escaped the stake, instead serving three years in prison, and hearing Mass and sermons on Sundays and feast days. In addition, he was to wear for the rest of his life the *sanbenito*, the penitential garment meant to mark and humiliate condemned people.[101]

Our discussion of how Moriscos perceived their bodies and how Christian authorities sought to protect themselves by punishing those bodies publicly provides insights that can be applied to all muted groups—not only in the past, but also in the present.[102] Just as Madalena's story is not merely that of a single woman, the Moriscos' story is not limited to one minority group in early modern Spain. When we consider the embodied knowledge of these people, we see that their story demonstrates how we perceive, oppress, and attempt to preserve

[99] Gracia Boix, *Autos de fe*, 73.

[100] AHN, Inquisición, libro 991, 119–119v: "cien açotes por las comunicaciones de carceles."

[101] García Arenal, *Inquisición y moriscos*, app. 2, 126; the phrase is "pudieramos relaxar su persona a la justicia y brazo seglar mas queriendo usar con el de hequidad y misericordia y no seguir el rigor de la justicia."

[102] Scholarly literature on the body in history has increased considerably. I wish to thank Aurora Morcillo for discussing some of the recent literature with me and for the very helpful bibliography in her book, *True Catholic Womanhood: Gender Ideology in Franco's Spain* (DeKalb: Northern Illinois University Press, 2000). Readers may want to see especially the following works: Leslie A. Adelson, *Making Bodies, Making History: Feminism and German Identity* (Lincoln: University of Nebraska Press, 1993); Judith Butler, *Bodies That Matter: On the Discursive Limits of "Sex"* (New York: Routledge, 1993); Kathleen Canning, "The Body as Method? Reflections on the Place of the Body in Gender History," *Gender and History* 11:3 (November 1999): 499–513; and Caroline Walker Bynum, *Fragmentation and Redemption: Essays on Gender and the Female Body in Medieval Religion* (New York: Zone Books, 1992).

difference—issues of tremendous importance in our own society of the present time. The broader theoretical possibilities of the body become more apparent if we complement historical studies with approaches by anthropologists and sociologists.

Consider, for example, the body as site of difference. As we have already seen in the case of Moriscos, they identified themselves and others defined them as different because of what they did with their bodies. Moreover, this difference became inscribed in purity of blood laws that treated their difference as a matter of blood and thus racialized it as biological inheritance. In a sociological view, such difference is inherited not through biology but through culture-based ethnicity, which preserves itself by boundary mechanisms such as endogamy, lack of intermarriage with other groups. The body acts as one of the major "building blocks" of ethnicity, according to sociologist Manning Nash. It is essential to the "core trinity of ethnicity," which consists of blood, substance, and cult—that is, kinship, material culture, and religion.[103] Notice that blood cannot be separated from the body, that substance is produced and used by the body, and that the sacred beliefs of cult are expressed through the body.

But Moriscos tell us about the body not only as site of difference, but also as site of deviance and oppression. Inquisitors, as we saw earlier, prosecuted Madalena not for her beliefs but for how she washed herself. Her early morning bath broke the boundaries of diversity allowed in her Christian-ruled city, and her deviant body threatened Spanish society with an impurity that Christian officials believed must be neutralized through punishment. In the view of sociologist Kai Erikson, every community identifies and punishes its own deviants as a way to define itself and maintain its boundaries.[104] Moreover, any "bounded system" can be viewed as a body, according to anthropologist Mary Douglas, and it seeks to protect itself from pollution or impurity that can attack inner as well as outer boundaries.[105] Christian authorities in the body politic of sixteenth-century Spain saw Moriscos as such a mortal danger that eventually they considered it necessary to expel them.

Moriscos tell us about the body as site of resistance, as well. Sometimes overt, as in open rebellion, more often covert, their resistance derived from an embodied knowledge of their own identity that they could not or would not forget. Anthropologist James Scott studies

[103] Manning Nash, *The Cauldron of Ethnicity in the Modern World* (Chicago: University of Chicago Press, 1989), 5, 10–11, 35.

[104] Kai T. Erikson, *Wayward Puritans: A Study in the Sociology of Deviance* (Jew York: John Wiley and Sons, 1966), 9–11.

[105] Douglas, *Purity and Danger*, 114–115.

what he calls "everyday resistance," which subordinate people carry out through individual acts such as foot-dragging, dissimulation, false compliance, and feigned ignorance. Lacking power to openly challenge a dominant order, these people—whom he characterizes as "history's losers"— nevertheless engage in a resistance that requires "little or no coordination or planning." The very "banality" of such resistance reveals the "normal context" and ordinary ways that social conflict occurs.[106] All historical resistance by subordinate classes begins, Scott proposes, "close to the ground, rooted firmly in the homely but meaningful realities of daily experience."[107]

As we review Morisco cases before the Inquisition, we see that the great majority of offenses involved ordinary daily experiences. We will probably never know for certain whether the offensive acts were intentionally resistant. Did Madalena, for example, consciously intend her early morning bath to be an act of resistance? Some of the Moriscos' acts may have been conscious behavior deliberately intended to resist the dominant Christians, but many others may have been unconscious repetitions of daily habits that had been inscribed in their bodies as children. Did Madalena have any control over how observers projected on her their fears and desires, concocted stories about her act of washing, and denounced her to the Inquisition? Like so many members of muted groups, Madalena presents very sparse historical evidence. Left with more questions than answers, we can conclude, nonetheless, that Madalena's bath represents a knowledge of the body which two of her neighbors perceived as resistance to Christianization and grounds for denunciation. But the bath is more than Madalena. It represents the identities of countless Moriscos and the dangers of embodied knowledge for minority people throughout the world.

[106] James Scott, *Weapons of the Weak*, 27, 29, and 33.
[107] Scott, *Weapons of the Weak*, 348.

3

DANGEROUS DOMESTICITY

NOT ONLY did embodied knowledge become dangerous for Moriscos in sixteenth-century Spain; so also did their homes. As we saw in the previous chapter, Christian authorities increased their attempts to prohibit any expression of Muslim culture and religion after expelling Muslims in 1502. In response, many Moriscos transformed their homes into a space of resistance. Within this domestic space, the women in particular taught their children the prohibited Arabic language as well as Muslim prayers.[1] Moriscas supervised their households in the observation of Muslim holy days and fasts, circumcision of male infants, dietary restrictions, and ritual washing of the body for daily prayer and for burial. Even when subjected to arrest, interrogation, imprisonment, and punishment by the Inquisition, these women continued to devise strategies of resistance.[2]

Morisco responses to Christians' prohibitions on their culture included both covert domestic resistance and overt armed rebellion. Their historical memory of armed conflicts with Christians during centuries of the Reconquest merged with knowledge that Ottoman Turks could provide armed help in the sixteenth century. Yet they also knew from living under Christian rulers in the later medieval period that

[1] Morisco historical memory may have included knowledge that in the medieval period children were taught in Hispano-Muslim homes as well as in mosques and schools attached to mosques. Boys and girls were both instructed, although they were separated after they became older. For more on the teaching of children before and after forced conversion to Christianity, see Anwar G. Chejne, *Islam and the West: The Moriscos* (Albany: SUNY Press, 1983), esp. 32; and Julián Ribera y Tarragó, *La enseñanza entre los musulmanes españoles. Bibliófilos y bibliotecas en la España musulmana* (Cordova: Real Academia de Córdoba, 1925), 72–73 and 84–86.

[2] See, for example, Galia Hasenfeld, "Women between Islam and Christianity: The Moriscos according to Inquisition Trial Records from Cuenca," (Ph.D. diss., Tel-Aviv University, 2002). Compare this with recent work on Judeo-conversas, such as Deborah S. Ellis, "Domesticating the Spanish Inquisition," *Violence against Women in Medieval Texts*, ed. Anna Roberts (Gainsville: University Press of Florida, 1998), 195–209; Melammed, *Heretics or Daughters of Israel?*; and three essays by Renée Levine Melammed: "Sephardi Women in the Medieval and Early Modern Periods," in *Jewish Women in Historical Perspective*, ed. Judith R. Baskin (Detroit: Wayne State University Press, 1991), 115–134; "Sixteenth-Century Justice in Action: The Case of Isabel López," *Revue des études juives* 145:1–2 (1986): 51–73; and "Women in (Post-1492) Spanish Crypto-Jewish Society," *Judaism* 41:2 (Spring 1992): 156–168.

they had been able to preserve their culture in their own homes. Frequently overlooked in studies that focus on the history of men and battles, covert resistance from the home actually played a major role in Morisco-Christian relations. A focus in particular on the experiences of Morisco women provides clear evidence of domestic resistance.

The political significance of gender, domestic space, and everyday acts becomes apparent as we examine Moriscos' domestic rituals and Christians' official attempts to prohibit them. Not all Moriscos and Christians engaged in this conflict, of course. Moriscos varied widely in their assimilation or resistance, with some consciously attempting to assimilate into the dominant Christian culture.[3] Nevertheless, evidence of Morisco resistance in their homes appears not only in Inquisition records—where it would be expected—but also in secular and ecclesiastical documents, in writings of both Christians and Moriscos, and in Aljamiado literature. These sources show that Morisco homes changed as they adapted to changing conditions in the sixteenth century. During this time Moriscos, most notably the women, became politicized as their homes were invaded, as they chose to resist the obliteration of their culture, and as their private rituals were transformed into public penance.

Politicization of the Morisco Home

The political significance of the home had long been recognized by Muslims of Iberia. In his treatise published in al-Andalus at the beginning of the twelfth century, Ibn ᶜAbdun described the importance of homes for municipal government. Homes should be "protected and watched," he declared, "since goods are deposited in them and lives are guarded."[4] Both a refuge and a depository, the Muslim home pro-

[3] For example, see discussion of the Moriscos who became Christian prelates and attempted to Christianize other Moriscos, in Borja de Medina, "La Compañía de Jesús," 3–136. Helpful studies of Muslims and Moriscos integrated into Christian society include Meyerson, *The Muslims of Valencia*; Tapia Sánchez, *La comunidad morisca de Avila*; the recent work on Moriscos of Aragon by Mary Halavais, *Like Wheat to the Miller: Community, Convivencia, and the Construction of Morisco Identity in Sixteenth-Century Aragon* (New York: Columbia University Press, 2002); James Tueller, *Good and Faithful Christians: Moriscos and Catholicism in Early Modern Spain* (New Orleans: University Press of the South, 2002); and James Tueller, "The Assimilating Morisco: Four Families in Valladolid prior to the Expulsion of 1610," *Mediterranean Studies* 7 (1997): 167–177.

[4] Ibn ᶜAbdun, *Sevilla a comienzos del siglo XII. El Tratado de Ibn ᶜAbdun*, ed. and trans. Emilio Gracía Gómez and E. Levi-Provençal (Seville: Servicio Municipal de Publicaciones, 1981), 112, also quoted in Bosch Vilá, "La Sevilla islámica," 242. I use the terms

tected the family, which acted as the core for the *umma*, or community of believers.[5] Whether the mud-walled, earthen-floored hovel of poor day laborers or the tiled and carved palace of the wealthy, the home provided the essential bedrock for the orderly Islamic community. Its strength derived from a fusion of spiritual, physical, and material concerns.

Ironically, Christians and Moriscos, who differed in many respects, shared common ideals of women and home. Domestic space, according to both cultures in early modern Spain, should provide protection for women and family honor. For Ibn ʿAbdun, "[H]omes are shelters in which souls, spirits, and bodies take refuge."[6] Not meant strictly to enclose women, the Muslim home nevertheless was a private space most closely associated with women, while men were expected to live actively in public spaces.[7] When Muslim women ventured out of the home in al-Andalus, they were directed to remain separate from men—not to sit with them on the banks of the river, nor even to take the same street to the river on festival days.[8] Traditional law and custom for Muslims encased women in marriages in which husbands would maintain and provide for them, while wives would bear children and care for their families.[9]

The Christian society that Moriscos were expected to adapt to in sixteenth-century Spain also idealized the protective home and a domestic politics based on the "natural domesticity" of women. Fray Luis de León, who wrote *La perfecta casada* (The perfect wife) in 1583, based

---

"politicization" and "political significance" here in the sense that the Morisco home and Moriscos themselves became increasingly entwined with a larger power system that viewed them as a danger to the political order.

[5] Ira M. Lapidus, *A History of Islamic Societies* (Cambridge: Cambridge University Press, 1988), 31.

[6] Ibn ʿAbdun, *Tratado,* 112. Mikel de Epalza, *Los moriscos antes y después de la expulsión* (Madrid: Editorial Mapfre, 1992), notes a "certain reclusion of the woman," especially in urban areas, 103; for more of his discussion of the Morisco family, see 103–105.

[7] A. Cano et al., "La mujer andalusi, elementos para su historia," in *Las mujeres medievales y su ámbito jurídico,* ed. María Angeles Durán and Cristina Segura Graiño (Madrid: Técnicas Gráficas, 1983), 183–189; Pierre Guichard, *Al-Andalus: Estructura antropológica de una sociedad islámica en occidente* (Barcelona: Barral Editores, 1976), esp. 79; and Julian Pitt-Rivers, *The Fate of Shechem, or the Politics of Sex: Essays in the Anthropology of the Mediterranean* (Cambridge: Harvard University Press, 1971).

[8] Ibn ʿAbdun, *Tratado,* lists many prohibitions on women in public places, esp. 142–146.

[9] *Leyes de moros del siglo XIV,* in *Memorial Histórico Español* (Madrid: Real Academia de la Historia, 1853), 5:11–246; and Margarita María Birriel Salcedo, "Notas sobre el matrimonio de los moriscos granadinos (1563)," in *Mélanges Louis Cardaillac,* ed. Abdeljelil Temini (Zaghouan: Fondation Temini pour la Recherche Scientifique et l'Information, 1993), 1:97–105.

his prescription for women on analogies with nature. The fish, he noted, swims in peace and security in water and cannot live outside it. Likewise, the good woman cannot live outside the peace and security of her home.[10] Juan de la Cerda, a Christian moralist writing in the sixteenth century, urged parents to keep their daughters enclosed in the home. Here parents could train girls to become virtuous women and guard their purity "as dragons."[11] Biblical verses and traditional proverbs in writings of this period emphasized a "natural" order of the sexes that required enclosure for females, in either home, convent, or brothel. This order had to be protected in particular from women who left the security of their enclosure to wander about the dangerous spaces outside where they could lose their virtue and cause their families to lose their honor.[12]

During the sixteenth century Morisco homes became politicized in response to Christian attempts to prohibit their culture. Following the rebellion of Muslims in Granada at the beginning of the sixteenth century, mass baptisms of 50,000–70,000 Muslims created a new group of converts who Christian authorities had good reason to believe were mostly Christian in name only.[13] At first, the Church and monarchy sought to catechize these new converts and to grant them an interim of six years during which they would be expected to gradually abandon their Muslim customs and Arabic language. Royal decrees extended this dispensation for another twenty years, although authorities required that all writings in Arabic and Aljamía be handed in for inspection. They then burned in public bonfires those writings relating to Islam.[14]

The forcible baptism of thousands of additional Muslims during the Germanía Revolt in 1520–1521 multiplied Christian suspicions of false converts. Five years later a junta of Church leaders formalized these

[10] Fray Luis de León, *La perfecta casada* (1583), in *Biblioteca de Autores Españoles* (Madrid: M. Rivadeneyra, 1855), 37:211–246.

[11] Juan de la Cerda, *Vida política de todos los estados de mugeres: en el qual se dan muy provechosos y Christianos documentos y avisos, para criarse y conservarse devidamente las mugeres en sus etados* (Alcalá de Henares: Juan Gracian, 1599), 242r.

[12] See, for example, Juan de Espinosa, *Diálogo en laude de las mujeres* (1580), ed. Angela González Simón (Madrid: Consejo Superior de Investigaciones Científicas, 1946), 258, who discusses the proverb "Ni espada rota, ni mujer que trota" (neither broken sword nor wandering woman).

[13] For an account of these baptisms, see Domínguez Ortiz and Vincent, *Historia de los moriscos*, 17–19; and Nykel, *Compendium*, 27. Note that efforts to catechize Moriscos continued almost up to their expulsion, beginning in 1609.

[14] José Capdevila Orozco, *Errantes y expulsados. Normativas jurídicas contra gitanos, judíos, y moriscos* (Cordova: F. Baena, 1991), 111–112.

baptisms, deciding that the new converts must be considered Christians and forbidding all Morisco "particularism," including songs, dances, bathing, and the ritual slaughter of animals.[15] All expressions of Muslim culture now became evidence of Islam and thus apostasy, although Moriscos were still able to buy some time from prosecution by the Inquisition. An edict of grace issued by the Inquisition in Seville in July 1548 assured Moriscos that they would not be prosecuted for past errors, nor would their goods be confiscated from them or their heirs. Nevertheless, the edict required that each Morisco family live apart from all others, perhaps an attempt to break the strength of Morisco kinship groups and extended families. Moreover, it required Moriscos to live among Old Christians and to marry their sons and daughters to Old Christians. The edict required Moriscos to follow burial practices of Old Christians, live faithfully as Catholics, and send their children to be instructed in the Catholic faith.[16]

From the late fifteenth century, Christian efforts to convert Muslims targeted their children, who they hoped would not only grow up to become a new generation of loyal Christian subjects, but would also invert the usual generational order by teaching the basics of Christian doctrine—and a love for it—to their parents. Clerics especially sought young Muslim children, whom they saw as least resistant to Christian proselytizing, presumably because they had not yet learned Muslim beliefs or internalized the abhorrence with which Muslim adults regarded Christians. Moreover, officials could treat young children as potential hostages, whom they could take away from parents who resisted conversion. Archbishop of Granada Pedro Guerrero declared that Morisco boys should be educated in Christian schools and cut off completely from contact with their families.[17] Such action was justified, both secular and ecclesiastical officials argued, to protect the souls of the newly converted children; they did not add that the threat that their small children might be taken also worked to discourage expressions of resistance by Muslim parents.

[15] Domínguez Ortiz and Vincent, *Historia de los moriscos*, 22.

[16] AHN, Inquisición, libro 1254. Undoubtedly, Old Christians varied in their responses to this edict. Some would oppose marrying their sons and daughters to those of Moriscos, recognizing that their grandchildren would then be barred from many privileges by purity of blood statutes; see chapter 2, above. In none of the documents that I have read does the Inquisition call for Judeo-conversos to intermarry with Old Christians as a means to better assimilate them, although some of its edicts warn that both Jews and "infidels" (*infieles*) could lead the faithful away from the Church; see, e.g., AHN, Inquisición, libro 1229, fol. 37.

[17] Vincent, *Minorías y marginados*, 26, discusses the instructions of the archbishop, which were issued in 1555–1560.

In the later sixteenth century, Jesuits established schools for Morisco children in Granada and Valencia. A report from the Jesuit school in the Morisco quarter of Albaicín in Granada tells of young children going with their older brothers and sisters into the church each morning to take holy water, make the sign of the cross, and say the basic prayers.[18] In the school, which was held outside in good weather in the cemetery next to the church, a youth whom the Jesuits had assigned to the pre-reading group would recite and drill the young children in basic articles of faith such as the Lord's Prayer, the rosary, and the creed. Attempting to teach to their children a religion and culture alien to most Morisco parents, these schools succeeded mostly in offending the parents.

Girls, who were assigned a section in the church for daily prayers separate from the boys, were not to stay to attend school with them.[19] For several years, girls returned home to their own parishes, where Jesuits came to teach them, but later Jesuits rented another house in a central location in Albaicín where they established a school for Morisco girls. They entrusted them to two older women, who were to train them for both domestic tasks and acculturation. The girls learned needlework, a typical household craft that reinforced their domesticity. In addition, they learned Christian doctrine and reading and writing in the Castilian language, which they scarcely knew.[20] Once a week a priest would visit to talk with the girls.

Jesuits took a more active role in teaching boys in this gender-specific school system, dividing the pupils into three groups based on age and ability. They taught the older boys to read, write, and count; and they provided them with paper, quills, and primers free of charge. Boys showing the most aptitude and receptivity were trained to accompany Jesuits and translate their Castilian words into Arabic when they went to preach to Morisco adults. Some of these Morisco boys went on to enter the Jesuit Order and carry on the tasks of converting other Moriscos, becoming in a sense "conquerors" of their own people. Not surprisingly, many Moriscos strongly opposed these schools as a usurpation of their parental role to teach their own children.[21]

As baptized Muslims could no longer freely visit a mosque or publicly observe Islam, many Morisco homes became refuges for Muslim traditions and expressions of faith. For centuries Hispano-Muslims

[18] Borja de Medina, "La Compañía de Jesús," 69–73.

[19] Borja de Medina, "La Compañía de Jesús," 69.

[20] Borja de Medina, "La Compañía de Jesús," 72.

[21] An account of the opposition of Moriscos, especially the opposition of the women, to these schools is in García Arenal, *Los moriscos*, 122.

had built their houses with few windows and with interior courtyards designed to accommodate the Mediterranean climate as well as protect women and family honor. In addition, this domestic architecture became useful during the sixteenth century as a means of shielding household activities from outside observation. Although some homes that also functioned as sites of businesses and artisanal services opened their doors and gates to the street during the day, many Morisco houses presented to the street blank whitewashed walls or shuttered windows and balconies. Such shutters allowed those inside to see the street and enjoy the movement of air, and they also protected them from the sun and from being seen by outsiders.[22] This domestic architecture veiled from public view activities in the home and the hidden doors that led to adjoining houses. It also hid small nooks and crannies where religious and cultural objects that were prohibited in the sixteenth century could be safe from view. Often clustered with other Morisco homes on slopes and narrow winding streets, these houses strengthened a sense of community even as their location discouraged visits from outsiders.[23]

It is easy to assume that Morisco homes that attempted to shelter such an intricate network of family relationships fit neatly into the center/margins paradigm discussed in the introduction. Clearly, these homes appear far from official centers of Christian power. Yet our observation of Morisco homes suggests that marginality offers certain advantages to women and other nonelite peoples. The margins are "much more than a place of deprivation," as one cultural critic notes; for they are also "the site of radical possibility, a space of resistance."[24] Paradoxically, the margin itself becomes a center—a "central location for the production of a counter-hegemonic discourse that is not just found in words but in habits of being and the way one lives."[25] In fact, marginality can become "a site of transformation" where oppressed people build "communities of resistance."[26] Meeting in the margins, these people begin to identify not merely in the terms the center elite uses to define them, but also in terms of their own cultural traditions.

[22] For more on the balcony or overhead projection closed by wooden shutters (called an *ajimez*), see Cano et al., "La mujer andalusi," 186.

[23] Caro Baroja, *Los moriscos del Reino de Granada*, 264–265.

[24] hooks, *Yearning*, 149. For Catherine Hall, *White, Male and Middle-Class* (New York: Routledge, 1992), margins are "very productive terrain—a space from which both to challenge establishments and develop our own perspectives, build our own organizations, confirm our own collectivities," 34.

[25] hooks, *Yearning*, 149. Note that this discussion of the development of a culture of resistance might be extended to other marginal groups, such as delinquents, Gypsies, and pícaros.

[26] hooks, *Yearning*, 213.

Yet even if we agree that marginality can become a center of power, it must preserve distance from the dominant center, protecting itself from being co-opted or absorbed. Moreover, it is only with this distance that those on the margins can develop power and carry out resistance to make an impact on the center, sometimes transforming it and sometimes moving the center to the margins. Muslims who wanted to remain in Spain after the defeat of their rebellion at the beginning of the sixteenth century accepted baptism, but many continued their own cultural practices in their homes, in *morerías* (urban Moorish quarters) or in isolated mountainous and rural villages where few Christians ventured. If an outsider came to one of these isolated areas, the residents would quickly and secretly warn each other against revealing their forbidden culture. Their strategy for survival became palimpsestic, conforming on the surface to obscure a deeper resistance and subversion of the dominant order.[27]

Women in their homes played major roles in the cultural resistance of these people.[28] As Christian authorities determined to destroy the hated Muslim culture, however, they sent sheriffs into Morisco homes unannounced and especially at mealtimes, when they could surprise a family eating food prepared in the Muslim manner, seated on the ground in traditional fashion. The Morisco home could no longer provide either a protective distance on the margins of official power or a female space safe from intrusion. Instead, it became the primary battlefield for the cultural and religious conflicts between Moriscos and Christians. Yet it is important to acknowledge that not all Morisco homes were the same, nor did all Moriscas play identical roles.

Despite their many differences, we see that in the sixteenth century the Morisco home and family changed in response to increasing prohibitions against their cultural and religious practices. Moriscos used the hidden doors and passageways between their houses to facilitate clandestine meetings and preserve their kinship networks.[29] They had to decide whether to hide their children or send them to Christian schools. As their religious leaders disappeared into exile, many Moriscos sought to find ways to preserve Islam and teach it to their children in their homes. Sometimes the men of this community left their homes to join groups of bandits or highwaymen, and in 1568 thou-

[27] Moi, *Sexual/Textual Politics*, discusses the palimpsestic strategy of women writers, but the strategy certainly is also employed by other oppressed groups, 59. For an anthropological approach to strategies of resistance, see James Scott, *Weapons of the Weak*.

[28] See Mary Elizabeth Perry, "Beyond the Veil: Moriscas and the Politics of Resistance and Survival," in *Spanish Women in the Golden Age: Images and Realities*, ed. Magdalena S. Sánchez and Alain Saint-Saëns (Westport and London: Greenwood Press, 1996), 37–53.

[29] Vincent, *Minorías y marginados*, 8–15.

sands of Moriscos in Granada joined an armed rebellion, the focus of the next chapter. Following the defeat of the rebels, many Morisco men were killed or captured as slaves.[30]

Just as Carcayona had assumed the traditionally male task of building a shelter in the wilderness, Moriscas took on the roles of their men in providing a shelter for their children and their faith. In countless everyday tasks, these women prayed, prepared food, consumed it with their families, laundered clothing and household linen, presenting it each week to replace soiled linen, drew water at a fountain or well for washing the body. Such ordinary private acts would become increasingly politicized, publicly and specifically announced in edicts of faith as grounds for denunciation of self or others to the Inquisition.[31]

Domestic Resistance

As we consider Moriscos' resistance to oppression, it is important to acknowledge the complexity of this resistance, the difficulty of proving it was carried out consciously, and the interjection of my own subjectivity. Personally, I would much rather regard Moriscas as strong determined women than as victims to be pitied, but historical evidence does not prove that all these women made a conscious choice to resist oppression. What it does suggest is that some Moriscas consciously chose to resist, some unconsciously resisted, and all of these probably resisted only because of the situation imposed on them. Some of their acts must be regarded as passive resistance rather than as active. And compounding all this are the interactive strategies that these women devised, which combined active conscious resistance with active conscious accommodation.[32] In my judgment, there is no question that Moriscas wanted above all to survive and to assure the survival of their families. Sometimes the imperatives of survival meant that they accommodated Christian regulations even though they might wish to resist them. These women dutifully presented their infants for baptism where they received Christian names, but often they gave them Arabic

[30] The absence of many Morisco men was compounded by the forced dispersion of the Moriscos of Granada throughout Castile; see chapters 4 and 5, below.

[31] For example, see the Edict of Faith in AHN, Inquisición, libro 1244, fols. 105–109.

[32] James Scott, *Weapons of the Weak*, discusses many strategies of resistance and accommodation used by people who lack access to official power, passim. Corteguera, *For the Common Good*, xiii, notes that we historians cannot fully claim to know the "minds and true intentions" of people who lived in the past.

names in clandestine Muslim ceremonies and continued to use these Arabic names in their homes.[33]

Moriscas, like so many other women, became politicized as they responded to threats to their homes and families. When Christians intensified their attempts to obliterate Morisco culture, both the women and men of this community had to become more aware of the context of power in which they sought to survive and to preserve their culture. Traditional Muslim ideals for women might prescribe marriage and homes for them in which men would make decisions and carry out all interactions with outsiders. In sixteenth-century Spain, however, this ideal became impossible to realize. Not only did women in less affluent households have to work outside the home, but Christian authorities visited Morisco homes to look for evidence of continuing observation of Islam.

Historical records show that these women were far more than passive victims powerless to help themselves or their families. As Christian officials moved to prohibit all writings in Arabic or Aljamía, regardless of their subject matter, many Morisco households began to engage in domestic subversion. Moriscos concealed these writings in hollow pillars and false floors, ceilings, and walls in their homes.[34] Morisco women and men hid these texts, the women in particular, perhaps to deflect attention from the men whom inquisitors usually treated as guardians of the written word. Moriscas could also use their clothing to conceal books and papers when outsiders came to look for incriminating evidence. In Jaén, for example, an official entered the house of Elvira Hernández, believing that she was hiding some papers, but she quickly passed a large bundle to Isabel de Aranda, who hid the writings in her skirts. As the official caught sight of her, Isabel de Aranda passed the bundle on to another Morisca, Isabel de Silva. In what must have seemed a desperate game of keep-away, Isabel de Silva concealed the papers in her skirts and swiftly took them to another room, where she hid them beneath a woven grass mat.[35]

Not all Moriscos had access to this Aljamiado literature, nor do we know how many would risk hiding these writings in their homes.

[33] Andrew C. Hess, *The Forgotten Frontier: A History of the Sixteenth-Century Ibero-African Frontier* (Chicago and London: University of Chicago Press, 1978), 144; and Vincent, *Minorías y marginados*, esp. 16.

[34] Nykel, *Compendium*, 29–30; López-Baralt, *Islam in Spanish Literature*, 171–174; and Ribera and Asín, *Manuscritos árabes y aljamiados*, v–xviii, 138, 156–157.

[35] These cases are presented in Gracia Boix, *Autos de fe*, 272–272. For more cases of Moriscas hiding forbidden writings on their bodies, see Ronald E. Surtz, "Morisco Women, Written Texts, and the Valencia Inquisition," *Sixteenth Century Journal* 32:2 (2001): 421–433.

Nonetheless, this forbidden literature may well have empowered the Morisco community that was struggling to survive under very difficult circumstances.[36] Reinforcing a belief that common people could invoke supernatural powers to protect themselves, Aljamiado literature also gathered together many popular beliefs and legends of a centuries-long oral tradition that helped to unify Moriscos in resisting Christian domination.[37]

An Aljamiado manuscript entitled *Caxtigox para lax gentex* demonstrates the great importance that Morisco households placed on the family as a network of mutual rights and responsibilities. One chapter describes the husband's rights over the woman, and another details the wife's rights over the husband. Subsequent chapters include children's obligations to obey fathers and mothers, and the legal issues involved in marriage between sisters and brothers.[38] The recent research of Margarita Birriel Salcedo has shown that in the middle of the sixteenth century, many of the marriage contracts for Moriscos in Granada still sought to preserve these rights and responsibilities.[39]

As one of their responsibilities, Morisco women worked. The domestic economy of most Morisco families required labor from all members except the very young and the very old.[40] Moriscas worked in fields

[36] For example, the legends of Joseph and of Job in this literature emphasized faith and endurance in the face of affliction, and the wife of Job presented a model for women of heroic patience and holy compassion. For the wife of Job, see Guillén Robles, *Leyendas moriscas*, 1:82–83; Antonio Vespertino Rodríguez, ed., *Leyendas aljamiadas y moriscas sobre personajes bíblicos* (Madrid: Editorial Gredos, 1983), 272–299; and chapter 5, below. For the legend of Joseph, which includes a temptress whom he ultimately forgives and finds true love with, see Guillén Robles, *Leyendas moriscas*, 1:xvi–xix. Prophecies explained present suffering as just punishment for moral degradation and irreligiosity among Moriscos, but they promised that the just and merciful God would grant them ultimate political victory over their enemies, as in García Arenal, *Los moriscos*, 55–62. Three of these legends were translated for the Inquisition in Granada and are included in Mármol Carvajal, *Historia del rebelión*, 169–174.

[37] Nykel, *Compendium*, 22, states that Arabic gradually became limited to an educated upper class; but he also overlooks the potential power of Aljamía, seeing it as merely reflecting "the resignation of a subject people, trusting not to its strength, but seeking refuge in superstitions, charms, divinations, and a vague belief that Allah will send someone to deliver them from the evils and persecutions of which they are the victims." For more on the political significance of language, see Antonio Gramsci, *Selections from the Prison Notebooks of Antonio Gramsci*, ed. and trans. Quintin Hoare and Geoffrey Nowell Smith (New York: International Publishers, 1972), esp. 21; and Miriam Ojeda Rentas, "Literatura de ficción como arma política de resistencia para los moriscos españoles del siglo XVI," in Temini, *Las prácticas musulmanas*, 151–159.

[38] See manuscript 8 in Ribera and Asín, *Manuscritos árabes y aljamiados*, 48–49.

[39] Birriel Salcedo, "Notas sobre el matrimonio," 97–107.

[40] Vincent, "Las mujeres moriscas," 598; and Vincent, "50,000 moriscos almerienses," 495–496.

and gardens of their families. Those with less wealth went out to work in small factories that produced soap and tile and gunpowder. They provided unskilled labor in construction and in hauling. Essential to sericulture, these women picked mulberry leaves to nourish silkworms, unwound the delicate filaments from cocoons, and spun and wove it into silk. They prepared food that they peddled in the streets or sold from their homes, and they earned some money from spinning cotton and wool. Some Moriscas worked as fish sellers, shopkeepers, and housekeepers; while others, risking the unwanted attention of suspicious inquisitors, earned a meager living through healing and love magic.[41] Figures 5 and 6 present prints of Moriscas at work cleaning house and spinning. For many Morisco families, women's work—both paid and unpaid—made the crucial difference between subsistence and destitution.

Women made the crucial difference for cultural survival as well. Despite official prohibitions of the Arabic language, Islam, and Muslim cultural practices, all of these aspects of Moriscos' lives survived. We know this because the Inquisition continued to prosecute Moriscos for apostasy. Women played prominent roles in many of these cases, such as that of Leonor de Morales, whose husband had testified against her that she had persuaded him to follow Muslim practices.[42] Moreover, other witnesses said that she danced and sang as a Muslim at weddings, and that she ate while sitting on the ground, cooked meat in oil, ate meat on Fridays, changed into clean clothing on Fridays, and communicated with "other Moors." Under torture she confessed to changing into clean clothing and fasting and praying as a Muslim; but she confessed to nothing more, even though she was

[41] See, for example, the case of Ynés Yzquierda, who was prosecuted by the Inquisition for healing and using an Arabic medical book, AHN, Inquisición, legajo 2075, no. 15. For more on Moriscas and healing, see Luis García Ballester, *Los moriscos y la medicina: Un capítulo de la medicina y la ciencia marginadas en la España del siglo XVI* (Barcelona: Editorial Labor, 1984); and Mary Elizabeth Perry, "Las mujeres y su trabajo curativo en Sevilla, siglos XVI y XVII," in *El trabajo de las mujeres: siglos XVI–XX*, ed. María Jesús Matilla and Margarita Ortega (Madrid: Universidad Autónoma de Madrid, 1987), 40–50. For more on love magic, see María Helena Sánchez Ortega, "Woman as Source of 'Evil,' " in *Culture and Control in Counter-Reformation Spain*, ed. Anne J. Cruz and Mary Elizabeth Perry (Minneapolis: University of Minnesota Press, 1992), 196–215; and Cardaillac-Hermosilla, "Quand les morisques," 477–505. The work of Moriscas is reported in several sources, including the 1589 census in AGS, Cámara de Castilla, legajo 2196; Caro Baroja, *Los moriscos del Reino de Granada*, 136–137; and Fournel-Guérin, "La femme morisque en Aragon," 525–528. For a discussion of women's work in rural Seville during the late medieval period, see Mercedes Borrero Fernández, "El trabajo de la mujer en el mundo rural sevillano durante la baja edad media," in Angeles Durán and Seguro Graiño, *Las mujeres medievales y su ámbito jurídico*, 191–199.

[42] AHN, Inquisición, legajo 2075, no. 11, dated 1601.

Fig. 5. Morisca Cleaning House. *Authentic Everyday Dress of the Renaissance: All 154 Plates from the "Trachtenbuch"* (New York: Dover Publications, 1994), plate 82.

Fig. 6. Morisca Spinning. *Authentic Everyday Dress of the Renaissance: All 154 Plates from the "Trachtenbuch"* (New York: Dover Publications, 1994), plate 81.

subjected on the rack to six turns of the cord, nor did she give names of any accomplices.[43]

In another case, witnesses accused Lucía de la Cruz, along with her husband and fifteen-year-old daughter, of living according to Islam.[44] Under torture she confessed to all she had been accused of and added, whether out of pain or defiance, that she washed five times each day in the Muslim manner and taught Islam to others. Inquisitors reported that she had communicated with other Moors about their proceedings against them. In both these cases, and countless others like them, inquisitors found Moriscas guilty of preserving Muslim practices in their homes, influencing others to follow Islam, and communicating with other Moors. The women, as Bernard Vincent has pointed out, "were the guardians of Muslim culture."[45]

Yet inquisitors identified some Morisco men as heads of apostate households. In Seville in the early seventeenth century, Joan Valenciano was accused of leading Muslim prayers at night in his home, where both family and friends gathered. According to witnesses, Joan Valenciano read from the Qurʾan and instructed some of them in how to pray and perform the ceremonies of Islam. They all prayed, lowering their heads and affirming, in Arabic, that God is great.[46] Luis de Castro evidently led similar Muslim meetings in his home in Murcia in the 1580s. He had Arabic books and papers that, according to his oldest daughter, he showed to many Moriscos who came to the meetings. His wife, daughters, sons, and daughters-in-law were all implicated with him.[47] María de Luna from the town of Fuentes voluntarily confessed to the Holy Office in Zaragoza that her father, Domingo de Luna, had persuaded her to live as a Muslim because she could not be saved if she lived as a Christian. From the age of eight, she had performed Muslim ceremonies with her father and many other Moriscos.[48]

In contrast to these cases, the great majority of those in which accused Moriscos identified the person from whom they had learned Islam named their mothers, grandmothers, or mothers-in-law. Angela

[43] As in much of medieval and early modern Europe, the Inquisition used torture not for punishment but to obtain "full proof," discussed in Edward Peters, *Inquisition* (New York: The Free Press, 1988), 65. In this case, it examined Leonor de Morales using the *potro*, a rack to which the body and limbs were bound, with the examiner tightening the cords by turning them. Six turns would have been very severe. For more on the Inquisition and torture, see Kamen, *Inquisition and Society*, 174–177.

[44] AHN, Inquisición, legajo 2075, no. 11, dated 1601.

[45] Vincent, "Las mujeres moriscas," 592.

[46] For Joan Valenciano and those accused of meeting in his home, see AHN, Inquisición, legajo 2075, no. 19.

[47] AHN, Inquisición, legajo 2022, no. 14.

[48] AHN, Inquisición, libro 991, fols. 117v–118.

Hernández, or Isabel Jiménez, called la Hardona in Cordova, not only taught Islam to her family members but was said to be a "teacher and dogmatist" and to advise others when the fast of Ramadan should be kept. Her house, witnesses said, "was like a mosque"—surely confirming the worst fears of inquisitors.[49]

It should be noted here that some Moriscos, both men and women, made genuine conversions to Christianity, and a smaller number even intermarried with Old Christians—yet all Moriscos remained subject to suspicion.[50] One Morisco response to Christian efforts to obliterate their culture was to conform externally to the dominant Christian culture, while hiding their internal loyalty to Islam. This longtime Muslim tradition of taqiyya, or "precaution," had developed earlier as Muslims tried to preserve Islam in situations where it was forbidden.[51] "God is not concerned with your exterior attitude, but with the intention of your hearts," the mufti of Oran had advised Moriscos of Spain in 1563. "And if they tell you to denounce Muhammad, denounce him by word and love him at the same time in your heart."[52] To such dissimulation, some Christian clerics responded harshly, seeing Moriscos not as obedient sheep of their flock whom they could lead, as the Dominican preacher Jaime Bleda noted, but "as flesh-eating wolves, and rabid dogs."[53] Decrying the obstinacy of Moriscos who refused to become true Christians, an *informe* from Madrid about the instruction of Moriscos warned that the women were the most "obstinate," particularly in keeping their children from Christian schools and preserving the daily ceremonies of Islam in their homes.[54] Moreover, Moriscas who

[49] Gracia Boix, *Autos de fe*, 246, presents this case: "maestra y dogmatista de la secta de Mahoma y su casa era como Mezquita y que avisaba a los demás cuando caía en el ayuno de Ramadán y las Pascuas de moros."

[50] The 1589 census reports very few cases of intermarriage, but for a very interesting case of intermarriage raising issues of assimilation, see AHN, Inquisición, legajo 2075, no. 31, "Relación de causas de fe," discussed below in chapter 7, and in Mary Elizabeth Perry, "Contested Identities: The Morisca Visionary, Beatriz de Robles," in *Women and the Inquisition*, ed. Mary E. Giles (Baltimore: Johns Hopkins University Press, 1998), 171–188. For Moriscos who became Christian prelates and attempted to Christianize other Moriscos, see Borja de Medina, "La Compañía de Jesús," 3–136. More recent work on assimilating Moriscos of Aragon is by Halavais, *Like Wheat to the Miller*; Tueller, *Good and Faithful Christians*; and Tueller, "The Assimilating Morisco," 167–177.

[51] Lammens, *Islam: Beliefs and Institutions*, 168–175; Galmés de Fuentes, *Los moriscos (desde su misma orilla)*, 108–113; and Cardaillac, "Un aspecto de las relaciones," 107–122.

[52] "Respuesta que hizo el mufti de Oran a ciertas preguntas que le hicieron desde la Andalucía," May 3, 1563, published in García Arenal, *Los moriscos*, 44–45.

[53] Bleda, *Corónica de los moros*, 882: "no eran ovejas, sino lobos carniceros, y perros rabiosos."

[54] "Informe de Madrid a Valencia sobre instrucción de los moriscos," in García Arenal, *Los moriscos*, 116–125, esp. 122. Perhaps the women's "obstinacy" was actually their traditionalism. It may also reflect the fact that many Morisco women had had less interac-

were sheltered from daily interaction with Christians continued to speak Arabic and to wear their traditional clothing. Yet what Christians saw as obstinacy could be seen by Moriscos as faithfulness to their own religion, their difficult circumstances not so different from the story of the handless Carcayona.

Morisco mentalities thus became contested space and the object of inquisitorial investigations. Confronted by inquisitors with sworn eyewitness testimony that she had met with other Moriscos for prayer and religious readings in the home of Joan Valenciano, her father, Floriana de los Reyes confessed that she had attended these meetings and had heard her father read from the Qurʾan. But she also declared that she had been unsure which was the true law, that of the Christians or that of the Moors, so she had observed both religions and asked God to receive the best. Since then she had learned that Christian law was "the true law," she added, and she had hesitated to testify against her parents and brothers because she did not want to condemn them. Inquisitors evidently did not accept her assurances that she was now a loyal Christian, for they ordered her to be reconciled to the Church in a public auto de fe. They confiscated all her goods, ordered her to wear the sanbenito and sentenced her to "perpetual prison."[55]

Perhaps the most cruel contestation between Moriscos and Christians invaded Morisco family and kinship bonds. When inquisitors interrogated Moriscos about their religious beliefs and cultural practices, they often tried to get them to implicate other family members. Diego Martín, for example, was denounced by a witness who said that Diego had declared he was a Moor and prayed the Qurʾan. Under questioning, he tried to defend himself by saying that he changed his shirt on Fridays only at the persuasion of his wife, Leonor de Morales, who was also arrested, interrogated, and condemned.[56] It is not clear whether she had actually persuaded him to follow Islam, or whether this couple, like Ana Albexite and Miguel Condres in the province of Zaragoza, had decided together to observe Islamic rites in their home.[57]

Even more tragically, María Jérez, a fifteen-year-old girl, was denounced to inquisitors by her own parents, who had been accused of observing Islam.[58] Her father died in the prison of the Inquisition, but mother and daughter survived to be reconciled to the Church. It is

---

tion with Christians and had not learned as well as Morisco men how to blend into Christian society. Morisco women seem to have preserved traditional dress longer than Morisco men, who were more likely to dress as Christian men did.

[55] AHN, Inquisición, legajo 2075, no. 19. As noted above in chapter 2, "perpetual prison" was not usually enforced because of lack of space and supervision.

[56] AHN, Inquisición, legajo 2075, no. 11.

[57] AHN, Inquisición, libro 991, fol. 114–114v.

[58] AHN, Inquisición, legajo 2075, no. 11.

doubtful that their family survived, however. Although María got the relatively light sentence of two years of instruction and seclusion in a monastery, her mother lost all her property to the Holy Office and was sentenced to perpetual prison. Under such circumstances, it would have been very difficult for them to be reunited or for María to have obtained a dowry so that she could later marry.

For years Moriscos had carried on this subversive but covert—and sometimes even unconscious—resistance to Christianization in the privacy of their homes. Women in particular determined cooking and eating practices and set the schedule for changing into clean clothing. They continued to speak Arabic in their homes and taught the Arabic language and Muslim prayers to their children, perhaps unconsciously falling back on traditional practices. However, as the Inquisition increased its efforts to prosecute Moriscos for speaking and praying in Arabic, it does not seem likely that women's persistence remained unconscious. Moreover, a conscious choice to resist seems clear in those cases of women who hid their children so they would not have to attend schools established to Christianize them. The Christian report that labeled Morisco women as the most "obstinate" in resisting Christianization reflected more than a biased view against them.[59]

Soon Morisco homes were no longer safe spaces of resistance, for by the mid–sixteenth century authorities had already determined that they would enter Morisco homes to look for evidence of Muslim practices.[60] They sent rectors and lay sheriffs to Morisco homes to find out whether the children were attending the compulsory Christian schools that had been established for them.[61] No longer the refuge that the home had represented for Moriscos, these spaces became the primary forum for the struggle over apostasy. While inquisitors found the commonplace heretical, Moriscas made the ordinary subversive.

Despite this dangerous and hostile world in which the very stones seemed to be watching them, some Moriscos continued their resistance. Even after inquisitors caught and condemned them, they found ways to communicate with other Moriscos in prison, and refused to name accomplices. One outraged cleric reported that a Morisca sentenced to wear a sanbenito asked inquisitors for a second sanbenito for

[59] "Informe de Madrid a Valencia sobre instrucción de los moriscos," included in García Arenal, *Los moriscos*, 116–125, esp. 122. For more on the resistance of women, see García Cárcel, *Herejía y sociedad*, 229; Monter, *Frontiers of Heresy*, 226–227; and Temini, *Las prácticas musulmanas*, 175.

[60] See the "Instrucción" and "Informe" reprinted in García Arenal, *Los moriscos*, 106–125.

[61] Borja de Medina, "La Compañía de Jesús," 69–73, for reports on schools established by Jesuits especially in Granada.

her young son "because he was cold."[62] Another Morisca requested a new sanbenito because her old one was wearing out.[63] Historical records do not tell us whether these women made their inquiries sincerely or in a conscious attempt to ridicule the power of the Inquisition.

From Private Rituals to Public Penance

Most confrontations of Moriscos and Christians took place in the contested space of home, church, mentalities, and family bonds. Usually these confrontations ended with Christian authorities taking charge to transform Moriscos' private rituals into public penance. By the mid–sixteenth century the Inquisition had become the primary institution to confront Morisco resistance. It sought to encourage Moriscos to denounce themselves by offering a period of grace in which those who voluntarily confessed to forbidden behaviors could receive more leniency. Gerónimo Galix not only voluntarily confessed to the Holy Office of Zaragoza that he had lived as a Muslim and performed Islamic ceremonies; he also named other persons who had carried out these ceremonies with him.[64] However, Moriscos who had been given lenient treatment for self-denunciation faced severe punishment for future offenses, as Gerónima de Ambaxil learned in Zaragoza in 1608. Twenty-three years after inquisitors had "reconciled" her to the Church following her voluntary confession, she was denounced for carrying out Muslim ceremonies in her own home. This time she was condemned to death.[65]

Most Moriscos punished by the Inquisition were arrested after they had been denounced by others. Many of the witnesses against them were Old Christians, but a large number were Moriscos who knew and implicated other Moriscos, usually under pressure to name their "accomplices" as they were being examined and tortured. Tragically, once inquisitors arrested any member of a family, they expected the prisoner to denounce other family members as "accomplices" for "living as a Moor" or teaching others "the sect of Muhammad." In Cordova, Pero Gómez denounced as Moors who "lived in observance of the sect of Muhammad" eleven other Moriscos, including his mother, brother, and sister-in-law.[66]

[62] Fonseca, *Justa expulsión*, 126.

[63] Memorial of Fray Nicolás del Río to Philip III from Valencia, June 13, 1606, quoted in García Arenal, *Los moriscos*, 127; also see Bleda, *Corónica de los moros*, 883.

[64] AHN, Inquisición, libro 991, fol. 113–113v.

[65] AHN, Inquisición, libro 991, n.p.

[66] Gracia Boix, *Autos de fe*, 242–245.

Moriscos caught by the Inquisition quickly learned of its power to interpret and transform their private actions or beliefs into public offenses. Authorities arrested Moriscos who had been denounced or caught with incriminating evidence, often in their homes, and imprisoned them where they could be watched and subjected to the private rituals of inquisitorial prosecution. Even before the auto de fe, which was the major ritual of penance, prisoners of the Inquisition had to participate in rituals of interrogation and confession. Cut off from friends and family, held in secret prisons of the Holy Office, and lacking legal counsel until the last stages of the case against them, all prisoners must have been very aware of their tremendous vulnerability before the power of the Inquisition. Interrogators had only to mention torture or show the instruments of torture to some of the prisoners to get the confessions they wished. In many cases, inquisitors seemed to put words into the mouths of prisoners, whose testimonies and confessions became little more than exercises in ventriloquism.[67] Any conclusion about how we can analyze such testimony, of course, has to consider the context in which it was given.

Despite enormous physical and psychological pressure, Moriscos did not always cooperate with rituals of interrogation and confession. Hieronymo Rodríguez de Guiomar, for example, confessed to charges against him and gave testimony against other Moriscos as "accomplices."[68] Later, however, he requested another audience with inquisitors. This time he declared that he had not seen at Morisco prayer meetings those he had previously testified against. Evidently such equivocation resulted in a more severe sentence: reconciliation in a public auto de fe, confiscation of goods, the sanbenito, four years of galley service, and then (if he survived) a prison for penitents.

Prisoners of the Inquisition were supposed to be kept in isolation from one another, but this was not always possible. We can only speculate on the messages that Morisco prisoners might have sent to one another, or the moments in which they dared to speak together. Those discovered in communication were often subsequently gagged. Lucía de la Cruz, mother of the adolescent María Jérez discussed above, was noted as having communicated with other Moors "in the discourse of their cause." Leonor Morales, another prisoner included in the same list of 1601, was reported to have "communicated with other Moors." It is not clear whether this offense increased the severity of the sentence

[67] For more on ventriloquism and confession, see Mike Hepworth and Bryan S. Turner, *Confession: Studies in Deviance and Religion* (London: Routledge & Kegan Paul, 1982); and Michel Foucault, *Discipline and Punish: The Birth of the Prison* (New York: Random House, 1995), esp. 35–42.

[68] AHN, Inquisición, legajo 2075, no. 19.

of each: perpetual prison for de la Cruz and a whipping of one hundred lashes for Morales.[69]

Christian authorities had developed a ritualized ceremony, the auto de fe, to announce the offense and punishment of each person convicted by the Inquisition. Those convicted were sentenced to appear in this ceremony, usually public, in the city in which the tribunal of the Inquisition had tried the prisoners. Processing together through city streets from the buildings of the Inquisition to a large church or plaza, prisoners became subject to public gaze. They had to wear symbols such as the corona, or pointed cap, and the sanbenito, often inscribed with the guilty one's name and offense. In some cases they also had to carry wax candles or wear a rope around their necks. Recalcitrant offenders or those who threatened to disrupt the solemn decorum of the ceremony had to wear gags.[70]

Significantly, the ritual of the auto de fe engaged the participation of not only the prisoners but also the larger public and leading officials. Onlookers witnessed the procession of ecclesiastical leaders and penitents following the green cross of the Inquisition to the site of the ceremony. In a church or plaza dignitaries and officials assumed their honored positions on a platform erected above the penitents and ordinary people. Together, officials and the larger public affirmed their faith and witnessed the offense and penance read for each penitent. Yet the ceremony did not level differences between officials and ordinary people. From their exalted position on the platform, officials enacted their power as leaders in an established order; in contrast, the attendance of the larger public demonstrated deference to this established order in which a partnership of Church and Crown had the power to define orthodoxy and condemn any deviance from it.

In this ceremony, prisoners could not hide themselves in an anonymous crowd. After Mass and a sermon, a notary called each prisoner by name; when the prisoner answered, the inquisitor read aloud for all to hear the offenses this person had committed. Announcing the punishment for each prisoner, the spokesman for the Inquisition effectively transformed the private acts of these people into a public demonstration of power that could impose control over them.[71] Inquisitors required them to be "reconciled" to the Church, and to swear that they

[69] Both of these cases appear in AHN, Inquisición, legajo 2075, no. 11.

[70] Inquisition records frequently describe the use of the gag, as in AHN, Inquisición, legajo 2072 and legajo 2075, no. 4. See Kamen, *Inquisition and Society*, 173, for the use of the gag in prisons to prevent communication among the prisoners, and 193 for a description of the gag used in autos de fe. For an excellent discussion of the auto de fe, see Ruiz, *Spanish Society*, 155–160.

[71] For a detailed account of an auto de fe in the city of Toledo in 1486, see Kamen, *Inquisition and Society*, 190–192.

would no longer commit their offense. Most had to continue to wear the sanbenito, the garment that publicly identified them as sinners punished by the Inquisition. Often inquisitors also sentenced Moriscos to pay fines and receive instruction "in the things of our Holy Catholic Faith."[72] Their goods were also confiscated to cover the expenses of the Holy Office in imprisoning and prosecuting them.[73]

Although a small minority of Moriscos caught by the Inquisition were "relaxed" to be put to death by secular officials, most Moriscos were sentenced to forms of penance that assured a long-continuing third act of the domestic drama we have been considering. Exile from their place of residence or confiscation of their goods undoubtedly made a permanent impact on their lives and families. Often inquisitors sentenced Moriscos penanced in the autos de fe to a year or more of instruction and supervision; they also sentenced to perpetual prison those Moriscos they considered less educable. Male Moriscos were increasingly likely to be condemned to galley service, especially as the royal navy required more galley slaves in the later sixteenth century.[74] Officials most commonly sentenced female Moriscos to reclusion in a hospital or institution where they would have to work under supervision for their food. Both males and females received sentences of whipping—usually one hundred lashes, to be inflicted in the streets of the city. These punishments provided visible evidence of the powerful presence of the Inquisition, which continued to impact the lives of not only the individuals they penanced, but also those people who observed them.

The Church, in fact, had power to reach beyond the grave. Prisoners unfortunate enough to die in prison would be brought in procession as effigies or as a box of bones to be penanced in an auto de fe—perhaps even to be handed over to secular authorities for burning. The father of María Jérez, whom we have already met, died in prison and appeared as an effigy in the same auto de fe with his wife and daughter. Moriscos sentenced to wear the sanbenito usually had to wear the garment for the rest of their lives; even after they died, their sanbe-

[72] Gracia Boix, *Autos de fe*, 104, for the case of Lorenzo Ardón: "en las cosas de Nuestra Santa Fe Católica."

[73] The oath would likely be "de levi" in the case of first or minor offenses; but it would be "de vehementi" for second offenses or those considered more serious. Those taking the latter oath would be subject to more severe punishment for any subsequent offenses. Kamen, *Inquisition and Society*, 186–189.

[74] *Don Luys Mendez de Haro y Sotomayor, Marqués del Carpio . . . Asistente deste ciudad de Seville y su tierra, y Capitan general de la gente de guerra della, por el Rey nro Señor, etc.* (Seville: Bartolomé Gómez, 1610), in Ignacio Bauer Landauer, *Papeles en mi archivo: Relaciones y manuscritos (moriscos)* (Madrid: Editorial Ibero-Africano-Americana, 19??), 165–166.

nitos, marked with their offenses and family names, would be hung from the rafters of the parish church. Eternal damnation followed for those who would not confess to their crimes and become reconciled with Mother Church. Their execution following the auto de fe might end the painful ordeal for the condemned person, but devout Christian onlookers believed that this was just the beginning of eternal pain and punishment. Moreover, the spectacle of the execution could traumatically scar members of the condemned person's family.

What was the power of the Inquisition for Moriscos? Its rituals of penance seemed intended to become a permanent part of penitents' lives, indelibly marking them and their families. Guilt by association made family members all the more vulnerable to accusations and prosecution. And yet the very records of the Holy Office show that the rituals of public penance imposed by this powerful institution could neither stop Moriscos' acts of resistance nor convert them to "true" Christians. As a ceremony of degradation that exposed convicted Moriscos to public scorn, the auto de fe presented itself as "reconciling" the offenders to the Church. However, it included no steps to reintegrate the penitent into society once the punishment had been completed.[75] In fact, public degradation and punishment that tore families apart widened the chasm of difference between Moriscos and Christians.

Considering the devastating effect that these measures had on Morisco homes and families, some Moriscos concluded that they had exhausted all peaceful methods of resistance and opposition. Violent confrontations, in fact, had already taken place between Moriscos and Christians in the sixteenth century, particularly through banditry and piracy.[76] In 1568 when a Morisco rebellion erupted in the Alpujarra Mountains, it quickly spilled out of Morisco homes to spread across much of southern Spain and defy the king's armies for nearly two years. For Morisco rebels and their families, military action would now replace the resistance and betrayal of dangerous domesticity.

[75] Erikson discusses reintegration and deviance in *Wayward Puritans*, esp. 16–17.

[76] Fernand Braudel, *The Mediterranean and the Mediterranean World in the Age of Philip II*, trans. Sian Reynolds (New York: Harper Torchbook, 1976), 734–754 and 864–891; Ruiz, *Spanish Society*, 200–201; Vincent, "50,000 moriscos almerienses," 490–491.

4

WITH STONES AND ROASTING SPITS

THE OUTBREAK of an armed Morisco rebellion in the Alpujarra Mountains on December 24, 1568, confirmed the suspicions of many Christians that Moriscos were dangerous internal enemies. For nearly two years the rebellious Moriscos would hold off the soldiers of Philip II, sometimes with the help of Turks and North Africans, often with the help of women. A Christian eyewitness to a January 1569 battle near Almería reported that Christians had killed between 1,500 and 2,000 of the enemy, "and among them some women because they fought as men although they had no weapons but stones and roasting spits."[1] Most historians who have noted this report have considered it as yet one more indication that the poorly equipped Moriscos proved no match for the Christians' forces. Moreover, some present a hostile viewpoint that these people were so desperate that the Morisco men had to call on the help of women, would-be amazons who readily violated gender prescriptions and deserved the deaths they suffered in battle.

In fact, an actual amazon appears in another account of the battle of Galera written by a soldier who had fought with Christian forces. "This Mora was called Zarçamodonia," Ginés Pérez de Hita reported, "large in body, with strong legs and arms, that attained a very great force."[2] More than merely a warrior, however, Zarçamodonia also acted as an envoy between the Morisco soldiers and a Turkish contingent that had come to assist them. Highly regarded by both Moriscos and Turks, she met separately with each group and was able to establish some peace between the quarreling allies. Although the rebels and their Turkish allies were able to withstand the siege of Galera for some time, Morisco and Turkish soldiers had begun to fight among themselves, with their leaders physically attacking one another. "Many women," Pérez de Hita wrote, "took part in the pacification, especially Zarçamodonia, for whose valor all had respect."[3]

[1] *Relación muy verdadera sacada de una carta*: "y entre ellos algunos mugeres porque peleavan como los hombres con que ellas no tienen mas armas q piedras y assadores."

[2] Pérez de Hita, *Guerras civiles de Granada*, 2:253.

[3] Pérez de Hita, *Guerras civiles de Granada*, 2:261.

By no means can we regard Zarçamodonia as typical of Moriscas, or "Moras," as the Christians called them in their reports. Not all of these women were as physically strong or as combative as Zarçamodonia in seizing a sword and killing others with it. Nor did all the Moriscas command enough respect to be able to effectively restore peace between Morisco and Turkish soldiers. Yet her story encourages us to recover her precedents, the many Morisco women prominent in times of war and peace alike; it shows how women played many active roles as wartime overturned the gender order. Through the story of Zarçamodonia and our glimpse of the women fighting with stones and roasting spits we can better understand the tragedy of the defeat of the Moriscos in 1570.

Precedents for Moriscas in War and Peace

Zarçamodonia's appearance as woman warrior in the battle of Galera cannot be dismissed as a strange abnormality, for Moriscas knew of many other women who had acted bravely in armed conflicts. The Morisco story "La batalla de Huzayma al-Bariqiyya," for example, tells of a non-Muslim "warrior maiden" fighting against the Muslim army of ᶜAli.[4] A woman "very honorable" and "very knightly," she challenged the Muslims to send out a warrior to face her in single combat. She quickly defeated him, and only ᶜAli could contend with her. But it took ᶜAli an hour to unhorse her and pin her to the ground with his sword. Faced with death, Huzayma decided to convert to Islam. Her story and other Morisco battle stories affirmed the certain victory of Islam, which one scholar sees as "the major theme of Muslim narrations."[5] At first, these stories were part of an oral tradition in Muslim Iberia that relied on rhyming and rhythmic prose.[6] Probably originating in evening gatherings during pre-Islamic times, the stories developed as circles of people came to Muhammad's mosque in Medina to listen to narrators talk about historical events and prophets and stories in the Qurʾan. In the early years, it was difficult to distinguish the storytelling from preaching, but gradually narrators came to be regarded less as learned Muslims and more as popular minstrels or jesters.[7]

[4] Alvaro Galmés de Fuentes, *El libro de las batallas. Narraciones é épico-caballerescas. Estudio literario y edición del texto por A. Galmés de Fuentes* (Madrid: Editorial Gredos, 1975), 1:61: "la doncella guerrera."

[5] Galmés de Fuentes, *El libro de las batallas*, 1:22.

[6] Galmés de Fuentes, *El libro de las batallas*, 1:18.

[7] Galmés de Fuentes, *El libro de las batallas*, 1:21–24.

Morisco battle stories offered not only examples of warrior maidens but also models of ordinary women who went to war. Another ancient story, "The Battle of the Valley of Yarmuk," is based on an actual battle between Syrians and Islamized Arabs in the seventh century.[8] It acknowledged the crucial role of women in the Muslim victory at the valley of Yarmuk. This story was finally written down in Aljamía and then hidden when Christians called in all writings in Arabic and Aljamía to burn. We do not know that Moriscas ever read this legend, for most of these women are believed to have been illiterate.[9] It seems very likely, however, that they knew the story and continued to tell it during the sixteenth century, when it could have inspired Moriscos desperately trying to defend their faith against an overwhelming adversary.[10]

In the battle in the valley of Yarmuk women and children accompanied Muslim soldiers, just as they later accompanied rebellious Moriscos in the War of the Alpujarras. Both the Muslims in the legend and Moriscos of the sixteenth century faced an enemy of great numerical superiority, so numerous as to appear in the legend "like locusts."[11] Concerned that the discipline of his soldiers might break in battle, the Muslim leader in the valley of Yarmuk commanded the women to take their children and position themselves at the foot of a hill—but not merely for their protection. "Take sticks," he told them, "and if you see

[8] For the legend, see BN, Batallas de los primeros tiempos del islamismo, ms 5337. It has been translated and published in Spanish by Guillén Robles, *Leyendas moriscas*, 3:83–184; and in Aljamía in Roman letters by Galmés de Fuentes, *El libro de las batallas*, 1:257–325. In this chapter, I will provide English translations from Galmés de Fuentes's edition.

[9] See the study by Bernard Vincent "Las mujeres moriscas," 589; but note that some Moriscas may not have "understood" or signed their names to Inquisition statements out of resistance rather than illiteracy. James C. Scott, *Domination and the Arts of Resistance: Hidden Transcripts* (New Haven and London: Yale University Press, 1990), suggests that subordinated people can pretend not to understand or to be able to read as a form of resistance; see esp. xxi–xxvi, 29, and 37. It is misleading to conclude that none of the Moriscas were educated; see, for example, Vincent, "50,000 moriscos almerienses," 504; and L. P. Harvey, "El Mancebo de Arévalo y la literatura aljamiada," in *Actas del Coloquia Internacional sobre Literatura Aljamiada y Morisca* (Oviedo: Editorial Gredos, 1972), 21–41; and Ribera y Tarragó, *La enseñanza entre los musulmanes españoles*.

[10] Mercedes García Arenal suggests that Aljamiado literature can be regarded as part of a collective memory, in "El problema morisco: propuesta de discusión," *Al-Qantara* 13 (1992): 499–503. But also see Alvaro Galmés de Fuentes, "El interés literario en los escritos aljamiado-moriscos," in *Actas del Coloquio Internacional sobre Literatura Aljamiada y Morisca* (Oviedo: Editorial Gredos, 1972), 189–209, who argues that this literature cannot be viewed as reflecting exclusively a Morisco or Muslim memory, for Christians also knew it, lived with it, and used it, 202–208. See the thoughtful "Estudio preliminar" of María Paz Torres in the 1994 edition of Guillén Robles, *Leyendas moriscas*, 1:lxxxii–cxvii.

[11] Galmés de Fuentes, *El libro de las batallas*, 1:278.

any of the Muslims fleeing, attack the faces of their horses."[12] Soon the right wing of the Muslim army broke ranks. "In high voices," the women called to the soldiers, gathering up their children in their arms and throwing stones at the faces of their horses. "You are not our husbands," they shouted to them, "for you are fleeing from the evil foreigners."[13] Again the Muslim soldiers regrouped, only to break again. "And the Muslims were overcome three times on that day," the story declares, and each time the women attacked them with sticks "and made them return to battle and they threw stones at the horses."[14] Holding their children in their arms, they shouted to the men, "Go back to the field, or you will see your children and women captives in the hands of the evil foreigners."[15]

The next morning in the valley of Yarmuk, the Muslim commander prayed and then ordered the women to go out again with sticks and attack those who tried to leave the battle. Again the women shamed and attacked the Muslim soldiers trying to flee in the heat of the battle. Finally, however, the Muslim soldiers held their ground and were able to defeat the Syrians and their Byzantine allies. Here in this story of an important victory for Islam, women played a critical role, not merely in shaming the men to return to battle, but also in strengthening their resolve in the struggle. And they did this by using the same strategy so often deployed by men to control women: into an overarching and compelling message they interwove gender prescriptions of honor with obligations of faith.[16]

Women used not only sticks and stones as weapons in this strategy but also words. For Arabs the word has a "magical value," according to literary scholar Alvaro Galmés de Fuentes, and it is the most important gift. "The Arab has received the gift of modeling in the word and with the word all that which others model in stone, matter, marble, silk, color."[17] In the battle of the valley of Yarmuk, Muslim women used

[12] Galmés de Fuentes, *El libro de las batallas*, 1:294: "Tomaréys palos; i si veréys // fuir a nenguno de los muçlims, ferirles-eys en la / kara del kaballo."

[13] Galmés de Fuentes, *El libro de las batallas*, 1:301: "No soys nuestros // maridos, puwes fuiys de los iljjes [extranheros] malos."

[14] Galmés de Fuentes, *El libro de las batallas* 1:307–308: "I jweron vençidos los muçlims en-akel diya / teres vezes, a kada vez hasta las mujeres. Y-ellas / ke les feriyan kon palos, i los feban [sic] volver a la batalla . . . i les a pedreaban a los kaballos, kon piyedras."

[15] Galmés de Fuentes, *El libro de las batallas*, 1:307–308: "i les sakaban sus kiruaturas en sus baraços, i les deziyan—Tornad al kampo, ke veres vuwestras kiriaturas i mujeres en poder de los /// iljjes [extranjeros] malos, i kativos."

[16] Galmés de Fuentes notes that the importance of women in the legends of these Muslim battles is rarely equaled in European epics, *El libro de las batallas*, 1:60.

[17] Galmés de Fuentes, *El libro de las batallas*, 1:54–55.

words to shame and exhort the men to greater effort. And in retelling the story, they used words to stir emotions, appeal for protection, strengthen faith.

This strategy came into play again in the last few days of the fifteenth century, when women participated in the rebellion that broke out among Muslims in the Albaicín quarter of Granada. Living together in a densely inhabited part of the old city, these people especially resented Christian zeal to convert Muslims to Christianity, in violation of the terms of their surrender in 1492. One day a servant of Archbishop Francisco Jiménez de Cisneros entered the Albaicín and attempted to take to prison the daughter of a Christian who had converted to Islam. Screaming that she was being forced to become a Christian, the woman triggered a mutinous uproar that spread quickly. Thousands of Muslims took up arms against their Christian rulers, saying that they no longer had to respect the terms of their surrender because the Christians had already violated them.[18] As their rebellion spread from Granada to Ronda and to the Alpujarra Mountains, atrocities escalated on both sides, with women and children as victims as well as perpetrators. In his account of this rebellion, Luis del Mármol Carvajal described how Christian forces responded to Muslim fortification of a castle in Andarax, blowing up the major mosque where women and children had taken refuge.[19] Christians killed rebel men whom they had captured and enslaved the women and children, although children younger than eleven were to be placed with Christian families and raised as Christians.[20]

As Christians put down the rebellion, authorities published decrees in 1502 requiring Muslims to convert to Christianity if they wanted to remain in Castile. At first, their intention seemed to be limited to simply prohibiting a religion. Soon, however, the enforcement of these decrees expanded to prohibit expressions of Morisco culture, such as their dress, language, and ways of butchering animals. These measures, according to Antonio Domínguez Ortiz and Bernard Vincent, "were the result of a deliberate policy of middle officials, determined to destroy the peculiarities of Morisco culture."[21] Finally, in 1526 a junta meeting in Granada agreed to forbid all Morisco "particularism." As we saw in chapter 3, countless Moriscos became embroiled in the conflict with Christians as they attempted to preserve their culture and faith in their homes.

[18] Mármol Carvajal, *Historia del rebelión*, 154.
[19] Mármol Carvajal, *Historia del rebelión*, 156.
[20] Mármol Carvajal, *Historia del rebelión*, 157.
[21] Domínguez Ortiz and Vincent, *Historia de los moriscos*, 21.

For a time, Moriscos were permitted to pay a special tax that could buy relief from the prohibition on all their cultural expressions. However, an edict of grace issued—for Muslims newly converted to Christianity—by Archbishop Don Hernando de Valdés of Seville in July 1548 made it clear that this loophole was disappearing, as ecclesiastical authorities no longer separated Morisco culture from their religion. Beginning in a conciliatory tone, the edict granted that Moriscos would not be sentenced for their "past errors," nor would they be punished for them by having their goods confiscated or taken from their heirs.[22] It went on, however, to prohibit newly converted Moriscos from living together and required them to live among Old Christians. Their servants must be Old Christians, and Moriscos must marry their sons and daughters to Old Christians. They must provide dowries for their daughters, and these dowries would not be confiscated unless the Morisca was convicted of heresy, the same privilege given to an Old Christian woman who married a Morisco. Furthermore, Moriscos must be buried in Christian cemeteries according to the specific manners and customs of Old Christians. They must live faithfully as Catholics and separate themselves from their errors. They must receive instruction in "our holy Catholic faith," and allow the Church to replace them as teachers of their own children.

By 1555 the rift between Moriscos and Christians had widened, especially as Christian authorities perceived growing threats from abroad. A Turkish and Berber presence dominated the western Mediterranean and took over many former Spanish outposts on the North African coast. Iberian Muslims and renegades, in fact, made up the bulk of elite units in the Moroccan army during the sixteenth century, and many Christians feared that Moriscos who fled to North Africa would return with Berbers to invade Iberia.[23] As Moriscos of Granada and Valencia maintained contact with Constantinople, Spanish Christians suspected them of acting as a treacherous fifth column. In 1560 the viceroy of Valencia prohibited Moriscos from fishing because they were believed to be aiding Morisco and Berber pirates. French Huguenots supported Morisco banditry in Aragon, and Moriscos helped *monfís*, those Moriscos who had become highwaymen in the mountains, elude forces that had been organized against them in Andalucia.[24] Christians who suspected that Morisco carriers and muleteers carried more than goods in Granada and Valencia believed that they organized and spread

[22] AHN, Inquisición, libro 1254.

[23] Hess, *The Forgotten Frontier*, 184–185; and Domínguez Ortiz and Vincent, *Historia de los moriscos*, 142.

[24] Domínguez Ortiz and Vincent, *Historia de los moriscos*, 28–30.

treasonable conspiracies.[25] Even Morisco ownership of African slaves concerned members of the *cortes* that met in Toledo in 1560. Asserting that Moriscos taught Islam to these slaves, the cortes warned that the Morisco nation was growing each hour, but confidence in its loyalty was declining.[26]

Morisco prophecies discovered by the Inquisition and by a soldier in a cave of the Alpujarras raised even more the questions as to the loyalty of these people. One prophecy spoke specifically of "the island of Spain" and a return to complete the conquest of unbelievers. With the sign of a comet would come "great armies of Turks," who would march into Rome and subdue all the Christians.[27] Another warned of the tumult that would come to the "island of Andalucia," identifying this apocalyptic period as part of God's plan. Some may dress in the humble skin of the lamb and speak with tongues sweeter than honey, but "their hearts will be those of wolves." This terrible time will end when God sends a cloud of birds, including two birds representing the angels Gabriel and Michael. Then "all the world will return to the law of the Moors." The prophetic documents also warned of a time of great disorder and sinfulness, of drought and Rome in flames. At this time a tyrannous king will arise in the West and "the evil old Antichrist will be born."[28] The king will be embroiled in wars with Lutherans, and Andalucia will be as an orphan, the prophecy continued. But a sign will come of a large cloud of birds flying over the Alpujarras, and then all their troubles will disappear.

Both secular and Church leaders signaled in the 1560s that they had run out of patience with these reluctant "New Christians." A synod of clerics meeting in Granada in 1565 deliberately replaced the previous policy of evangelical persuasion with a call to prohibit every aspect of Morisco culture. In addition, they asked Philip II to order that leaders of the Morisco community send their sons "to serve in Old Castile at

[25] Henry Charles Lea, *The Moriscos of Spain: Their Conversion and Expulsion* (1901) (New York: Burt Franklin, 1968), 187–188.

[26] Mármol Carvajal, *Historia del rebelión*, 159.

[27] These and following quotations are taken from Mármol Carvajal, *Historia del rebelión*, 169–172. Mármol Carvajal read translations of the prophecies that were originally written in Arabic. For more on Morisco prophecies of victory and aid from the Turks, see García Arenal, *Los moriscos*, 55–62. The Mancebo de Arévalo's *Breve Compendio* and chapter 58 of Iça de Segovia's *Brevario Sunni* contain strong apocalyptic messages that are discussed in Wiegers, *Islamic Literature in Spanish and Aljamiado*, esp. 168 and 240–242.

[28] Mármol Carvajal, *Historia del rebelión*, 17. Note that "Anticristo" seems an unusual term for Muslims to use; one explanation is that the Christian translator of the text that Mármol Carvajal read chose this term as an Arabic word for an evil leader, but another explanation is that the use of this term may suggest cultural synthesis among Christians and Moriscos.

the cost of their parents so that they acquire customs and Christianity from them."[29] The king accepted most of the prelates' proposals and issued a pragmatic in 1566. Demonstrating increased determination to obliterate the faith and culture of these people, Christian officials again condemned Morisco "particularism" and decreed that those continuing to use the Arabic language and express Hispano-Muslim culture would be subject to prosecution by the Inquisition.

The pragmatic of 1566 did not simply leave the prohibition of Morisco culture to the Inquisition, however. It also declared null and void land agreements written in Arabic and imposed fines on those who no longer had acceptable title of ownership. Unable to pay the fines, many Moriscos in Granada lost any claim to the land that they and their forebears had used for generations.[30] A marked increase in taxes in 1561 and 1564 and a depression in the silk trade that supported so many Moriscos of Granada compounded the severity of these measures. Both secular and Church leaders ordered priests and curates in 1567 to inform their Moriscos that after the end of the year they could no longer wear silk. Moreover, priests and curates must "register all the children, boys and girls, of Moriscos in Granada, from the age of three years to fifteen years, in order to place them in schools where they would learn the language and Christian doctrine."[31]

Moriscos protested many of these measures. They sent one of their own, Francisco Nuñez Muley, to use his long experience in negotiating on their behalf to ask the president of the Audiencia of Granada to soften the measures. Speaking "with low and humble voice," according to Mármol Carvajal, he nonetheless pointed out that when they had converted to Christianity, Moriscos had not been obliged to replace their language, dress, or other customs. The present attempt to enforce rules against their culture would benefit no one, he argued. Moriscas' dress was not Moorish or Islamic but provincial in the same way that women in other regions, such as Castile, had their own kinds of head coverings, skirts, and footwear. Likewise, he said, the zambra was neither Moorish nor Muslim but a provincial custom of Moriscos in Granada. Previous archbishops, such as Hernando Talavera, had

[29] Domínguez Ortiz and Vincent, *Historia de los moriscos*, 32.

[30] Ciezar Nicolás Cabrillana, *Almería morisca* (Granada: Universidad de Granada, 1982), 115–125; Caro Baroja, *Los moriscos del Reino de Granada*, 152; Domínguez Ortiz and Vincent, *Historia de los moriscos*, 31–32; and Hess, *The Forgotten Frontier*, 145. The 1566 pragmatic is published in Bleda, *Corónica de los moros*, 657–659, and is also in *La Nueva Recopilación*, libro 8. For a Morisco response to this pragmatic, see BN ms 6176, Francisco Nuñez Muley, "Memoria al presidente," 311–330, also published in Mármol Carvajal, *Historia del rebelión*, 163–165.

[31] Mármol Carvajal, *Historia del rebelión*, 167.

accepted Morisco music, and "the zambra was in the choir with the clerics . . . and some words in Arabic were spoken in the Mass."[32] Point by point, he disputed the attempts to deny Moriscos the legitimacy of their own culture.

Yet despite the eloquence of this former page to Archbishop Hernando Talavera and the respect that he had earned from Old Christians and Moriscos alike, Nuñez Muley failed in his attempt to pacify escalating tensions. His argument that Morisco culture should be treated simply as another regionalism ran headlong into opposition from those who insisted that Moriscos must be entirely assimilated into Christian culture, as well as from those who simply feared that Moriscos had found allies in the Ottoman Turks. Nuñez Muley's plea for the easing of the new regulations brought only the response that they would remain in force because they "were so holy and just, and had been made with such deliberation and agreement."[33]

In contrast, the president of the Audiencia listened in April 1568 as Moriscos of Granada came to him after a Christian captain ordered Moriscos in the Albaicín region of Granada to shelter and feed his soldiers. To force them to quarter soldiers in their homes, where they had wives and daughters, would lead to "the destruction of the Albaicín," the Moriscos warned.[34] The president took their warning seriously and prevailed on Philip II to change the orders for quartering soldiers. Apparently he recognized that Moriscos could not be regarded as an insignificant minority in Granada, for they accounted for 43 percent of the population, the highest proportion of Moriscos in any of the Spanish kingdoms.[35] Moreover, the Moriscos of Granada were largely farmers who owned their own land, very rarely vassals dependent on a lord or city dwellers assimilating to urban Christian life.[36]

Philip II expressed concern that Moriscos not be pushed into rebellion, and local officials sought to reassure him that Moriscos of Granada were attempting to follow the new directives despite their protests. In a striking example of association between veiling and closed doors, twin symbols of Morisco otherness, Alonso de Granada Venegas wrote to the king in the spring of 1568 that the women were going about without veils, just as they now were leaving open the doors of

[32] Nuñez Muley, "Memoria," 319v: "estava la zambra en el coro con los clerigos . . . y dezia en la mysa en algunas palabras en arabigo."

[33] Mármol Carvajal, *Historia del rebelión*, 163–165.

[34] Mármol Carvajal, *Historia del rebelión*, 176.

[35] Domínguez Ortiz and Vincent, *Historia de los moriscos*, 78, citing a study by Felipe Ruiz Martín. Note, however, that Domínguez Ortiz and Vincent believe Moriscos accounted for more than half the population of Granada.

[36] Domínguez Ortiz and Vincent, *Historia de los moriscos*, 80.

their houses on Fridays and festival days, as they had been instructed.[37] Enforced obedience to imposed rules did not add up to assimilation, however, and Moriscos of Granada found few options for either negotiation or survival.

War and the Gender Order

When the call to arms echoed throughout the Kingdom of Granada in the last days of 1568, Moriscos seized arms long prohibited to them. The men "went to the mountains with their women and children," according to a Christian report from the city of Marbella, and that same day the people of the city "went out against them and followed them for several days. They routed them," the report goes on to say, "and took the women and children, capturing some of them."[38] Historical documents do not tell us whether the women of the Morisco community had played any role in the decision to go to war, but as this report makes clear, women became a part of the war from the beginning.

Moriscas who went with their husbands and children to the caves of the Alpujarras must have hoped to find protection there. Many already knew that Moriscos had made comfortable homes in the hamlets and villages of these mountains where so few Christians lived, regions that had been described as "very fertile," with "many fountains of fresh water" and "beautiful groves of fruit trees."[39] Rebels in these isolated communities often reverted to Islam, openly following Muslim customs, engaging in polygamy, and marrying within degrees prohibited by the Church.[40] In the words of a character in Calderón de la Barca's play *Amar después de la muerte*, the "first thing" the Morisco rebels ordered was opposition to the pragmatic that had forbidden expression of their culture.[41] Moriscos such as Ysabel Fernández would later confess to inquisitors that they had learned to observe Islam when they

[37] Mármol Carvajal, *Historia del rebelión*, 178.

[38] AGS, Cámara de Castilla, legajo 2811, report of the city of Marbella to Philip II: "se fueran a las sierras con sus mugeres y hijos y luego el mismo día salió gente de la dicha ciudad contra ellos y al cabo de avelos seguido algunos días. Los desbarrataron y quitaron los mugeres y hijos prendiendo algunos dellos."

[39] For example, see the description of the regions of the Alpujarras in Mármol Carvajal, *Historia del rebelión*, 202.

[40] Mármol Carvajal, *Historia del rebelión*, 189; Caro Baroja, *Los moriscos del Reino de Granada*, 178–179, notes that hatred and derision of Christianity accompanied the Morisco reversion to Islam; for polygamy and marriage among Moriscos during this war, see Vincent, "Las mujeres moriscas," 586.

[41] Calderón de la Barca, *Teatro Selecto*, 2:491: "La primera cosa que ordena / Fue, por oponerse en todo / A las pragmáticas."

had joined the rebels.[42] As Christian troops made their way into the mountains, however, once lovely havens became battlefields and scenes of slaughter.

Even those Moriscas who remained in their homes below while their husbands went to join the rebels in the mountains would have little security. With the outbreak of war, Christian soldiers and neighbors burned Morisco homes, stole their belongings, and captured the women and children to sell into slavery.[43] Some people opposed the enslavement of Moriscos, who were at least nominally Christians. After many consultations, however, it was decided that Moriscos could be enslaved because they were false Christians who had forfeited any protection from the prohibition against Christians' enslaving other Christians. A precedent had been established for this when Christians had enslaved rebellious Jews in Toledo, for Moriscos called upon Muhammad and called themselves Moors.[44] Even though Philip II had decreed that girls under 9½ years and boys under 10½ should not be enslaved, reports indicate that younger children had been taken and branded on the face as slaves.[45] Other accounts told of Christians taking Morisco children from battle areas and then keeping them not as slaves, but as servants whom they were expected to "Christianize."[46]

Some of the Morisco men decided not to join the rebels, and they tried to remain in their homes with their families as "Moriscos of peace." Declaring in letters and petitions to local and royal officials that they were "good Christians," these Moriscos said they wanted only to remain in their homes to carry out the work that benefited their Christian neighbors. The Marqués of Mondéjar agreed to protect those who came to him. He certified that even if these Moriscos had rebelled, they had done so only because they were forced to by foreigners or by Morisco outlaws.[47] Yet many Christians suspected that "Moriscos of peace" provided support for the rebels, and they rounded up many of these men, transporting them to places where they could not be con-

[42] AHN, Inquisición, legajo 2022, no. 14.

[43] Mármol Carvajal, *Historia del rebelión*, 343, who blamed these attacks on undisciplined Christian soldiers. For more on the slaves taken during the war, see Martín Casares, *La esclavitud*, 110–115.

[44] Mármol Carvajal, *Historia del rebelión*, 247.

[45] *Pragmática y declaración sobre los moriscos del Reyno de Granada;* and Mármol Carvajal, *Historia del rebelión*, 247.

[46] See the study of Morisco children captured in the war and taken to Málaga, in Rafael Benitez Sánchez-Blanco, "Guerra y sociedad: Málaga y los niños cautivos, 1569," *Estudis: Revista de Historia Moderna* 3 (1974): 31–54.

[47] Mármol Carvajal, *Historia del rebelión*, 224.

tacted by the rebels.[48] Moriscas tried to defend their homes and children in the absence of their husbands, assuming many of the customary roles of men. Countless petitions to Philip II told of the suffering of these people caught between rebels of their own community and the Christians determined to put down the rebellion. Doña Brianda Vanegas, for example, petitioned the king to return the property taken from her Morisco family, declaring that neither she nor her dead husband nor her children "had any guilt whatsoever in the rebellion but served Your Majesty in it and before it and after it with much loyalty as good vassals."[49]

Whether they stayed home or went into the mountains, Morisco women and children could not escape the war. Yet to assume these people were mere victims is to ignore the fact that they also made decisions and acted to carry them out. Motivated by loyalty to their faith and fear for their families, these women pushed aside traditional gender restrictions. Consider the situation in the town of Alozaina in the mountains near Ronda. Moriscos who did not want to surrender to approaching Christian troops in 1570 gathered in an ancient castle whose walls also enclosed a church and some houses. Only seven men were there to join the women and children, and the women took on "the defense of the weak walls," disguising themselves "with hats and cloth caps on their heads and wearing short capes" so that "the enemies understood that they were men."[50] María de Sagredo, a Christian woman in this same battle, took similar action on the other side when her father was shot dead by a Morisco. Taking a short cape from the body of her father, she put it on along with a helmet. Then with a crossbow in her hands and a quiver of arrows at her side, she mounted the wall and fought as "a brave man, defending a small opening, and killed one Moor and wounded many others by arrow."[51]

[48] For the rounding up of Moriscos who said they were not rebels, see Mármol Carvajal, *Historia del rebelión*, 323–324.

[49] AGS, Cámara de Castilla, legajo 2169, n.p.: "supplicando a V Mag sea servido de mandar la bolver y restitución [de] la hacienda que se le tomó en el reyno de Granada atento que su marido ni ella ni sus hijos que en aquella sazon el mayor hera de seis años no solo no tubieron culpa ninguna en la rebelion pero servieron en ella y antes y después a V Mag con mucha lealtad como buenos vasallos." This legajo contains petitions from both "Moriscos of peace" and Christians asking for special consideration or compensation for the losses they suffered during the war.

[50] Mármol Carvajal, *Historia del rebelión*, 352.

[51] Mármol Carvajal, *Historia del rebelión*, 352. As a member of the winning side, María de Sagredo could request for her marriage dowry estates that had once belonged to Moriscos. Compare these examples of women warriors with that of the Christian women of medieval Avila described in María del Carmen Carlé, *La sociedad hispano medieval. Grupos*

Disguise could work for both men and women. In the winter of 1569–1570, Morisco soldiers donned women's head coverings and waited in ambush for Christian soldiers. Believing they were women, a Christian squadron approached them, expecting to take them prisoner or kill them. Instead, the disguised Morisco soldiers opened fire and killed many of the unsuspecting Christians. Morisco women fought in this skirmish, as well. A Christian captain, according to Hurtado de Mendoza, died after a Morisca hit him in the head with a stone.[52]

In his description of the battle of Galera, Pérez de Hita wrote of Morisco women and children who joined the fight to save their besieged city. After Christians dug tunnels and set off explosives beneath the city, they quickly entered Galera and found women and children "with a very great diligence" carrying stones to hurl at them.[53] Among the women, two especially distinguished themselves "with such courage that it was marvelous to see how they fought so bravely and defensively."[54] One took command and inspired the defenders with her spirit and bravery under fire. The other, whom he identified as Zarçamodonia, fought with a sword in her hands. She

> attacked a soldier who climbed up the fortification very confident of his own bravery, and with the sword she wounded him badly, and not content with this she grappled with him so powerfully that she knocked him off his feet and in one instant without anyone's being able to defend him, she beheaded him and seized the armor and helmet that the soldier was wearing, and the first wound that she gave him, as the soldier came over the fortification, went to the point beneath the armor for the groin, with such ferocity that the soldier could not regain his feet.[55]

Donning the slain soldier's armor and helmet, Zarçamodonia continued to fight, killing "by her hand eighteen soldiers, and not the worst of the field."[56]

More than merely imitating the actions of male warriors, Zarçamodonia also tried to bring peace between Morisco rebels and Turkish soldiers who had arrived to support them against the Christians.

---

períficos: Las mujeres y los pobres (Barcelona: Editorial Gedisa, 1988), 74–75. These women decided to undertake the defense of Avila when Moors appeared and all their men had died or disappeared; they, too, disguised themselves as men and stationed themselves on the city walls. In this case, according to Christian tradition, they tricked the Moors into leaving in the belief that the city was armed.

[52] Hurtado de Mendoza, *La guerra de Granada*, 109.

[53] Pérez de Hita, *Guerras civiles de Granada*, 2:253.

[54] Pérez de Hita, *Guerras civiles de Granada*, 2:253.

[55] Pérez de Hita, *Guerras civiles de Granada*, 2:253.

[56] Pérez de Hita, *Guerras civiles de Granada*, 2:253.

Working with many other women, Zarçamodonia was able to get the allies to settle their quarrel. Then, in the time-honored fashion reported by Pérez de Hita, a beautiful Moorish woman was married to the Turkish commander, "and thus was all pacified."[57]

An unusual individual, Zarçamodonia personified a tradition known to many people living in early modern Spain. The "manly woman" appeared in both fiction and nonfiction. Sometimes a figure of ridicule, she was also esteemed as a model. Reformed Carmelites such as Teresa de Jesús and María de San José exhorted nuns to emulate the courage and purposeful action of the manly woman.[58] The Jesuit Juan de Sandoval wrote of historical amazons in his treatise on Ethiopia. According to Justinian, he wrote, these women were so brave that "with great courage they seized control of all Asia."[59] Members of religious orders had reported their presence in a "Province of Amazons" near the Kingdom of Gorage in the Ethiopian Empire, as well as in areas of South America. Carrying arms for hunting and participating in wars and disputes, "they demonstrated more a spirit of warlike men than that of weak women." From a young age, he wrote, "they burn the right breast in order to wither it" so that they can use the right arm to draw the bow to shoot arrows.[60] No report suggests that Zarçamodonia belonged to such a group of warlike women; instead, available evidence implies that she and the other Moriscas who participated in the battles of the War of the Alpujarras did so in order to survive.

In the final throes of fierce fighting in Galera, stones "rained down" on Christian soldiers, the Moriscas and children fighting along with the men.[61] They defended the town house by house, but Christian soldiers continued to enter, setting houses on fire and breaking down the walls of the city. Noting the bravery of Zarçamodonia, Pérez de Hita praised "many other Moras [who] also fought courageously and died fighting as men."[62] He described one young woman who died that day. This

[57] Pérez de Hita, *Guerras civiles de Granada*, 2:261.

[58] See, for example, BN ms 3537, María de San José, "Carta que escribe una pobre, y presa descalça consolándose a sus Hermanas, y hijas que por berla así estaban afligidas, del año 1593."

[59] BN ms R 12.179, Juan de Sandoval, S.J., *De Instauranda Æthiopium Salute* (Cartagena, ca. 1642), 342–347: "mugeres tan esforçadas, que segun Justinio, señorearon con gran valor toda la Asia."

[60] Sandoval, *De Instauranda Æthiopium*, 342–343: "muestran un animo mas de hombres belicosos, que de mugeres flacas. Y para este efeto desde pequeñas las queman el pecho derecho, para que secandoseles, y no les creciendo, puedan usar del braço derecho, y del arco, y flechas ligeramente." Note that the author uses the verb "quemar" to describe what they did to the right breast in order to be able to use their right arm for the bow.

[61] Pérez de Hita, *Guerras civiles de Granada*, 2:281.

[62] Pérez de Hita, *Guerras civiles de Granada*, 2:281.

> very beautiful maiden, who had lost her mother earlier, knew that her father had died in the bombardment, and taking by the hand her two little brothers she left her house and . . . gathered the two children with her left arm and brandishing a sword with the right hand, she went out to the battle and fought bravely with the Christians until they killed her and her two brothers together. It is certainly a thing deserving to be remembered and to be written down, for understanding the force of love.[63]

Zarçamodonia fought so valiantly on this day that her courage frightened Christian soldiers. One, finally realizing the importance of getting rid of her, shot her dead. Those women who did not die in the desperate defense were enslaved. For Pérez de Hita, the victorious Christians at the end of this battle used "such rigor and severity with the women and children that it seems to me that the destruction there was much more than that permitted by justice . . . death reaching not only the women but also the baptized babies."[64] This was done by order of Don Juan de Austria, commander of Christian forces. According to Pérez de Hita, Don Juan wanted the punishment to serve as an example to other rebels, but he also sought to temper the severity of the order and pardoned the lives of women and children younger than five years old. In his description of the Alpujarras rebellion, Mármol Carvajal reported that Christians killed 400 women and children at the end of the battle of Galera, sparing another 4,500 of them.[65]

Even after the defeat of Galera, the rebellion sputtered on sporadically. To hasten an end to the war, Philip II ordered that all Moriscos who had remained in Granada be sent elsewhere so they could no longer give information and aid to Aben Humeya, the rebel leader, and those who continued to fight with him. Philip II also directed that the war be proclaimed as one of "fire and blood" rather than as a mere punitive action against rebels.[66] Christians sought to end the war more quickly by planting copies of a letter, written in Arabic, where Moriscos could find them. Supposedly written to the rebels by a Muslim religious leader (*alfaquí*) or hermit (*morabito*), the letter told Moriscos that it was foolish to continue to believe they could win the war. They might receive help from Turks and the kings of Africa, the letter warned, but they could never defeat the king of Spain "because he is invincible."[67]

[63] Pérez de Hita, *Guerras civiles de Granada*, 2:286.
[64] Pérez de Hita, *Guerras civiles de Granada*, 2:285.
[65] Mármol Carvajal, *Historia del rebelión*, 314.
[66] Mármol Carvajal, *Historia del rebelión*, 292.
[67] Mármol Carvajal, *Historia del rebelión*, 320–321.

Historical Significance of Women in War

Although some women joined actively in the fighting against Christian troops, it is likely that their presence among the rebellious Moriscos slowed the pace and mobility of these men. Much more familiar than most Christians with the trails and strongholds of the Alpujarras, Moriscos could have fought a lengthier and perhaps more successful guerrilla war against their adversaries if they had had fewer concerns about protecting the women and children with them. Christians often forced Moriscos out of their hiding places by attacking the women and children whom they had left behind when they saw Christian soldiers approaching. Sometimes Moriscos left the women and children in protective caves for periods of time. Yet to "win" this war, Moriscos had to be able to leave their mountain strongholds, connect with Turkish troops, and defeat Christians holding the towns and cities of Andalucia.

At the same time, the presence of women and children probably stiffened the fighting resolve of the Morisco men. In the War of the Alpujarras, the women did not have to make the men return to the battlefield by throwing stones or wounding the faces of the men's horses, as they had done in the battle of the valley of Yarmuk. Instead, they joined with the men in the fighting, using whatever they could find as weapons, even stones and roasting spits. Some women, such as those in the ancient castle of Alozaina, held off the enemy by disguising themselves as Morisco soldiers. In a few cases, Moriscas seized sword, armor, and helmet to fight as women warriors. Perhaps their determination to protect their families augmented the determination of the men to defend their faith and culture and their right to their own identity.

Unfortunately, the presence of women and children in this war deepened its tragic consequences. Some evidence suggests that Christians expected to be able to put down the Morisco rebellion rather quickly, but by summer of 1569 any optimism had been replaced by genuine concern and a hardening attitude toward the rebels. On July 15, 1569, Don Juan de Austria had written to Philip II about the problems he was having in subduing the rebellion and warned of "the damage that is growing" and "the fire that is spreading there."[68] Moreover, Moriscos had sought aid from the Ottoman Turks and from North Africa. In the early months of 1570 the Ottoman ruler Selim II finally dispatched men

[68] AGS, Consejo de Cámara, legajo 2052: "al daño que yba cresciendo, y . . . el fuego que alli van encendiendo."

and arms from Algiers to aid the Morisco rebels. A company of about 200 of these soldiers landed in Spain just north of Almería. Aben Humeya, the Morisco leader, sent his brother to Algiers to plead for more soldiers and arms and to assure Muslims there that Spanish Muslims would accept the rule of the Ottoman sultan.[69]

In the final months of the war when Christian soldiers relentlessly pursued them, Moriscos took their wives and children into large caves that became primary battle sites. In just two of these caves, an eyewitness reported, Christian soldiers found some 800 people.[70] At another place, they found more than 3,000 Moriscos "and a great quantity of women, baggage, and stock animals."[71] They captured the women and children and killed most of the Morisco men. Then, to compensate themselves for some of their own hardships and their lack of salary, the Christian troops sold their captives into slavery. One scholar estimates that a minimum of 25,000 people were enslaved during this war, predominantly women and children.[72] The exact number of Morisco slaves taken in this war will never be known, but the slave population clearly increased in Andalucia following the war, particularly in the cities of Seville and Lisbon, which were major slave markets at this time.[73]

Moriscos also captured Christians whom they sought to sell as slaves. By June 1570, they had nothing to feed them and wanted to kill them. The Turks who had come to the aid of the Moriscos opposed their plan, however. They argued that it was inhumane to kill captives, and they urged Moriscos to wait for three days. If within that time no boats came from North Africa to take the captives and sell them as slaves in Berbery, they agreed that Moriscos could kill the captives or do whatever they wished with them.[74] We do not know precisely what happened to these captives, but it is unlikely that Moriscos were able to move and sell them in the last few months of the rebellion, when they were coming under increasing fire from the Christian soldiers pursuing them. In some cases, they may have turned the captives over to Morisco women for execution. After "extracting their eyes with knives," the Moriscas "finished killing them with stones," a pattern of the uprising noted in the history written by Mármol Carvajal.[75]

The presence of Moriscas and their children in the War of the Alpujarras brings the reality of battle into sharp contrast with the old ideal

[69] Hess, *The Forgotten Frontier*, 88–89.
[70] Mármol Carvajal, *Historia del rebelión*, 360.
[71] Mármol Carvajal, *Historia del rebelión*, 338.
[72] Aranda Doncel, *Los moriscos*, 133–134.
[73] Domínguez Ortiz, "La esclavitud," 369–428.
[74] Mármol Carvajal, *Historia del rebelión*, 348.
[75] Mármol Carvajal, *Historia del rebelión*, 203.

of warfare as an orderly chivalric contest between male combatants, neatly fought according to rules, and carefully choreographed by men of honor. Even in the twentieth century, a military historian has declared that "warfare is . . . the one human activity from which women, with the most insignificant exceptions, have always and everywhere stood apart."[76] Yet women in the Morisco rebellion had no opportunity to stand apart. Like most wars, that of the Alpujarras was messy, dirty, bloody, and cruel. Moriscas' roles in the war of 1568–1570 show that far from being the game of kings or powerful men, war almost obscenely seizes and arms the disempowered—the poor men rounded up to serve in the infantry, to be sure, but also the women and children who must fight for their lives, who snatch a sword, a poker, or a stone to maim an enemy who is lunging to kill them.

Not surprisingly, atrocities escalated on both sides of the war, and accounts of these barbarities stirred even more people to act out of hatred and fear. Moriscos feared Christians who burned their homes, captured and enslaved or killed their women and children. Christians feared capture by Moriscos who could torture them and then turn them over to their women to brutally mistreat before killing them.[77] They told of Morisco soldiers who had killed a twelve-year-old boy by cutting him into pieces before the eyes of his mother.[78] Their enemies were not only brutal, Christians said, but deceitful in using disguise and trickery to kill them. One Morisca tricked a Christian soldier into believing that a nearby hut contained great riches. When the soldier entered the hut, the Morisca killed him by running a poker through him.[79]

In this "war without quarter," both sides killed or enslaved huge numbers of women and children, leaving some towns with no survivors whatsoever.[80] The Marqués of Mondéjar led troops that finally took Grajar from Morisco control, and executed every person found within the town, regardless of age or gender. Moriscos, too, could be very brutal. After they conquered Serón, they took 80 women as slaves and killed 150 men and 4 old people, despite their promises otherwise.[81] When Christian forces found a large number of Moriscos near the river

[76] John Keegan, *A History of Warfare* (New York: Knopf, 1993), 75.

[77] Mármol Carvajal, *Historia del rebelión*, 203.

[78] AGS, Cámara de Castilla, legajo 2169, the petition of Doña Margarita de Trevino and Doña Beatriz de Moya asking Philip II for compensation for their losses in the War of Alpujarras, which included for Beatriz "un hijo solo que tenia de doce años se le hicieron pedaços delante sus ojos."

[79] Mármol Carvajal, *Historia del rebelión*, 121.

[80] Domínguez Ortiz and Vincent, *Historia de los moriscos*, 37–38.

[81] Domínguez Ortiz and Vincent, *Historia de los moriscos*, 38.

of Bolodui, they chased them into nearby mountains, killed 200 of the men, and captured some 800 women and children.[82]

Monfís committed many atrocities against Christians during the war. They gathered in the Albaicín quarter of Granada, leaving by night to attack people, "tearing their faces to pieces, ripping out their hearts with their swords and cutting them apart limb from limb."[83] They captured women and children of the city and took them to sell as slaves in Berbery. Shocked though he was at monfí brutality, Mármol Carvajal noted that the Christian soldiers going after the monfís had no fear of God and committed more crimes than the delinquents they sought.

In fact, Christian accounts of the war often blamed atrocities on the lack of discipline among Christian troops. Diego Hurtado de Mendoza, for example, referred many times to the fact that Christian soldiers were not paid but were only given some food and organized into small undisciplined groups.[84] Mármol Carvajal described an incident near Ronda when Christian soldiers "as inexperienced and badly disciplined people began to rob and load themselves down with clothing and to collect slaves and livestock, wounding and killing without difference anyone who in some manner obstructed their greed."[85] As Moriscos saw what was happening to the women and children they had left in their homes, they quickly returned to engage the Christian soldiers in battle, but they could not prevent the soldiers from taking the women, children, livestock, and clothing to sell in nearby Ronda. Although Spain's professional and well-disciplined *tercios* were renowned as a military force, the Crown had to levy soldiers for this war by an archaic system of requiring each town to provide a certain number of men. In many places, men fled their homes to avoid conscription. Those who could not escape military service would receive little training or food and even less payment.[86]

In the closing months of the war, Philip II chose to regard Moriscos who continued to fight not as rebels but as people responding to the wrongs committed against them by Christian soldiers. He called for the return of the women, children, and property that Christian soldiers had taken from them, and he entrusted their "subjection" to Luis Cristóbal Ponce de León, Duke of Arcos. Negotiations for their surrender fell through, however, and another Morisco leader convinced them to

[82] Mármol Carvajal, *Historia del rebelión*, 303–304.

[83] Mármol Carvajal, *Historia del rebelión*, 160.

[84] Hurtado de Mendoza, *La guerra de Granada*, 90, for an example.

[85] Mármol Carvajal, *Historia del rebelión*, 343.

[86] Domínguez Ortiz and Vincent, *Historia de los moriscos*, 40.

rebel. The Duke of Arcos then hanged some of them and sent others to galley service.[87]

Morisco rebels who held out against Christian soldiers defended their mountain strongholds to the death. The commander left in charge of clearing out the rebels held to a policy of "iron, hunger, and calamity."[88] The rebel leader, Aben Aboo, continued with about 400 men, going from cave to cave. One of his followers negotiated with Christians in March 1571. After Christians killed the leader, they brought his body back to Granada, where it was quartered. His head was placed on the arch of the Rastro gate that leads to the Alpujarras; this marked the end of the war of Granada, which had succeeded in "destroying the Morisco nation that had remained in [Granada]."[89]

No explanation can excuse atrocities, nor does vengeance die quickly after such wars. The peace following the War of the Alpujarras inflamed still raw wounds rather than healing resentments and suspicions between Christians and Moriscos. Even before the final Morisco surrender, Philip II ordered all Moriscos of Granada, whether rebels or not, to report to relocation centers. Under armed guard, some 50,000 men, women, and children would be uprooted from their homes and dispersed throughout Castile. More than one-quarter of them would die during the journey.[90]

Moriscos who survived the War of the Alpujarras had much to mourn. Defeated by the armies of Philip II, they now had to leave their homes and follow royal orders to travel to other parts of the Spanish kingdoms for relocation. Many families had lost to the war members who had been killed or captured and sold into slavery. Those Moriscos who knew the prophecies contained in Arabic books that the Inquisition had found in Granada may have thought in particular of the foretelling of the destruction of the family. Describing the punishments inflicted on the people, one prophecy declared that the scarcity of "charity and mercy, and the little fear of God in committing every evil and offense never appeared in any family, but that God would punish them with not hearing their prayers and pleas in their tribulations and fatigues; because when sin appears in the land, the sovereign Lord sends the punishment that must come from heaven."[91]

[87] Mármol Carvajal, *Historia del rebelión*, 355.

[88] Mármol Carvajal, *Historia del rebelión*, 363.

[89] Mármol Carvajal, *Historia del rebelión*, 364–365.

[90] AGS, Cámara de Castilla, legajo 2157, includes a letter from Cristóbal del Aguila to Philip II, November 3, 1570, describing the process of relocating the Moriscos. See also Domínguez Ortiz and Vincent, *Historia de los moriscos*, 50–56.

[91] Quoted in Mármol Carvajal, *Historia del rebelión*, 171.

Zarçamodonia and most of the nameless women who fought in the War of the Alpujarras died in battle before the surviving victims of the war began the long journey of exile. Yet the stories of these Moriscas inform us not only about the world of the sixteenth century but also about our own time. We learn from them how religious ideas combine with and empower economic, political, social, and cultural interests. And we see how such powerful combinations can motivate and justify actions, negotiate and define human identities, construct and preserve social institutions. Stories of the Moriscas corroborate the experience of many women and men who have found in warfare suffering and devastating loss, as well as an opportunity to challenge the usual social order.[92] They also show us how religious beliefs can combine with gender ideology to challenge a traditional gender order, if only for a time. Whether amazons or victims, the women of the War of the Alpujarras can teach us many lessons.

[92] As examples of historical scholarship on women, war, and violence see Linda Grant De Pauw, *Battle Cries and Lullabies: Women in War from Prehistory to the Present* (Norman: University of Oklahoma Press, 1998); Susan R. Grayzel, *Women and the First World War* (New York and London: Longman, 2002); Olwen Hufton, "Women and Revolution," *Past and Present* 53 (1971): 90–108; and Sheila Rowbotham, *Women, Resistance and Revolution: A History of Women and Revolution in the Modern World* (New York: Vintage, 1974).

5

PATIENCE AND PERSEVERANCE

ROUND UP THE "Moriscos of peace," Philip II ordered his soldiers in March 1570. Months before the War of the Alpujarras had ended, he sought to relocate these Moriscos of Granada who maintained that they had not fought against his armies. The king wanted them far from where they might provide support for the rebels. They had to leave their homes and farms, which they had struggled to maintain during the nearly two years of the war. And they were to bring their wives and children with them. Soldiers took them to churches in Granada where they would be kept under guard so that they would not try to flee to the Alpujarras.[1] As the war ground to an end, Philip II expanded this order to cover all Moriscos of Granada. "You know and ought to know," the king wrote, "how after the Moriscos of our Kingdom of Granada had risen up, rebelled, and taken up arms, they were subjected by us, defeated, and brought to our obedience." He understood, he continued, that "it was suitable for the complete security, pacification, and quiet of this kingdom, and for this and other considerations we order that all the said Moriscos of the Kingdom of Granada be gathered up with their children and women and taken to other parts and places of these our kingdoms."[2]

Soldiers enclosed the Moriscos in churches of Granada on All Saints' Day in 1570 and then began organizing their transportation by land or sea to relocation throughout Castile. A mutiny broke out among the Moriscos, which Christian soldiers put down by killing 200 and enslaving the women and children. Nevertheless, some of the mutinous Moriscos escaped into the mountains of Bacáres, and many made their

[1] Mármol Carvajal, *Historia del rebelión*, 323–324: "los moriscos de paces" is the phrase used many times to denote those Moriscos who did not join in the rebellion.

[2] AGS, Cámara de Castilla, legajo 2166: "Ya sabeis y debeis saber como despues que los moriscos del nuestro reyno de Granada que se avian alçado y tomado las armas, fueron por nos subjectados, reduzidos y traydos a nuestra obediencia, entendiendo nos convenia para la entera seguridad pacificación y quietud de aquel Reyno, y por lo que a los mismos moriscos tocaba, y por otras justas consideraciones mandamos sacar del dicho Reyno de Granada todos los dichos moriscos con sus hijos y mugeres y llevar los a otras partes y lugares destos nuestros reynos."

way to Berbery where the men served the king of Fez and his militia as "Andaluces."[3]

Spawning a sequel of yet more violence, as so many wars do, the War of the Alpujarras ended with the forcible uprooting of some 50,000 Moriscos from their homes in Granada and their relocation in cities and towns of Castile.[4] Hurtado de Mendoza described them as they moved to the points of embarkation with "a manner of forced obedience, their faces on the ground with greater sadness than repentance."[5] The women remained a day or two in their homes "to sell things and seek money to follow and maintain their husbands. They left, their hands bound, tied to a rope, guarded by infantry and horse soldiers . . . so that they would not flee and so they would not be harmed."[6]

The soldiers who accompanied them to their various destinations had been told to keep family units together as much as possible.[7] "Take great care," instructions from Madrid warned, "for the honor of the women and children of the said Moriscos and that they go together with their husbands and fathers."[8] Such an idealized notion of the gender order, of course, could not be applied to those families that had lost husbands and fathers in the War of the Alpujarras. During their journey of exile Moriscos struggled to keep their families together, but hardships along the way challenged their resolve. With only a limited number of wooden carts available to carry children and the elderly on overland routes, the ships for travel by sea became overloaded with the very young, the old, and the ill or disabled.

Even when they reached a town or city where they were to be relocated, Moriscos had no assurance that they could find shelter for entire families or livelihoods to support them. Their years as internal exiles would require that they summon all of their patience and perseverance simply to survive. Documents that describe the experiences of the uprooted Moriscos, together with their own stories and prophecies, reveal a deepening chasm between Old Christians and Moriscos. Surviv-

[3] Mármol Carvajal, *Historia del rebelión*, 360–362.

[4] Note that exact numbers for those uprooted and relocated are not known. Hess, *The Forgotten Frontier*, 147, estimates the number to be 70,000 to 80,000.

[5] Hurtado de Mendoza, *La guerra de Granada*, 92.

[6] Hurtado de Mendoza, *La guerra de Granada*, 92.

[7] For example, see AGS, Cámara de Castilla, legajo 2157, letter from Cáceres to Philip II, November 26, 1570.

[8] AGS, Cámara de Castilla, legajo 2171, "Instrucción para sacarlos moriscos de todas y otras partes, de Madrid 14 marzo 1572": "Aveis de tener gran cuidado . . . por la honor de las mugeres y hijas de los dichos moriscos y de que juntamente vayan con sus maridos y padres y no apartadas dellos para los inconvenientes que podia aver."

ing a journey of tears and the challenges of making new homes, Moriscos faced even more difficulties with an abortive uprising in 1580 and the evolving power of a central monarchy.

Journey of Tears

To justify the uprooting and relocation of the Moriscos of Granada, Christian authorities had only to point out that rebels must be punished and their power neutralized. If they were scattered throughout Castile, they could be more closely watched and would not be able to join together in defiance. These were disobedient people quick to escape and survive by robbing Christians. As local leaders of the village of Villa Robledo del Mar pointed out to Philip II, Moriscos who tried to escape must be captured and punished as an example to the rest.[9] Yet many Christians felt compassion when they saw the banished Moriscos walking overland or crowded into overloaded boats. According to Hurtado de Mendoza, many Moriscos died along the way, "from work, weariness, burden, hunger, by violence at the hand of those same people who were to guard them, robbed, sold as slaves."[10]

Officials charged with accompanying groups of the Moriscos to relocation centers in Castile reported to Philip II how they organized Moriscos and moved them in the early months of the dispersion.[11] Whenever possible, they were kept together in family units and turned over to local officials as families. From local centers in Granada, Moriscos were taken to two major embarkation centers, Albacete and Almería. Some 21,000 Moriscos arrived in Albacete to be marched north and westward to places in Castile. Ships took Moriscos gathered in Almería to other ports, such as Seville. Some 5,500 Moriscos arrived in Seville, 12,000 in Cordova, and 6,000 in Toledo. From these cities they would be further dispersed.[12]

Cristóbal del Aguila wrote from Albacete of the overland transportation that he and other Christian officials had arranged. Moriscos would be sent off in groups of 500, each led by a captain and two officials. In this embarkation center it was difficult to find buildings large enough to shelter so many people, however, or provisions to

[9] AGS, Cámara de Castilla, legajo 2169.

[10] Hurtado de Mendoza, *La guerra de Granada*, 92.

[11] See, for example, the report from Cáceres to Philip II, dated November 26, 1570, in AGS, Cámara de Castilla, legajo 2157.

[12] Domínguez Ortiz and Vincent, *Historia de los moriscos*, 50–52.

feed them. "Moriscos have come so rapidly that in two days 4,000 have entered Albacete and then 6,000 on a following day."[13] As Moriscos flooded into Albacete, plans for moving them had to be quickly adjusted. Consequently, eleven groups were sent off, each of about 600 people. Two weeks later, Cristóbal del Aguila wrote again to the king that they had sent off another group of more than 400 men and two additional groups of men, women, and children that numbered more than 1,100.[14]

From Granada Rodrigo de Monsalve reported taking charge of almost 2,500 Moriscos.[15] He had turned them over to Juan de Almirante, a resident of Albacete, who had traveled with them to several places in Castile. Responsible for feeding them, Juan de Almirante was also instructed to keep order during the journey. More than 560 Moriscos had already been left at towns for relocation, handed over to the local officials. However, the rest of them could not continue to travel by foot, and they had no carts. Each day, Monsalve noted, women and children were dying.

In early December 1570, Cristóbal del Aguila reported to Philip II on the 1,700 Moriscos he had accompanied from Albacete northward.[16] He did not leave any of them in Ciudad Real, he wrote, because he found that 4,000 Moriscos had already been left in that city. He continued with his group to Segovia and then to León. Now the king had ordered him to ameliorate their poverty and lack of clothing and to bury the dead. "The winter in Castile is more severe," he noted, "and the equipment of carts and baggage is more difficult and the road longer."[17] What could be accomplished with ease in a different season was causing great distress now. With little food, clothing, or shelter, the Morisco groups crossed high plateaus and mountain passes, burying their dead along the way.

[13] AGS, Cámara de Castilla, legajo 2157, letter of Cristóbal del Aguila to Philip II, November 3, 1570: "Y tambien an venido los moriscos tan aprisa que en dos dias entraron en Albacete quatro mil y luego otro dia siguiente seis mil."

[14] AGS, Cámara de Castilla, legajo 2157, letter of Cristóbal del Aguila to Philip II, November 14, 1570. Sizes of these groups varied considerably; Domínguez Ortiz and Vincent, *Historia de los moriscos*, 50–51, reported that the Moriscos were moved in groups of 1,500.

[15] AGS, Cámara de Castilla, legajo 2157, letter of Rodrigo de Monsalve, November 24, 1570. The name of the person to whom he turned the Moriscos over for transporting is nearly illegible and may not be "Juan de Almirante."

[16] AGS, Cámara de Castilla, legajo 2157, letter of Cristóbal del Aguila to Philip II, December 9, 1570.

[17] AGS, Cámara de Castilla, legajo 2157, letter of Cristóbal del Aguila to Philip II, December 9, 1570: "Asi que en castilla es el invierno mas recio y el aparejo de carros y bagajes mas dificultoso y el camino mas largo."

Reports of more deaths came from other parts of Castile. Don Miguel de Eraso wrote in mid-December that he had turned over 2,035 Moriscos to the *corregidor* (crown-appointed magistrate) of the city of Toledo. He noted that 127 Moriscos in his care had "died from their illnesses."[18] A report from the governor of Mérida said that 300 Moriscos had been taken there, but "more than half of them have died." Things had gone "very badly," the report continued, "and the residents of the land do not apply themselves to provide charity. They especially flee from them because this land of Estremadura is full of illness and they understand that evil has come from them. I have taken care," the author asserted, "as your majesty has ordered that they die as Christians."[19] Some Moriscos who died during the journey left possessions that sparked conflict, such as the jewelry claimed by several parties after it was left by two elderly women who died en route.[20] Typhus in particular afflicted the travelers. At least one-fourth of the Moriscos who set out on the journey of relocation died, their lives ended by exposure and hunger as well as disease.[21]

Deaths during the journey brought many difficulties, especially for children left without parents and elderly people without adult children to help care for them. The corregidor of Palencia addressed the problem of orphans when he reported a boy of ten or eleven years who had arrived with other Moriscos from Granada but with no parents or relatives.[22] He had taken in this boy named Hernando, and he had been teaching him the Catholic faith. Now he would have to be absent from the city and wrote to ask Philip II for permission to take the boy with him, even though these Moriscos were supposed to stay in the place where they had been resettled.

Travel by sea seems to have been no less arduous for the Moriscos, yet some reports indicate that women and the very young and old were taken to Almería where ships would take them to resettlement locations. In December 1570 the mayor of Molina de Mosquera reported that 10,550 Moriscos were to be taken by sea to Seville, includ-

[18] AGS, Cámara de Castilla, legajo 2157, letter of Don Miguel de Eraso to Philip II, December 14, 1570: "murieron de sus enfermedades."

[19] AGS, Cámara de Castilla, legajo 2157, report of the governor of Mérida, January 4, 1571: "an muerto mas a la mytad. . . . lo pasan muy mal y los vecinos de la tierra no se aplican a les hacer caridad. Especialimente que huyen dellos porque esta tierra de Extremadura esta muy enferma y entienden que les a venydo dellos el mal. Yo e tenido cuydado . . . como V. Md me lo tiene mandado y de procurar que muerdan como Xianos."

[20] AGS, Cámara de Castilla, legajo 2170.

[21] Domínguez Ortiz and Vincent, *Historia de los moriscos*, 52.

[22] AGS, Cámara de Castilla, legajo 2169, report from Licenciado Toro, corregidor of Palencia.

ing "the oldest and women and people unable to walk."[23] Transporting such a large number of people from Seville to other parts of Castile would be difficult, for these were "the most poor and miserable of the Kingdom of Granada," he wrote. "Men and women and children all come without clothing or any protection and all with extreme need for coats and sustenance . . . so that I have understood it is an impossibility to be able to sustain such a number of Moriscos." And, he continued, "I have warned two captains of those who brought these Moriscos of the bad way that they and their soldiers had treated them, and many youths had wounded them and taken their money and clothing." He had detained nine or ten of these offending youths and asked Philip II if he wished to punish them or make them pay restitution for the goods they had stolen.

Ironically, the soldiers hired to guard the Moriscos during their journey sometimes robbed them of the little that they had been able to bring along. Perhaps it was easy for some soldiers to rob these people who had so recently been their enemies in the War of the Alpujarras. Undoubtedly, the soldiers developed certain attitudes about Moriscos, such as that expressed by the Conde de Priego when he reported that twenty-four ships had landed in the port of Seville carrying "5,500 head of New Christians."[24] People in such large numbers, forced to leave their homes and subjected to such appalling travel conditions, must have seemed similar to sheep or cattle—less than human, but live creatures that had to be herded.

With the relocation of Moriscos underway, Philip II established a Junta de Población, or population board, which would take on the question of which Moriscos of Granada could be exempt from the relocation order. Many nobles asked the king to exempt certain Moriscos who had served them and continued to serve them. The Duke of the Infantado wrote in alarm to the king, protesting that among the Moriscos gathered up from his estates for relocation was Diego de la Torre, who had the responsibility of collecting the rents from his lands. Not

[23] AGS, Cámara de Castilla, legajo 2157, report of the alcalde of Molina de Mosquera in Albacete, December 8, 1570: "los mas viejos y mugeres y gente inpedida para poder caminar . . . la mas pobre y miserable que del Reyno de Granada sea sacado y asi hombres y mugeres como niños todos vienen desnudos y sin ningun amparo y con toda estrema necesidad de abrigo y de ser sustentados . . . que tengo entendido es tan imposibilitados a poder sustentar tanta cantidad de moriscos como espera. . . . Yo tengo prevenido [?] dos capitanes de los que an traydo estos moriscos por el mal tratamiento que ellos y sus soldados avian hecho y aver hurtado muchos muchachos y robadoles los dineros y ropa."

[24] AGS, Cámara de Castilla, legajo 2157, report of the Conde de Priego, November 29, 1570: "cabezas de cristianos nuevos."

only did the duke ask that this Morisco be allowed to remain in Granada for four months to collect the rents and give an accounting for them, but he also reminded Philip in a second letter that it was important that he act quickly to exempt this Morisco because harvesttime was at hand.[25] Nonnoble Christians also resisted the loss of Moriscos who had been very useful to them, but Christians who retained Moriscos in Granada despite the order of relocation faced prosecution.[26]

Pleading for funds, towns and religious corporations wrote repeatedly to Philip II, telling him that they could not survive without the tithes and taxes that resident Moriscos had paid them.[27] In despair the city of Almería wrote to the king that the city is "lost and lacking population and all things necessary for its conservation and protection and defense from its enemies . . . because it loses population through not having commerce or any business."[28] Ecclesiastical leaders of Almería wrote of "the great poverty of that church since the rebellion of the Kingdom of Granada" and asked Philip II to grant them at least eight hundred ducats, as he had in the past year.[29] Convents and monasteries also asked the king for funds because without Moriscos to work their lands, they had little income. The Convent of the Conception suffered "extreme necessity," according to the abbess, "because it does not earn a thing from its estate."[30] From Granada the abbess and nuns of the Monastery of Our Lady of the Angels of the Order of Saint Clare wrote that they were "very poor and do not have income to sustain forty nuns . . . nor to be able to rebuild the house in which they live that is falling apart."[31]

Individual Moriscos also petitioned the king to exempt them from relocation because they had served him and not the rebels in the War of the Alpujarras. Martín Forrano, for example, said that he had been brought from Berbery at the age of four and had served his majesty in

[25] AGS, Cámara de Castilla, legajo 2189.

[26] AGS, Cámara de Castilla, legajo 2166, "Procesos contra algunos cristianos que retienen moros en el Reyno de Granada contra lo ordenado."

[27] AGS, Cámara de Castilla, legajo 2170, contains many petitions from convents, monasteries, churches, and the Hospital de San Juan de Dios in Granada.

[28] AGS, Cámara de Castilla, legajo 2171: "tan perdida y falta de poblacion y de todas las cosas necesarias para su conservacion y guarda y defensa de los sus enemigos . . . porque se va despoblando por no aver comercio ni trato alguno."

[29] AGS, Cámara de Castilla, legajo 2180.

[30] AGS, Cámara de Castilla, legajo 2170: "El abadesa y convento de la concepcion de la ciudad de Almeria dicen que padecen estrema necesidad porque no goçan cosa alguna de su hacienda."

[31] AGS, Cámara de Castilla, legajo 2169: "es muy pobre y que no tiene renta con que poderse sustentar quarenta monjas que ayen el ni con que poder redificar la casa en que viven que esta cayendo."

the army in Flanders as well as in the War of the Alpujarras. He asked permission to remain in Murcia, where he had lived since childhood and had married.[32] Many Moriscos declared that they were "Old New Christians" because their parents had converted to Christianity before the rebellion of 1568–1570, and they had always been treated as Old Christians and had served the king faithfully.[33] Royal archives contain lists of Moriscos allowed to remain in Granada, some because they were crippled or blind, others "for the quality of their persons."[34] Usually they were given an official document or certificate stating that they were Moriscos with permission to remain in Granada.

The exile of tens of thousands of Moriscos from Granada left much of this kingdom depopulated. Recognizing the need to move new residents into Granada, Philip II announced special benefits for anyone willing to repopulate the places left by Moriscos. He would give permission to settle in Granada to anyone "of whatever state, condition, and quality" so long as they were not Moriscos from Granada. He promised the new settlers that they could live in Granada "with complete security, without being offended, harmed, or molested by monfis, highwaymen, thieves, and other bad men."[35] For those settling in the regions of the Alpujarras, he made special grants that they could own a house in perpetuity with a small tax, a period of complete tax exemptions, and then low taxes overall, and that they would be exempt from quartering soldiers. Those owing debts, he added, would be protected from having their arms seized, or their clothing, wives, or beds.[36] Responding to the rumor that Moriscos ordered to leave Granada had buried their valuables there, Philip also offered to split fifty-fifty any treasure that Christians repopulating this area might find.[37] Two Mo-

[32] AGS, Cámara de Castilla, legajo 2169.

[33] See examples in AGS, Cámara de Castilla, legajo 2169: "cristiana nueva del viejo" is a term used to describe many of the petitioners.

[34] For example, see AGS, Cámara de Castilla, legajos 2158 and 2172.

[35] AGS, Cámara de Castilla, legajo 2166, letter from Philip II, February 24, 1571: "de qualquier estado, condicion y qualidad que sean. . . . con entera seguridad, sin que sean ofendidos dañificados ni molestados de los monfies, salteadores, ladrones y otros malos hombres." See also appendix 64, "Pragmática, o major Real provision, dada en Aranjuez por D. Felipe II a 24 de febrero de 1571," in Florencio Janer, *Condición social de los moriscos de España. Causas de su expulsión, y consecuencias que ésta produjo en el órden económico y político* (Madrid: Real Academia de la Historia, 1857), 246.

[36] For more on the repopulation of Granada, see Margarita María Birriel Salcedo, "Las instituciones de la repoblación del Reino de Granada (1570–1592)," in *Hombre y Territorio en el Reino de Granada (1570–1630). Estudios sobre repoblación*, ed. Manuel Barrios Aguilera and Francisco Andújar Castillo (Almería: Instituto de Estudios Almerienses, Universidad de Granada, 1995), 89–132. Note that in addition to the royal Junta de Población, a Consejo de Población was also established in Granada.

[37] AGS, Cámara de Castilla, legajo 2161, pt. 1, memorial of Philip II, February 4, 1571.

riscos tried to stretch this offer, writing the king from their relocation destination in Aragon that they had buried eight or nine thousand ducats when they had had to leave Granada. They would give Philip II a third of this treasure, they proposed, if he permitted them to return to Granada to find it.[38] We have no record of his response.

Many Christians petitioned the king to grant them a house or lands vacated by the exiled Moriscos. Some requests came from Christian soldiers wounded or disabled in the war, and others came from Christian widows of the Alpujarras, whose husbands had been killed and homes or estates destroyed in the war. María Rodríguez wrote that she and her four children had been taken captive after her husband was killed, and now she and her children remained "with much poverty."[39] When Moriscos killed her husband and her son, Doña Ysabel de Malgares lost an estate of more than ten thousand ducats, and now she was reduced to asking for "something with which she could sustain herself given that she had extreme necessity."[40] Beatriz de los Arcos had lost her husband in the war and opened up her home to shelter and feed as many soldiers as possible. She healed them when they were ill, she wrote, and she furnished them with bows, pikes, arquebuses, "and other necessary things" at a cost of two thousand ducats.[41] Because of all this, she asked very directly for the estate of Aben Hadens, a Morisco who had participated in the rebellion. The repopulation of Granada would take many years, for responses to these petitions and recruitment of new settlers required collaboration between the royal government and local officials.[42]

The relocation of Moriscos took many years, as well. Some towns asked Philip II to send the exiles to other destinations, such as Guadalajara where the mines needed more workers. But the city of Ubeda petitioned the king to allow Leonor de Toledo and Gonçalo Pérez, Morisco silk-dyers, to remain because "they are so necessary in this city."[43] In addition, Moriscos found ways to escape the relocation. Repeatedly in the 1570s, the Crown sent orders to Almería to expel its Moriscos, but only a small number were actually deported. They may have been able to disappear into remote areas of the mountains when authorities

[38] AGS, Cámara de Castilla, legajo 2180.

[39] AGS, Cámara de Castilla, legajo 2169.

[40] AGS, Cámara de Castilla, legajo 2161, pt. 1: "se le de alguna cosa con que se pueda sustentar attento a que pasa necesidad extrema."

[41] AGS, Cámara de Castilla, legajo 2161, pt. 1.

[42] AGS, Cámara de Castilla, legajo 2164, fols. 30–88, reports of Rodrigo de Monsalve, who had been commissioned by Philip II to find new settlers to live in depopulated areas of Granada.

[43] AGS, Cámara de Castilla, legajo 2169: "son tan necesario en esta ciudad."

came to gather them together for relocation. Or they may have been able to get the support of Christians who believed their presence was essential to the economic recovery of Granada.[44]

Difficulties in New Homes

Moriscos who survived the journey of relocation faced even greater challenges in making new homes in the towns and cities where they had been taken. In most cases local authorities regarded the newcomers as an unwelcome burden, for they required food, housing, and work so they could support themselves. For many towns and cities, 1570 was a time of dearth. As the Conde de Priego wrote Philip II after some 4,300 Moriscos had been handed over to him in the port of Seville, the city "is in such need of bread" that it was difficult to know how to provide food and shelter for them.[45]

The resettlement journey did not end quickly for many Moriscos. On paper, the plan was to settle family groups in towns and cities where they were carefully registered with authorities who would become responsible for them. Soldiers who accompanied a resettlement group to a town turned the Moriscos over to a Crown-appointed magistrate, who then "ordered the men and boys under pain of galley service, and the women under pain of public shame that they not go or leave from this town nor its jurisdiction without express license and that every first Sunday of the month they would come to be listed."[46]

However, many Morisco families had been separated during the relocation journey, and after being registered in their new dwelling place, some Moriscos attempted to locate other family members who had been sent into exile in a different contingent. If they were able to find them, they petitioned the king for permission to move so the family could be reunited. Some of these petitions were simple matters of asking that a husband or wife be allowed to move so that the nuclear family could be maintained. Luis Alcora, for example, had been settled in Almedir, but he asked license to go to live with his wife and children, who had been taken to Alcalá.[47]

[44] Vincent, "50,000 moriscos almerienses," 508–509.

[45] AGS, Cámara de Castilla, legajo 2157: "por estar esta ciudad tan necesitada de pan."

[46] AGS, Cámara de Castilla, legajo 2163: "el dicho señor corregidor les mando a los hombres y mozos que so pena de galeras, y a las mugeres de verguenza publica no se bayan ni ausenten desta villa ni su jurisdición sin espresa licencia y que cada domingo primero del mes se vengan a listar."

[47] AGS, Cámara de Castilla, legajo 2169, "Memoriales de moriscos a la Junta de población."

Some Moriscos petitioned authorities to allow them to reunite with siblings and parents. Lorenço de Medina declared that he was a "Morisco of peace," as were his mother, brother, and sister. He had been sent to Toledo, where he was a *hortelano*, or orchard worker. However, his mother and siblings had been sent to Almuarin, "a land very poor and where they die of hunger." Now he asked the king to allow his mother and siblings to move to Toledo, where they could live with him.[48] Gracia de la Paz asked permission for her sick husband to move from Guadalajara to be reunited with her and her brothers, who had rescued her from captivity and would be able to help support the couple and their children.[49] Evidently, the relocated Moriscos did not favor Guadalajara and work in its nearby mines, for others also asked to be moved from that city. Luis de Bolanos wrote, for example, that he had been taken to Guadalajara, but his "very old and very poor" mother was in Jaén. He could better take care of her, he wrote, if he could live with her in Jaén.[50]

Children became separated from their families when parents died during the relocation journey or were taken captive. Many of these children were branded as slaves and sold to masters in the slave markets of Seville and North Africa. Philip II had decreed that young Morisco children captured during the War of the Alpujarras should not be enslaved but instead should be distributed among Old Christians who would bring them up as good Christians. For food and shelter, the children were to "serve" these Old Christian masters until the age of twenty.[51] Evidently, many of these children were taken in as servants and slaves by Churchmen, for later the king would ask them to report to him how many Morisco slaves and servants they had in their households.[52]

As Moriscos from Granada arrived in towns and cities of Castile, Philip II made it clear that they should be kept under surveillance. He sent instructions to his corregidores about separating the newcomers. They should not be allowed to live only among themselves or with other Moriscos already living in the area. Instead, no more than one or two of the new families should be placed in each parish of each town.[53]

[48] AGS, Cámara de Castilla, legajo 2169, "Memoriales de moriscos a la Junta de población": "dize quel fue de los moriscos de pas . . . Almuarin, tierra muy pobre y donde mueren de anbre."

[49] AGS, Cámara de Castilla, legajo 2169, "Memoriales de moriscos a la Junta de población."

[50] AGS, Cámara de Castilla, legajo 2169, "Memoriales de moriscos a la Junta de población."

[51] Lea, *The Moriscos of Spain*, discusses the decree and the children, 265. Also see *Nueva Recopilación*, title 2, law 22, section 14.

[52] AGS, Cámara de Castilla, legajo 2196.

[53] AGS, Cámara de Castilla, legajo 2161, pt. 1.

He also ordered in 1572 that local officials in all communities that had received relocated Moriscos must send a report on them. "Because the Moriscos of the Kingdom of Granada and their wives and children were brought and distributed in diverse parts and places of these our kingdoms, and it is beneficial that there be particular notice and report of them, we order that in all the places, whether jurisdictional capital or villages and outlying areas, a list and register be made of all the Moriscos from Granada, whether free or slave."[54] He went on to require information as to where in Granada they had come from, their ages, identifying details of height and countenance, their positions and jobs, the houses and parishes where they lived. Later Philip II directed archbishops and bishops to compile periodical census-based reports on the Moriscos from Granada who lived in their jurisdictions.[55]

Ecclesiastical authorities issued directions for parish priests to monitor the newly relocated Moriscos. Now required not only to attend instruction by a cleric on Sundays and feast days, Moriscos were also to pay each time for the instruction and to pay a fine if they missed it. Priests of parishes in which Moriscos had settled were made responsible "to know how they live, and not to consent to their speaking Arabic, nor that they teach it to their children; and they must see that they do not live too many together, nor that they meet together, because in this way they hide their language and customs."[56] Clearly, the new homes of these relocated Moriscos would not afford them the refuge and space of cultural identity and resistance that they had found in their former homes.

Despite royal attempts to make ecclesiastical and local lay officials responsible for reporting on where and how all the relocated Moriscos were living, Philip II could not force them to assimilate as obedient Christians in their new homes. They found many ways to gather together, whether at a fountain or courtyard, an orchard or other place of work. Francisco Quixano, for example, complained on behalf of the people of Carmona about Moriscos from Granada who had been living among them for two, three, and four years. In the orchards and other places where they worked, they got together and created disturbances,

[54] AGS, Cámara de Castilla, legajo 2196: "porque los moriscos del Reyno de Granada y sus mugeres y hijos fueron traydos y repartidos en diversos partes y lugares destos nros Reynos y conveniene que haya particular noticia y relación dellos, mandamos que en todos los lugares assi principales cabeça jurisdición como en las aldeas y eximidos dellas se haga lista y registro de todos los moriscos assi libres como esclavos."

[55] AGS, Cámara de Castilla, legajo 2183 for census reports of 1581, and legajo 2196 for these reports in 1589–1590.

[56] See the "Instrucción" and "Informe" reprinted in García Arenal, *Los moriscos*, 106–125.

so Quixano asked for a letter and "royal provision" forbidding the said Moriscos from gathering and disturbing the town.[57]

Other Moriscos escaped from the places where they had been relocated to return to the mountains of Granada. An official in the Alpujarras reported that "some Moors still walk through the mountains and more along the coast, and from some who have been taken it is understood that many of them have returned from Castile, and it is believed that others could return."[58] He urged the king to reinforce the presidios of the Alpujarras and provide supplies that they lacked. Another official wrote to both the king and the Duke of Arcos complaining of Moriscos who were going about in gangs in the mountains committing crimes and cruelties.[59] Hernan Martín, a resident of Jubique under the jurisdiction of the Duke of Arcos, reported that thieves had robbed his house and taken his wife and five children. They had sold some as slaves and deposited others in Andalucia. The culprits were identified as "Antonio the One-Armed" and his gang of three hundred thieves.[60] Clearly, the relocation of Moriscos had not yet brought about the "quiet and pacification of the Kingdom of Granada" that Philip II had sought.[61]

Nine Morisco slaves escaped to the region of the Sierra Morena, where they turned to theft. The residents of the village of Moral who reported them said that the slaves had armed themselves and fled, robbing the houses and estates and causing "much damage."[62] When the outlaws arrived near their village, the people called for help, and the governor of the Order of Calatrava authorized armed pursuit. They went after the renegade slaves for more than twenty-six leagues, fighting with them at "great danger of our lives." As they attacked the runaway slaves, they took four as prisoners. Then they wrote to ask the king for permission to keep the slaves as reward for their service.

Most Moriscos did not run away from their new homes, however, but turned their attention to other modes of resistance. In 1580 authorities in Seville uncovered a network in which many Moriscos had planned to begin another rebellion. The head of the city council of Se-

[57] AGS, Cámara de Castilla, legajo 2180.

[58] AGS, Cámara de Castilla, legajo 2157, Francisco Gutierrez de Cuellar to His Majesty from Granada, January 30, 1571: "todavia andan algunos moros por las sierras y mas por la costa y de algunos que sean tomado se entiende que muchos dellos son de los de castilla sean buelto y es de creer que se pudieren bolverse otros de los que alla están."

[59] AGS, Cámara de Castilla, legajo 2157, letter of the Duke of Arcos to His Majesty, January 29, 1571, letter of Pedro Bermudez to the Duke of Arcos, January 28, 1571, and letter of Pedro Bermudez to His Majesty, February 2, 1571.

[60] AGS, Cámara de Castilla, legajo 2170; the phrase is "Antonio el Manco."

[61] For example, see his justification for the relocation in his letter to corregidores in AGS, Cámara de Castilla, legajo 2161, pt. 1.

[62] AGS, Cámara de Castilla, legajo 2170: "muchos daños . . . en gran peligro de ntras vidas."

ville announced on June 20 that Moriscos who had been relocated in Seville from Granada had been holding meetings to prepare for an armed uprising that would begin in just eight days.[63] Under the leadership of Fernando Muley Enríquez, these Moriscos had contacts in Cordova, Ecija, and Jaén. They expected victory with the aid of Turks and North Africans. Mobilized by this news, the city council of Seville issued special instructions for city residents. Old Christians could go to the Plaza de Armas to get weapons and instructions when an alarm was sounded, and they were also subject to being drafted to stand watch in the city. In contrast, Moriscos were now to become prisoners in their own homes, the men forbidden to leave by night or day. Morisco women could go out only during daylight and then only to get provisions for their households.[64] Despite these precautions, the rebellion did take place, but on a very small scale, its leader and his son soon captured.

Partly in response to the uprising of 1580, Christian authorities took measures to maintain better control over Moriscos. The Crown directed local officials to remove any Moriscos still remaining in Granada, adding that guards must accompany these people to protect Moriscos' wives and daughters and property from attack.[65] One official who reported on carrying out this task noted that some of these people were widows with children, and all were poor and had been raised from childhood in Christian homes where they had never learned Arabic. He asked the Crown for money to provide warm clothing and food for their journey.[66] Between 1581 and 1589 Church leaders in towns and cities that received the relocated Moriscos directed their parish priests to carry out a census of them.

The 1589 census of resettled Moriscos in Seville shows that many of them lived in homes far different from those idealized by either Muslim or Christian officials. Slaves often lived together in the same household without any blood or marital relatives, and so did widows. Although nuclear families appear in the census, female adults outnumber male adults by 35 to 31. This population imbalance can be explained by the numbers of adult men who went into captivity, galley service, slavery, or voluntary emigration to mountain hideouts or North Af-

[63] Celestino López Martínez, *Mudéjares y moriscos sevillanos* (Seville: Rodríguez, Giménez y Compañia, 1935), 57.

[64] López Martínez, *Mudéjares y moriscos*, 58–62.

[65] AGS, Cámara de Castilla, legajo 2186, Philip II's order to Francisco de Molina, December 17, 1583.

[66] AGS, Cámara de Castilla, legajo 2187, report of Don Esteban Nuñez, January 26, 1584.

rica.[67] Many widows and women without husbands lived together in *corrales*, those courtyards surrounded by buildings that shared water from a fountain, the company of a common bench, a play area for children, and the vigilance of caring neighbors.[68]

Although Christian officials declared that Moriscos should live scattered among Old Christians, they must have found it difficult to enforce such regulations. In practice, Moriscos tended to congregate in three or four parishes in Seville, with one-third of them living in Triana, a section of the city across the river from the rest of the parishes.[69] Availability of affordable housing probably played a major role in decisions concerning where to live, and the cost of living undoubtedly kept many Moriscos living together in a single structure even when they shared no blood or marital ties. In the eyes of Christian authorities, these households sheltered potential conspirators of rebellion and spies for the Turks.[70] When they arrested one person from these dwellings, they viewed the home as a snare in which they could catch other culprits through the detainee's betrayal of them under interrogation and torture.

Facing so many difficulties as they struggled to keep their families alive and intact, Moriscos must have found comfort and inspiration in their own legends. Many knew stories of Old Testament figures who had been acknowledged in the Qur'an and recorded in Arabic and Aljamía. These writings about Abraham, Moses, Joseph, and Job told of

[67] Vincent, *Minorías y marginados*, 140, refers to voluntary emigration as "a masculine phenomenon."

[68] The census report of Moriscos in Seville for 1581 is in AGS, Cámara de Castilla, legajo 2183, and that for 1589 is in legajo 2196. Decreed by Philip II, the census reports were compiled in most cases by parish priests. Lack of male heads of household is also evident in the earlier lists of relocated Moriscos made by Rodrigo de Monalbe in 1571, legajo 2164. Juan Aranda Doncel has found a similar pattern of missing male Moriscos in his study of Moriscos relocated in Cordova, *Los moriscos*, esp. 67. Lists of Moriscos in Ciudad Real, however, indicate that the great majority of Morisco households resettled there in 1571 were headed by a man or a married couple; see Carla Rahn Phillips, "Morisco Household and Family Structure in the Late Sixteenth Century," in *Estudios en homenaje a don Claudio Sánchez-Albórnoz en sus 90 años*, Anexos de Cuadernos de Historia de España (Avila: Seimagen, 1990), 373–388.

[69] The regulation against Moriscos' living together is in AGS, Cámara de Castilla, legajo 2196, and is also repeated in *Constituciones del Arçobispado de Sevilla. Hechas i ordenadas por el ilustríssimo i reveredíssimo Señor, Don Fernando Niño, de Guevara, Cardenal i Arçobispo de la S. Iglesia de Sevilla, en el synodo, que celebro en su cathedral año 1604* (Seville: Alonso Rodríguez Gamarra, 1609). See the population figures reported in AGS, Cámara de Castilla, legajo 2196; and also the discussion in Francisco Morales Padrón, *Sevilla: La ciudad de los cinco nombres* (Madrid: Turner, 1987), 92.

[70] Two contemporary examples are Bleda, *Corónica de los moros*, 891; and Pedro de Valencia, *Obras varias.*

hardship and faith and promised the ultimate triumph of the faithful.[71] Passing them on orally, Morisco women and men could have told the tales simply for diversion, or they may have chosen to tell them as a form of consolation, encouragement, or even resistance. When Morisco women gathered to tell tales, few Old Christians would suspect that these familiar Old Testament stories might carry messages of subversion—messages even more effective, perhaps, than the whispers of rebellion from the few clandestine gatherings of Morisco men who dared to ignore prohibitions on their meetings.

In contrast to Jewish and Christian versions, the Morisco story of Job extols, in particular, the patience of his wife, Rahma, who personifies the hopes and struggles of Moriscos.[72] Rahma suffers with Job the loss of all his possessions, his children, and his home. With him she endures the well-meaning friends who insist that he must have done something wrong to bring down such punishment. When Job is reduced to a stinking mass of oozing sores, she weeps for him and tries to find help. She refuses to abandon him after their village orders him to leave. Instead, Rahma prepares a garment with a bag or sling that she can wear against her back. She tells Job that she wants to take him to a village of the Israelite tribe, because "perhaps they will be more charitable and compassionate for you than our neighbors."[73] She lifts her husband into the sling and carries him as the worms and pus from his ruined body run down her back. Job apologizes to her for the mess and its bad odor. "O my love," she replies, "O Job! for me your odor is better than the fragrance of musk."[74]

When they finally arrive at a village of the tribe of Israel, the people marvel at Rahma, her beauty, and the strange garment on her back. They weep in compassion for her when they see what she has done, her great patience, and her suffering for her husband. They invite her to bring him to their homes where they can eat and drink and rest. But she asks them to bring her a hoe so she can make a shelter for her husband. She builds it using stones for its main support, and here she places the bread that the Israelites have brought her. Then she cries in a loud voice, "Have mercy on this poor, weak, wounded, unfortunate

[71] For more on these biblical stories, many of which also appear in the Qur'an, see Vespertino Rodríguez, *Leyendas aljamiadas y moriscas*.

[72] Francisco Guillén Robles has published this story as "Estoria y Recontamiento de Job," in his *Leyendas moriscas*, 1:225–263. Note that Job's wife's name is spelled both "Rahma" and "Rajma."

[73] Guillén Robles, *Leyendas moriscas*, 1:225: "por ventura serán más caritativos y más piadosos para tú que nuestros vecinos."

[74] Guillén Robles, *Leyendas moriscas*, 1:251: "Oh mi amado! oh Job! tu olor para mí es meyor que la olor del almizcle."

wife of Job, the tested one; and if someone wants clothing washed, I will wash it for them; and if there is someone who wants bread kneaded, I will knead it."[75] She also sells her hair to earn their food. Small wonder that in negotiating with Satan about testing Job's faith, Allah orders Satan not to harm Rahma, "because she is his aid and support with my help."[76]

Although the Old Testament story of Job seems an unlikely text to hide from Christians, Moriscos concealed an Aljamiado version of this story, not only because it was written in a forbidden script, but also, I would argue, because it had become a subversive text of resistance. On the surface, the story could be read as merely a benign reminder that the faithful must accept suffering and maintain their faith. Yet in this Morisco version, we meet Rahma, the wife of the unfortunate Job. Throughout all the misfortunes that strike Job and his family, Rahma remains faithful to her husband. More than patient and submissive or a mere helpmate for Job, she shows courage, determination, faith, and intelligence in finding ways for them to survive their afflictions. Rather than becoming bitter or simply abandoning this man consumed by worms and disease, Rahma holds fast to her faith and takes direct action to assure their survival. Carrying Job on her back, she symbolizes thousands of Morisco women who took on the burden of preserving their culture and carried it with them into internal exile following the War of the Alpujarras.

Although we can never ascertain how many Moriscos actually knew the story of Rahma and Job, we can use it as a metaphor to understand better the suffering and persistence of Moriscos in early modern Spain. This story must have appealed to many Moriscos who lived under increasing oppression in sixteenth-century Spain. As Christian officials moved to forbid all expressions of their Muslim culture, the story of Job and Rahma demonstrated to Moriscos the importance of maintaining their faith even as they suffered afflictions. When the Moriscos of Granada were forcibly uprooted from their homes to be relocated following their unsuccessful rebellion in 1568–1570, the story of Job and Rahma promised them that their suffering would end, and that Allah would reward them for their faith.

In countless Morisco homes, women emulated the patience and perseverance of Rahma, becoming heads of households as husbands dis-

[75] Guillén Robles, *Leyendas moriscas*, 1:252–253: "Apiadadvos de esta pobre, flaca, ferida, desdichada, muyer de Job, el probado; é si quiere alguno que le labe ropas, lavárselas he; y si hay alguno que l'amase el pan, amasarle he."

[76] Guillén Robles, *Leyendas moriscas*, 1:238: "porque ella es su ayuda y sostenimiento con mi ayuda." Note that the story refers to Satan or the Devil as "Eblis."

appeared into slavery, hiding, or captivity. Quietly, Moriscas replaced expelled Muslim leaders as they taught their children the prayers and beliefs of Islam. They went about the domestic tasks of caring for their families, washing the family's laundry, carrying water for bathing, preparing food as their mothers and grandmothers had done. Surely it is possible that in addition to those men identified in the abortive uprising of 1580, Morisco rebels included thousands of women who lived out the story of Rahma in their homes and in exile.[77]

Rebels and Royal Power

After the rebellion of 1580 broke out in the mountainous regions of Jérez de la Frontera, the Crown and local officials increased their vigilance over those Moriscos of Granada who had been relocated in the towns and cities of Castile nearly a decade earlier. The archbishop of Seville issued another version of his *Constituciones* that now required a cleric to be named as responsible for guarding and instructing Moriscos, preventing them from speaking Arabic or teaching it to their children, and enjoining them from gathering together. These instructions also ordered that church doors be guarded so that those Moriscos who came late to Mass could be punished. All Morisco children from five to eight years of age must now attend school to learn Christian doctrine and, for those who wished it, reading and writing.[78]

To further discourage future stirrings of rebellion, the Crown initiated a second phase of rounding up Moriscos in the Kingdom of Granada for dispersion and relocation. In December 1583, Philip II ordered that all Moriscos, regardless of age, be gathered up from Granada, except those to whom he had given particular license to remain for spinning silk.[79] He instructed the corregidor responsible for this task to transport them under guard, recommending twenty guards for every five hundred people. "You must take great care and look out well for the honesty of the women and daughters of the said Moriscos and that the money, clothing, and the rest that they brought with them is not taken from them and that they be brought completely and securely,

[77] For more on the significance of this legend for Moriscos, see Mary Elizabeth Perry, "Patience and Pluck: Job's Wife, Conflict and Resistance in Morisco Manuscripts Hidden in the Sixteenth Century," in *Women, Texts and Authority in Early Modern Spain*, ed. Marta Vicente and Luis R. Corteguera (New York and London: Ashgate, 2003), 91–106.

[78] Antonio Domínguez Ortiz, *Orto y ocaso de Sevilla. Estudio sobre la prosperidad y decadencia de la ciudad durante los siglos XVI y XVII* (Seville: Diputación Provincial de Sevilla, 1946), 57–58.

[79] AGS, Cámara de Castilla, legajo 2186.

and take much precaution in conformity with your commission, punishing as an example those who did these things."[80]

As in 1570, this order of dispersion also prompted a flood of requests for exemption. On behalf of "the Morisco maidens who from their childhood have served in the houses of Old Christians," one letter asked that they be allowed to remain in Granada with their masters.[81] Other requests came from poor Morisco widows with children who begged to be able to remain in the places where they worked as servants. Some Moriscos with grave illnesses requested that they be allowed to die in Granada, among them "Lucía Morisca": "I cannot travel," she declared, "except with danger to my life." One man asked permission for himself, his wife, and their daughter to remain in Granada because his wife had so recently given birth.[82] In response to the torrent of petitions, Philip II countered with a stern warning that some Moriscos remaining in Granada claimed to be Old Chistians so they could carry arms and move about without passports and avoid the laws governing Moriscos.[83]

As authorities began to implement the dispersion order, some sent letters to the Crown that counseled moderation and caution. "It appears to me better for the benefit of the silk [industry] of this kingdom, which is its principal business and of much importance for the wealth of your majesty, to leave a number of free Moriscos," Don Luis de Mercado wrote to Philip II.[84] Then, perhaps after getting the ear of the king through financial considerations, Mercado added that it would also be advisable to exempt some of the ailing Moriscos who could not travel without risk to their lives, and those of eighty and ninety years in age. Pushing even further, Mercado suggested that the exemption should include those Moriscos who claimed to be Old Christians and Morisco

[80] AGS, Cámara de Castilla, legajo 2186, order of Philip II to Francisco de Molina, December 17, 1583: "Haveis de tener gran cuydado y mirar mucho por la onestidad de las mugeres y hijas de los dichos moriscos y que el dinero, ropa y lo demas q consigo truxeren no se les tome y lo traygan entera y seguramente y porneis en ello mucho recaudo castigando exemplarmente a los q lo hicieren conforme a vta comision."

[81] AGS, Cámara de Castilla, legajo 2187: "las doncellas moriscas que desde su niñez se[rvian] en casas de xs'anos viejos para que quedan con sus amos."

[82] AGS, Cámara de Castilla, legajo 2187, for all these requests.

[83] BN ms R 7.673, *Provisión real de su Magestad, sobre la orden que se ha de tener en los negocios tocantes a los moriscos del Reyno de Granada, que pretendieren ser Christianos viejos* (Madrid: Guillermo Droy, 1585).

[84] AGS, Cámara de Castilla, legajo 2187, memorial from el licenciado Don Luis de Mercado, January 24, 1584: "Parecio mas conbiniente para el beneficio de la seda de este Reyno que es el principal trato y de mucha importancia para la hacienda de su magd se a dejado numero de moriscos sueltros . . . por parecer conforme a razon no apartar las de sus maridos."

women married to Old Christians. It seems reasonable, he wrote, "not to separate them [the Morisco women] from their husbands."

Towns such as Antequera responded to the dispersion order with protest. The corregidor had gathered up all the Moriscos of Antequera, enclosing "in one house all the Moriscos, men and women, youths, maidens, and children, that there were in the said city."[85] But, the report continued, the dispersion order is a "universal damage" for the city and its citizens because "the said Moriscos are very necessary" for agricultural labor, the raising of silk, and domestic service. Pointing out that the majority of the Moriscos of Antequera had died from the recent plague and other illnesses, the city asked that the king exempt from dispersion the youths, maidens, and children and orphans who had been under the administration of Old Christians and did not know and had never known the Arabic language. The Old Christians "were raising them as their own children, teaching and indoctrinating them in the things of the holy Catholic faith, and if they were taken with the other Moriscos of their nation, they would be perverted and lose the good customs and doctrine in which they were taught and the females would be bad and dishonest, which would offend our Lord." In particular, the city asked that the deportation of Moriscos exempt slaves "and leave them with their owners for their farm work and their service in their houses and for the raising and curing of their horses." Without their Morisco slaves, these owners would remain without services "because in that land those who are free do not want to serve and the peons and day workers are very expensive and cost an exorbitant price."

Despite the many requests for exemption, officials proceeded to gather up and transport the Moriscos. Don Esteban Nuñez, for example, reported that he had received more than 630 "head" of Moriscos that accounted for 90 households, "and some of them without husbands, widows with their children," all very poor.[86] Some of these Mo-

[85] AGS, Cámara de Castilla, legajo 2187, letter of the city of Antequera, January 17, 1584: "tiene reclusos y encerrados en una casa todos los moriscos hombres y mugeres muchachos donzellas y niños que habia en la dicha ciudad . . . lo qual es en daño universal . . . porque los dichos moriscos son muy necesarios. . . . los tienen como hijos proprios bien enseñados y dotrinados en las cosas de nra santa fe catolica, y si fuesen llevados con los otros moriscos de su nacion se perbertiran y perderan las buenas costumbres y dotrina en que están enseñados y las hembras seran malas y desonestas de que nro sr sera ofendido . . . con los moriscos que son esclavos cautibos y se dejen a sus dueños para sus labranzas y el servicio de sus casas y para la cria y cura de sus cavallos . . . porque en aquella tierra los q son libres no quieren servir y los peores y jornaderos son muy caros y a peso de dinero."

[86] AGS, Cámara de Castilla, legajo 2187, report of Don Esteban Nuñez, January 26, 1584: "cabeças . . . algunas dellas sin maridos viudas con sus hijos . . . muy pobres . . . medio desnudas y muchas vienen sin tener mantos ni mantellinas con q cubrirse."

riscos had been servants in Old Christian houses, and many of these did not know Arabic. Their masters let them go now without anything, "half-naked and many come without having cloaks nor clothes to cover themselves." Don Esteban asked for six hundred ducats to sustain these people as he took them to Castile.

As in the earlier dispersion, Moriscos of Granada faced a very difficult journey into Castile, one made even worse by the winter weather. To justify payment of salaries to five constables who accompanied Moriscos on the relocation journey, Francisco de Molina sent a careful report to the Crown in 1584. The men had begun their work on January 27, gathering up Moriscos in Malaga, Antequera, and Archidona. Some six weeks later, on March 9, they delivered the last of the Moriscos in Salamanca.[87]

Relocation in this case was no simpler than it had been in 1570–1571. Poverty seems to have prompted many Moriscos to request permission to move to a place other than that to which they had been consigned. Some poor women among the relocated Moriscos of Granada went to Valladolid and others to Segovia, telling authorities that they had relatives there who could help to support them. Don Martín de Çamudo reported that "some poor old women go about here, dying from hunger." They told him that in Valladolid, Pastrana, and other places "they have relatives who could sustain them and they ask license to go to the said places; I have not given this to any, nor will I," he added, "without order of Your Majesty."[88]

Special labor needs of the mine and factory of Almadén prompted more negotiations over where the Moriscos of Granada would be resettled. As the relocation began in 1584, authorities in Almadén wrote Philip II of their labor shortage and asked the king to direct Moriscos to be resettled there. Philip responded by authorizing the settlement in Almadén of fourteen households of those of the "best age and disposition for working."[89] Evidently this did not provide enough workers, for Almadén again wrote to Philip II, this time requesting that city officials of Ciudad Real and Campo de Calatrava permit Moriscos already settled there to be relocated to work in the mines.[90]

[87] AGS, Cámara de Castilla, legajo 2187, report of Francisco de Molina.

[88] AGS, Cámara de Castilla, legajo 2187, letter of Don Martín de Çamudo, March 27, 1584: "Andan algunas mugeres viejas aqui pobres muriendose de anbre . . . tienen deudos que las sustentarian y piden licencia para yrse a los dichos lugares y no las dado a ninguna ni la dare sin orden de V M."

[89] AGS, Cámara de Castilla, legajo 2187, letter of Almadén and response of Philip II, February 1, 1584. Although lead, copper, zinc, and other minerals were also mined in Almadén, it was probably the mercury mine that most needed workers in this period, as mercury had become an important material for the production of silver in Peru.

[90] AGS, Cámara de Castilla, legajo 2190.

Quietly Moriscos left these jobs and others as they attempted to sail from the Iberian Peninsula, especially for North Africa. Slaves as well as free Moriscos contacted boatmen who would take them from an unwatched beach, usually for a substantial fee. Authorities who apprehended them turned them over to inquisitors for prosecution. For example, Juana, the slave of Francisco de Piña of Gibraltar, faced charges of attempting to go to Berbery to live as a Moor.[91] In 1604 inquisitors sentenced her to appear in an auto de fe, abjure de vehementi, be whipped with one hundred lashes, return to her master, and take instruction in "things of our Holy Faith."[92] Forty years old, she was a native of the Alpujarras, presumably enslaved during the War of the Alpujarras, when she would have been a child.

Some nobles protested royal orders for dispersion and sought to protect the Moriscos of their jurisdictions, but they could not stop relocations in either 1570 or 1584. The Duke of Alva wrote to the king in January 1571 about the state of the lands under his jurisdiction in the Kingdom of Granada. Huesca, he declared, was "lost and ruined," suffering damages that it had received from both enemies and friends. With bitter sarcasm he identified these friends as "the most felicitous army of your majesty," who had ruined the vines and orchards and stolen the livestock.[93]

A year later the duke's wife responded to Philip's request that nobles with lands in Granada report to him on their vassals still living in the Alpujarras.[94] The duke had not replied, she wrote, because he had no land or vassals in the Alpujarras. They had defended Huesca at their own cost, she tartly observed, which was a great service to the king because it contained 300 households of Moriscos "who were the best and most useful vassals." But the king had ordered that these vassals leave the land. Because the Moriscos had not participated in the rebellion, however, they had assumed that they would be allowed to remain

[91] AHN, Inquisición, legajo 2075, no. 14.

[92] AHN, Inquisición, legajo 2075, no. 14. As noted above in chapter 2, inquisitors could require prisoners found guilty to swear to avoid this sin in the future (abjure), "de levi" for a lesser offense and "de vehementi" for a more serious offense; see Kamen, *Inquisition and Society*, 186.

[93] AGS, Cámara de Castilla, legajo 2171, letter from the Duke of Alva to His Majesty, January 23, 1571: "tan perdida y a ruinada, y assi por los daños que an rescibido de los enemigos, como el que les an hecho los amigos, de el felicisimo exercito de Vta Md, tatandoles las vinas y arboledas y robandoles sus ganados."

[94] AGS, Cámara de Castilla, legajo 2171, letter from the Duchess of Alva to His Majesty, March 24, 1572: "300 casas de moriscos, que eran los mejores y mas utiles vasallos. . . . se an confiscado sus haciendas para la real camara de V Md y quedan pobres mendigas que es causa de añadir en daño de nta tierra. . . . vino un juez de comision y tomo la posesion y arrendo los terminos muy en deservo de V Md."

on their land and help to recover part of the damage that they had suffered. Instead, their lands had been "confiscated for the royal chamber of Your Majesty and they remain poor beggars, which is the cause of additional damage to our land." In his jurisdiction the duke also had the village of Castilleja, which had some 250 Morisco households. These Moriscos had lost their lands, which fell under the law of repopulation. However, a judge came and took over the land "very much in disservice to Your Majesty." Later this land was confiscated for the royal chamber, she added, and now there were no more than 30 residents on it.

In response to these and similar complaints, Philip acknowledged that it was "almost impossible" to repopulate certain places in Granada until more security and provisions could be assured.[95] He directed nobles to report to him on how their lands could best be repopulated, and received letters expressing great concern over the slow pace of repopulation. Some nobles wrote to him asking that he order the prelates and churches not to collect all the tithes from the new settlers who had come to replace the Moriscos.[96] The Marqués of Vélez wrote a detailed report of how he was trying to get along with only 30 Moriscos in service to him. Some of those whom he was allowed to keep in 1571 had since died and had been replaced. He listed those in his service in 1571, 1574, 1579, 1583, and finally in 1584. But he ended his report with the sad statement that his Moriscos "have been taken from the kingdom [of Granada] except the said García . . . and his wife and children, who remain because of illness, and are ordered to leave within thirty days, as the rest [of the Moriscos]."[97]

For many nobles, the second phase of the relocation of Moriscos from Granada dealt a devastating blow to their financial status. The Duke of Bejar noted the departure of Moriscos from his lands as he plaintively wrote of his "need for things for planting and agriculture."[98] The Marqués of Zeneto complained vociferously that the royal confiscation of the property and possessions of Moriscos from his lands was "a great prejudice" to his jurisdiction and would cause "inconveniences and

[95] AGS, Cámara de Castilla, legajo 2161, pt. 1, letter of Philip II to the Duke of Arcos, March 1571.

[96] AGS, Cámara de Castilla, legajo 2171, letters of the Marqués of Vélez, Conde de Puebla, Marqués del Carpio, Don Diego de Cordova.

[97] AGS, Cámara de Castilla, legajo 2187, "Relación del marqués de los Vélez sobre los moriscos que pretende tener en los lugares de su estado," 1584: "los quales se sacaron del reyno excepto el dicho Garcia . . . y su muger y hijos que quedo por enfermo y sea hordenado salga dentro treinta dias como los demas."

[98] AGS, Cámara de Castilla, legajo 2188: "el tiene necesidad para cosas de pantios y agricultura."

confusions that can be repaired afterward only with difficulty."[99] Yet later, in 1589, he appealed almost apologetically to Philip II to allow the Morisco in charge of collecting his rents to stay for four months so that he could carry out this important task for the marqués. As recounted above, he then sent a reminder that he had asked Philip to act quickly because the harvest of silk and wheat was imminent and rents had to be collected.[100] In all these messages, royal power appears in the ascendant over that of the nobles or local jurisdictions.

Although it would be easy to conclude that in the continuing exile of Moriscos from Granada, royal power also eclipsed the power of this minority group, the survival of these people suggests that they were developing another kind of power. For nearly four decades following the defeat of the War of the Alpujarras, Moriscos accommodated the requirements imposed on them without losing their own identities. In fact, the dispersion and increased oppression seem to have increase their determination to preserve what they could of their culture. The forced relocation of Moriscos from Granada undoubtedly impeded their assimilation, for it deepened the chasm between Moriscos and Christians. As the dispersion scattered less assimilated Moriscos throughout Castile, it subjected all Moriscos to increased suspicion and surveillance. Despite the hardships of relocated Moriscos, however, some of them appear to have succeeded, especially in retail and trade. Their very success led members of the cortes of Madrid in 1592 to voice the exaggerated generalization that Moriscos had gained such wealth and power that they scarcely bothered to pretend to live as Christians.[101] Perhaps these circumstances prompted Moriscos to remember especially the patience of Job and Rahma, who taught them that all things can be endured given faith, mutual compassion, and a willingness to work to earn their living and build a new home.

[99] AGS, Cámara de Castilla, legajo 2188: "gran perjuicio . . . ynconvenientes y confusiones que despues con dificultad se podrian reparar."

[100] AGS, Cámara de Castilla, legajo 2188.

[101] "Representación hecha á Felipe II en las Cortes de Madrid del año 1592," app. 78 in Janer, *Condición social de los moriscos*, 270–271.

6

THE CASTIGATION OF CARCAYONA

MORISCOS NEEDED all the help they could find in their own culture during the first decades of the seventeenth century. In 1609 Philip III declared that all Moriscos healthy enough to travel should be expelled because they "are the most obstinate of their evil sect" and inflict their children "with their bad doctrine and example."[1] His decrees to expel these people from the Spanish kingdoms between 1609 and 1614 came after years of debate over the question of what to do with the Moriscos. He defended his decision, stating that he had reached it through consultation with theologians and "learned persons."[2] Some Moriscos desperately appealed for permission to remain in their Iberian homes, seeking support from the Christian nobles who depended on their vassalage.[3] A few would attempt to return, but more than 300,000 left Spain and sought to make their homes elsewhere.[4]

In Valencia, where the expulsion began in the autumn of 1609, Moriscos gathered at the ports of Alicante, Denia, and Valencia. They came to these points of embarkation "voluntarily" and "quickly," according

[1] *Declaración del Bando que se a publicado de la expulsión de los moriscos* (Seville: Alonso Rodríguez Gamarra, 1610), n.p.

[2] BN ms VE 36-4, *Traslado de la cédula real que se publicó en la ciudad de Córdova a diez y siete días del mes de enero* (Cordova: n.p., 1610); this decree is available also as BN ms VE 195-19, *Cédula real sobre los moriscos;* and as a royal pragmatic directed to Seville, in Archivo Histórico de Sevilla, Siglo XVII, 4 sección, Escribanías de Cabildo, tomo 23, no. 35. The phrase is "doctos hombres."

[3] AGS, Estado, legajo 213, for example, includes a letter to Philip III from the Marqués de los Vélez dated December 7, 1609, in which he reminds the king of the need to repopulate those places in his jurisdiction where Moriscos were expelled. Nobles of Valencia depended on Morisco vassals for the skilled labor that made possible the income they could earn from their land. When they realized that the Crown was actually going to expel Moriscos, nobles asked that they be allowed to keep a certain number of their Morisco vassals, and then, as the expulsion progressed, they petitioned the Crown to help replace lost vassals with "repopulation" programs. See also chapter 5, above; and Fonseca, *Justa expulsión*, 259–264.

[4] For numbers involved in the expulsion, see Henri Lapeyre, *Geografía de la España morisca*, trans. Luis C. Rodríguez García (Valencia: Diputación Provincial de Valencia, 1986), esp. 252–256; Domínguez Ortiz and Vincent, *Historia de los moriscos*, 200; and Bunes Ibarra, *La imagen de los musulmanes*, 81–94.

to one Christian account, as happily as Christians go to their churches.[5] The women wore their best clothing, this cleric reported; and one woman gave birth at the port, then said she was ready to leave and walked on board the boat. Another Christian writer declared that the Moriscos took much gold and silver as they left, although this was forbidden. Women, he added, wore most of it sewn into their clothing, particularly in the bands around their waists.[6]

Neither Moriscos nor Old Christians underestimated the serious consequences of their expulsion. Whether full of hope or simply defiant, Moriscos knew that they must now seek refuge in a distant place. "With these Moriscos all the world is in tumult," as the Marqués of Vélez wrote to Philip III from the village of Mula in November 1609. But this was not a problem for Moriscos alone, he added, for in the tumult "shamelessness and liberty" had undercut traditional principles. The Moriscos of his jurisdiction, he continued, "are sad and melancholy and sell what they have, all at reduced prices in exchange for gold and silver." Far from sympathizing with the Moriscos, however, the marqués acknowledged that the expulsion brought an economic disadvantage for Old Christians. "Now," he wrote, "a [silver coin] cannot be found in all these places, except in the hands of Moriscos who have extracted all the treasure." Moreover, Moriscos preparing to depart posed an even more immediate threat to Spanish Christians. "All the Moriscos of this village band together in groups of eight or ten, very happy and satisfied, mocking and making fun of the Old Christians by night," he observed. More ominously, however, he added that "it is said also that they have gathered arms and other things for their guard and defense."[7]

Wary and suspicious, many Christians viewed the expulsion as the final act in a centuries-long drama of conflict and coexistence. Christian attitudes, however, ranged from great relief to be rid of this troubling people to stiff opposition to expelling them, whether from sympathy or from economic interests. For Moriscos this was the final act in a tragedy involving both a failed assimilation and a triumphant poli-

[5] Bleda, *Corónica de los moros*, 1001.

[6] Fonseca, *Justa expulsión*, 273.

[7] AGS, Estado, legajo 214, letter dated November 30, 1609, n.p.: "con estos moriscos todo el mundo esta alborotado y es tanta ya la desberguenza y libertad que . . . andaban tristes y melancolicos y dieren en bender quanto tenian todo a menos precio a trueco de plata y oro. . . . y no se halla un Real que todo lo tienen los moriscos y lo mismo es en todos los lugares que sacan todo el tesoro de ellos. . . . todos los dichos moriscos enbandas todo el dia de ocho enoche y de diez en diez muy alegares y contentos fisgando y haziendo burla de los christianos biejos de noche . . . y se dize que tanvien han sacado Armas y otras cosas para su reparo y defensa."

tics of exclusion. The complexities of this momentous event and reactions to it become more apparent as we explore the debate over the "Morisco question" and the factors leading Philip III to issue the decrees of expulsion. The tragic consequences of the expulsion become especially clear as we consider Moriscos' experiences of a banishment which must have seemed even more cruel than that which Carcayona suffered in their ancient story of that Handless Maiden.

Debate over the "Morisco Question"

A "Morisco question" did not even appear until the last days of 1499, when Muslims in the Albaicín region of the city of Granada rebelled against Christian officials. As we have seen, these rebels protested against increasing pressure to convert to Christianity and, in particular, the imprisonment of *elches*, former Christians who had converted to Islam and refused to return to the Christian fold.[8] The revolt spread quickly to other parts of Andalucia and resisted "pacification" for nearly two years. Stung by this challenge to their authority, Christian leaders abandoned any pretense of toleration. They agreed to follow the imperative of expulsion that they had earlier established for Jews: convert to Christianity, or leave Iberia. And, just as their earlier directive to Jews had created a group of new converts whom Christian authorities regarded with distrust, so, also, did the decree of conversion for Muslims.

It would be easy to regard the beginning of this debate as a simple matter of religious difference between Christians and Muslims, but in fact a complex politics of religion was already developing in Iberia. During the Reconquest, Christian leaders had used religion as a means to unify supporters and justify their campaigns against Muslim rulers. Some Muslims and Christians lived together peacefully, however, and neither group could maintain internal homogeneity.[9] Although no Muslim rulers remained in Iberia after the fall of Nasrid Granada in

[8] Harvey, *Islamic Spain*, points out that the conditions of the capitulations clearly protected the rights of elches, but Archbishop Francisco Jiménez de Cisneros's "stubborn intransigence" about forcing them to return to Christianity brought about the crisis that led to the armed rebellion, 330–331. Nicolás Cabrillana, *Almería morisca*, 16, emphasizes Jiménez Cisneros's dislike of elches as triggering the rebellion.

[9] For example, see the important study by Robert Ignatius Burns and Paul Edward Chevedden, *Negotiating Cultures: Bilingual Surrender Treaties in Muslim-Crusader Spain under James the Conqueror* (Leiden: Brill, 1999); and Meyerson, *The Muslims of Valencia*, esp. chapter 1.

1492, Christian leaders still struggled to unify their subjects in the many diverse regions of Spain.

Ferdinand and Isabel, in particular, sought to maintain their positions of power in the Crowns of Castile and Aragon that they had brought together in their marriage of 1469. Covering a wide variety of cultures and peoples, the "Union of the Crowns" represented a move away from the smaller segmented political units of medieval times toward the larger and increasingly centralized political states of the early modern period.[10] Ferdinand and Isabel sought to institutionalize their power in a state that could mobilize resources and impose order. The Church provided a supporting ideology, a theology of worldly power, and a bevy of ecclesiastical leaders who would advise and collaborate with a growing royal state. With papal approval, Ferdinand and Isabel established an Inquisition in 1478 that became the first institution bridging the two Crowns of the Spanish kingdoms.[11]

In the first half of the sixteenth century, the Inquisition focused its efforts far more on Judeo-conversos than on Moriscos, and assimilation of the former Muslims seemed to be a real possibility. For Muslims who continued to use Arabic as their first language, Christian clerics developed materials for preaching and teaching them the basics of Christianity in Arabic.[12] Moriscos were permitted to pay a tribute to protect their community from prosecution by the Holy Office and allow them some time to change their customs. In 1526, for example, they agreed to pay a tax of forty thousand ducats for freedom from prosecution by the Inquisition, and for a ten-year grace period during which they could use their own language, dress, and cemeteries and receive recognition of consanguine marriages already consummated.[13] Charles V even promoted intermarriage between Moriscos and Old Christians as a means of assimilation, but this was to be strictly a one-way assimilation so that no Morisco influences would penetrate good Christian homes.[14]

[10] J. H. Elliott, *Imperial Spain 1469–1716* (London: Penguin, 1990), describes this union, 15–44. For discussion of the changes in tolerance and political units in the medieval perod, see Moore, *The Formation of a Persecuting Society.*

[11] Kamen, *Inquisition and Society,* esp. 18–23.

[12] BN ms R 8782, Arzobispo Martín de Ayala, "Doctrina Christiana, en lengua araviga y castellana" (Valencia: Joan Mey, 1566), provides an excellent example of these efforts. See also the "Informe de Madrid a Valencia sobre instrucción de los moriscos," quoted in García Arenal, *Los moriscos,* 116–125. Note that Moriscos in Granada were probably the last group to maintain Arabic as their first language.

[13] Domínguez Ortiz and Vincent, *Historia de los moriscos,* 24.

[14] See chapter 2, above; Vincent, *Minorías y marginados,* notes that this *cédula* of Charles V actually produced few mixed marriages, 25–27.

By the mid–sixteenth century, assimilation—whether mutual or one-way—no longer seemed a hopeful prospect in the debate about Moriscos. Muslims in the rest of the Spanish kingdoms had been required to convert to Christianity or leave Iberia, and the forcible conversions of Muslims during the Germanía Revolt of 1520–1521 had been declared legal. Many Moriscos responded to Christian efforts to obliterate their culture by conforming externally to the dominant Christian culture while hiding their internal loyalty to Islam. To suspicious priests, these Moriscos appeared to be merely false Christians.[15] The Church, under pressure to respond to Protestant attacks and carry out its own internal reforms, sought to protect itself from the heterodoxy of such people as Moriscos.

Clerics grew impatient with trying to Christianize people who seemed so resistant. For example, Archbishop Don Hernando de Valdés of Seville issued an edict of grace for newly converted Muslims in July 1548.[16] As a public enumeration of the sins and heresies that must be denounced to inquisitors, the edict began in a conciliatory tone. As noted in chapter 4, this edict granted that Moriscos would not be sentenced for their "past errors," nor would they be punished for them by having their goods confiscated or taken from their heirs. It went on, however, to prohibit newly converted Moriscos from living together and required them to live among Old Christians. Their servants must be Old Christians, and Moriscos must marry their sons and daughters to Old Christians. They must provide dowries for their daughters, and these dowries would not be confiscated unless the Morisca was convicted of heresy; Old Christian women who married Moriscos received this same privilege. Furthermore, Moriscos must now live faithfully as Christians and separate themselves from their errors. Required to receive instruction in "our holy Catholic faith," they also must send their children to be instructed in this faith. In sum, ecclesiastical authorities now would not permit baptized Moriscos to continue any aspect of their Muslim culture, which they saw as evidence of apostasy. They no longer distinguished between Morisco culture and religion.

By the mid–sixteenth century, the chasm widened between Moriscos and Christians. Christian authorities perceived growing threats from a Turkish and Berber presence that dominated the western Mediterra-

[15] "Informe de Madrid a Valencia sobre instrucción de los moriscos," in García Arenal, *Los moriscos*, 116–125, esp. 122. For more on taqiyya and conflict, see Cardaillac, "Un aspecto de las relaciones," 107–122.

[16] AHN, Inquisición, libro 1254; also see chapter 3, above, for more discussion of this edict of grace.

nean and the North African coast. As Moriscos of Granada and Valencia maintained contact with Constantinople, Spanish Christians suspected they were acting as a treacherous fifth column. For their part, Moriscos circulated prophecies of imminent assistance by the Turks.[17] At the same time, however, they agreed to pay a special tax so that they could have a few more years to speak their own language, observe their own customs, and wear their own costumes. Christian nobles who depended on the labor of Morisco vassals supported their petitions for more time to adjust to the requirements of "Christianization" and avoid prosecution by the Inquisition.

Social, economic, and political issues complicated debates over the Moriscos. Clerics, in particular, warned that "the Moriscos were growing each day in number and in wealth, and we were becoming less in everything."[18] Yet the increase in Morisco population benefited some cities and towns that had become depopulated, because Morisco numbers fed a labor pool and helped to keep down the cost of labor. Moreover, Morisco participation in local economies promoted their general acceptance in rural areas in La Mancha and Zaragoza.[19] The immigration of Moriscos to cities, whether voluntary or coerced, troubled urban officials who feared the outbreak of Morisco rebellions.[20] On the one hand, Christian nobles in Aragon, Valencia, and Granada opposed the expulsion of Moriscos as economically detrimental—not simply for landowners dependent on Morisco vassals for producing income from their land, but for all people of the empire.[21] In contrast, commoners resented the economic success of Moriscos whom they saw as retailers

[17] Domínguez Ortiz and Vincent, *Historia de los moriscos*, 28–30. An excellent source on the concerns about Turks and Moriscos is Hess, *The Forgotten Frontier.* Morisco prophecies of victory and aid from the Turks are in García Arenal, *Los moriscos*, 55–62; three of these prophecies were translated for the Inquisition in Granada and are included in Mármol Carvajal, *Historia de rebelión*, 169–174.

[18] Bleda, *Corónica de los moros*, 890: "los moriscos yvan creciendo cada día en número, y en hazienda, y nosotros disminuyendo en todo."

[19] For example, see Halavais, *Like Wheat to the Miller*, and Carla Rahn Phillips, "The Moriscos of La Mancha," *Journal of Modern History* 50:2 (1978): D1067–D1095, esp. D1085.

[20] Braudel, *The Mediterranean and the Mediterranean World*, 2:334–335.

[21] See the Memorial of P. Sobrino of September 1609, about the Conde de Castellar's message to the king in which he argued that expulsion of Moriscos would be detrimental to many, quoted in García Arenal, *Los moriscos*, 247–250. Domínguez Ortiz and Vincent, *Historia de los moriscos*, 146–147, discuss nobles of Aragon, Valencia, and Granada as defenders of Moriscos. The 1589 census of Moriscos in AGS, Cámara de Castilla, legajo 2196, noted the livelihoods for many of the people, both women and men. Barred by guild restrictions and purity of blood statutes from many offices, occupations, and professions, Moriscos worked primarily as retailers, nonskilled artisans, and day laborers. Morisco women specialized in preparing and selling food, and some made hats and kept shops.

eager to make money that they hid or took out of Spain.[22] Nobles in particular wanted to limit powers of the growing central state that infringed on their own regional powers. However, many ecclesiastical leaders urged the central monarchy to expel the Moriscos.

In the 1560s, the government of Philip II signaled that it was no longer willing to grant more time to these reluctant "New Christians." Demonstrating increased determination to obliterate the faith and culture of these people, Christian officials again condemned Morisco "particularism" and declared that the Arabic language and Hispano-Muslim culture would be grounds for prosecution by the Inquisition. As we saw in chapter 4, all land agreements written in Arabic were now considered null and void, and many Moriscos lost any claim to the land that they were using.[23] Intensifying the severity of these developments, a depression in the silk trade at this same time undercut the livelihood of many Moriscos of Granada.[24]

Hopes for peaceful assimilation seemed to end with the War of the Alpujarras. Atrocities on both sides deepened suspicions and hatred so that even those people who called themselves "Moriscos of peace" could find few Old Christians who believed that they truly desired peaceful coexistence. Moriscos from Granada found more suspicion than welcome in their new homes after relocation throughout Castile. A conspiracy for another Morisco uprising discovered in 1580 seemed to indicate that hope for assimilation was all but dead. As early as 1582, Philip II considered the possibility of expelling the Moriscos.[25]

Yet some clerics continued to believe that Moriscos could be Christianized. They asked how these people could possibly understand Christianity when they had not received instruction and did not understand the language in which priests spoke and preached to them.[26] Archbishop Martín de Ayala published *Doctrina Christiana, en lengua aráviga, y castellana* as a tool for clerics preaching to and teaching Moriscos who primarily used the Arabic language.[27] Jesuits established schools for Morisco children. At the request of the Duke of Gandía,

[22] For example, see Bleda, *Corónica de los moros*, 905–906.

[23] Caro Baroja, *Los moriscos del Reino de Granada*, 152; and Domínguez Ortiz and Vincent, *Historia de los moriscos*, 31–32. The 1566 pragmatic is published in Bleda, *Corónica de los moros*, 657–659. For a Morisco response to this pragmatic, see Nuñez Muley, "Memoria," also published in Mármol Carvajal, *Historia de rebelión*, 163–165.

[24] For more on the silk industry, see Nicolás Cabrillana, *Almería morisca*, 115–125; and Hess, *The Forgotten Frontier*, 145.

[25] Hess, *The Forgotten Frontier*, 154.

[26] For example, see the arguments presented by the Jesuit Ignacio de las Casas, in Borja de Medina, "La Compañía de Jesús," 3–136, esp. 14.

[27] Arzobispo Martín de Ayala, "Doctrina Christiana," presents a statement of Christian doctrine and ends with instructions on how to pronounce Arabic words, 22–24.

Ignacio de Loyola in 1545 agreed that the Jesuits would take responsibility for a school in Gandía to educate the newly converted.[28] Although many Moriscos resisted sending their sons to the schools established for them, Jesuits continued to try to work with them. In one of their schools in the Albaicín of Granada, they agreed to take in Morisco orphans whom they would train to carry out the ministry of Christianization among their own people. Here Morisco boys learned their first letters, and Jesuits also learned Arabic.[29] As one of the boys trained in this school, Ignacio de las Casas later became a Jesuit and a leading spokesman for the need to truly convert Moriscos through schools that respected their culture and their own language.[30]

Jesuits broadened the scope of their efforts, but with mixed results. After 1562, they visited Morisco homes to teach Christianity to older Moriscos and to young ones whose work prevented them from attending school. In Zaragoza Jesuits placed in Old Christian homes three young Morisco women whom they described as having recognized past errors and wanting to leave their people. Another Morisca, who had been abandoned by her own people because she lived as a Christian, refused to marry a rich Morisco. Jesuits stepped in to raise a dowry for her to marry an Old Christian.[31] Ignacio de las Casas and other Jesuits urged Christian clerics to learn Arabic so they could effectively preach to Moriscos, but Archbishop Juan de Ribera opposed this because, he asserted, the Arabic language was inadequate for expressing the mysteries of the Christian faith.[32] Until his death shortly before the expulsion, Ignacio de las Casas continued to call for Arabic instruction for Moriscos, whom he described as "baptized and not converted" because no one had instructed them in Christianity.[33]

Results of Jesuit efforts seemed disappointing, but Ignacio de las Casas urged Philip III and the pope to support the schools for Moriscos and erect two new schools in Salamanca and Alcalá for Moriscos relocated from Granada.[34] He called for the increasing integration of Moriscos, especially those from Granada who had been dispersed throughout Castile in 1570. Intermarriage with Old Christians could promote this integration, he believed, and he also proposed equal access for Moriscos to ecclesiastical positions and religious orders. In ad-

[28] Borja de Medina, "La Compañía de Jesús," 32.

[29] Borja de Medina, "La Compañía de Jesús," 67.

[30] Borja de Medina, "La Compañía de Jesús," esp. 77.

[31] Borja de Medina, "La Compañía de Jesús," 59.

[32] Borja de Medina, "La Compañía de Jesús," 48–49.

[33] Borja de Medina, "La Compañía de Jesús," 14. García Cárcel, *Herejía y sociedad*, 234, notes that Moriscos prosecuted by the Inquisition in Valencia were often completely ignorant of Christian doctrine and did not even know the Lord's Prayer or the Ave Maria.

[34] Borja de Medina, "La Compañía de Jesús," 20.

dition, he urged the pope to curb the Inquisition and burn all of its records of past cases as well as the sanbenitos that condemned people had to wear. Inquisitors should not be allowed to label as "New Christians" those believers whose ancestors had been baptized a hundred years ago or more, he argued.[35]

Although Jesuits attempted to integrate Moriscos into Christian life and teach them in their own language, the *Constituciones* of Cardinal Archbishop Niño de Guevara published in 1604 in Seville called for a harsher line. The responsibility for Christianizing parishioners, he declared, extended to all clerics.[36] Echoing many of the earlier instructions of Archbishop Cristóbal de Rojas, the *Constituciones* directed all members of the clergy to teach Christian doctrine, warning them that they would be fined if they did not. The directives gave clerics primary responsibility to instruct Moriscos, baptize their children, and punish them for not attending Mass. They must visit Moriscos, he added, to be sure that they were not continuing Muslim customs.

In contrast to these efforts to make Moriscos more like Christians, some believed in the possibility of a genuine synthesis between Islam and Christianity. A syncretic relationship had already developed between people of these two religions, especially in popular beliefs and mystical movements, such as Sufism.[37] Earlier, when Christians had lived under Muslim rule, their customs became Arabized or Berberized.[38] Then, when Muslims had to accept baptism in the sixteenth century, they could remember Qurʾanic passages that treated Jesus as a prophet. Their legends praised the life of Jesus as a "perpetual miracle," including stories of his boyhood when he is said to have made little birds out of clay and breathed on them to bring them to life.[39]

[35] Borja de Medina, "La Compañía de Jesús," 21.

[36] *Constituciones del Arçobispado de Sevilla*, esp. 17–21.

[37] Sufism, which developed much earlier, is described in Lammens, *Islam*, 117; López-Baralt, *Islam in Spanish Literature*, 42–43; and Ibn Khaldun, *The Muqaddimah: An Introduction to History*, trans. Franz Rosenthal, 3 vols. (New York: Pantheon, 1958), esp. 3:100 and 176.

[38] Américo Castro, *The Spaniards: An Introduction to Their History*, trans. Willard F. King and Selma Margaretten (Berkeley and Los Angeles: University of California Press, 1971), wrote that Christians living under Muslim rule in medieval Iberia brought Arabic or Muslim practices and mentalities into Christian kingdoms because their "customs were strongly Islamized," 58, but it is probably more accurate to say "Arabized" or "Berberized" because Berbers who came into Iberia from North Africa had a very different culture from Arab Muslims. See Maya Shatzmiller, *The Berbers and the Islamic State* (Princeton: Markus Wiener Publishers, 2000); and Thomas F. Glick, *Islamic and Christian Spain in the Early Middle Ages: Comparative Perspectives on Social and Cultural Formation* (Princeton: Princeton University Press, 1979). For a discussion of the mixing of popular forms of Islam and Christianity, see Jiménez Lozano, *Judíos, moriscos y conversos*, 99.

[39] Guillén Robles, *Leyendas moriscas*, 1:30.

Moreover, scholars have found in the writings of Cervantes implications of possible syncretism between Islam and Christianity through the figure of Mary, the mother of Jesus.[40] Some Aljamiado stories described Mary as a virgin who conceived the child Jesus when the Angel Gabriel approached her and blew on her breast. They compared her with Aixa, the beloved wife of Muhammad, for Muslims saw the two women as the sources of all purity.[41]

Moriscos' hopes for a reconciliation between Islam and Christianity peaked in 1588 with the discovery in Granada of writings that became known as the *Libros Plúmbeos*, or leaden books. Written in Arabic and crude Latin, these writings were believed to be ancient testaments of the common ground between Islam and Christianity, presenting an Islamic version of the Trinity: "There is no God but God and Jesus, the Spirit of God."[42] Demonstrations of popular enthusiasm for the writings were so strong, according to one writer of the period, that it was impossible to get through the streets around the archbishop's residence. At night people celebrated the discoveries with torches, trumpets, flutes, and special fires.[43] After he had ordered a careful study of the writings, the archbishop of Granada announced that they were holy relics that fulfilled prophecies of Saint John with commentary by Saint Cecilio, an Arab who wrote in Arabic.[44] Much later, in 1682, Pope Innocent XI would declare them to be forgeries, condemning the Arabic passages as attempts to defile the Catholic faith.

Decision for Expulsion

The "Morisco question" had acquired urgency by 1599, when Philip III ascended the throne, but his decision to expel Moriscos would not come for another decade. At first, the new king seemed to favor in-

[40] See, e.g., Delgado Gallego, "Maurofilia y maurofobia," 32; Francisco Márquez Villanueva, *El problema morisco (desde otras laderas)* (Madrid: Prodhufi, 1991), 132–133, also finds in Cervantes a belief that the expulsion abruptly ended the assimilation of the Moriscos that was in process, 181, and he discusses the attraction of the Marian cult for women of the Morisco community. See chapter 7, below.

[41] Guillén Robles, *Leyendas moriscas*, 1:20–22, 28–29.

[42] López-Baralt, *Islam in Spanish Literature*, 200. Some of the "Libros Plúmbeos" were found in 1588 and others in 1595. An interesting description of the Libros Plúmbeos and their discovery is by a contemporary, Adam Centurion, *Información para la historia del Sacromonte, llamado de Valparaiso y antiguamente Illipulitano junto a Granada*, pt. 1 (1632), which is in the Biblioteca Capitular de Sevilla. See the more recent essay by A. K. Harris, "Forging History: The Plomos of the Sacromonte of Granada in Francisco Bermúdez de Pedraza's *Historia eclesiástica*," *Sixteenth-Century Journal* 30:4 (1999): 945–966.

[43] Centurion, *Información para la historia del Sacromonte*, 31v–32v.

[44] Centurion, *Información para la historia del Sacromonte*, 12–12v.

creased evangelization rather than expulsion. He wrote to the archbishop of Valencia, Juan de Ribera, directing him to continue evangelizing Moriscos. "Since it has been worthwhile to institute a brotherhood that tries to find a place for daughters of new converts to serve in convents of nuns and in houses of Old Christians," he wrote, "I ask you together with the viceroys and their women in my city of Valencia that you attend personally and support such a holy and pious work."[45]

In fact, the decision to expel Moriscos would not come quickly or easily to Philip III. He depended upon the support of his nobles; and many of them had become staunch defenders of the Moriscos, particularly the nobles of Aragon, but also those in Valencia and Granada.[46] Although they had economic motives for opposing the expulsion of the Moriscos, at least some nobles opposed it because they made the humanist assumption that standards of behavior, knowledge, and aesthetics are universal rather than governed by religion.[47] Others sought to ease their consciences in defending Moriscos, for Jesuits had pointed out to them the miserable condition of their vassals and the need to evangelize and teach them Christian doctrine.[48]

Unlike previous decisions to expel Jews and Muslims, the proposal to expel Moriscos presented a problem for the Church because these people were baptized Christians, even if they were not "Christianized." Some Moriscos had become sincere Christians, and the Christianity of some women converts could even be described as fervent.[49] Ignacio de las Casas was not the only Morisco who joined a holy order and became a Christian cleric. To expel these people implied the failure of the Church to convert Muslims and make them into true Christians. Even more seriously, expulsion acknowledged the failure of the Inquisition to protect the Church from false converts and to prevent Moriscos from preserving Islam.[50]

As he pondered whether to expel Moriscos, Philip III had to consider several counterproposals for addressing "the Morisco question." Possible approaches included killing off the Moriscos, as Pedro de Valencia wrote in 1606.[51] This could be a just solution considering the risk they presented to Spain, he argued. Yet it probably was not sufficient cause

[45] Quoted in Domínguez Ortiz and Vincent, *Historia de los moriscos*, 165.

[46] Domínguez Ortiz and Vincent, *Historia de los moriscos*, 146–147.

[47] Helen Nader found humanist assumptions in the powerful Mendoza family, for example; see her study, *The Mendoza Family in the Spanish Renaissance 1350 to 1550* (New Brunswick: Rutgers University Press, 1979), esp. 99.

[48] Borja de Medina, "La Compañía de Jesús," 57.

[49] Domínguez Ortiz and Vincent, *Historia de los moriscos*, 150.

[50] Cardaillac, "Un aspecto de las relaciones," 119.

[51] Pedro de Valencia, "Tratado acerca de los moriscos de España," in his *Obras varias*, 57 ff.

to engage in a just war against all the Nation of Islam, which the expulsion of Moriscos could very well entail. Or, he continued, punishment and renewed evangelization could solve the problem, but only if bishops and other clergy took responsibility for teaching Moriscos and giving them the sacraments. "It is very strange," he observed, "that Spain, which encircles the sea and the land, from the ends of the East and those of the West, to Chile, to China, to Japan," looks to convert the infidels in these places "and does not take care or diligence to convert and confirm the faith of these people within their own houses who are baptized and should be taught and confirmed."[52]

Enslaving all Moriscos could be another solution, for it would prevent their multiplying so rapidly. Yet, as Pedro de Valencia noted, enslavement of so many enemies ran the risk of a rebellious uprising. It could be better to simply transport all of them to live in colonies in other parts of the Spanish Empire, such as Naples, Sicily, Lombardy, or Flanders. However, he added, "in no way is it advisable to [send them to] the Indies because their lack of loyalty would damage . . . the doctrine and the peace of the land."[53]

Others proposed ghettos to confine Moriscos in Spain. Alonso Gutiérrez, for example, sent a proposal in 1588 from Seville that Moriscos be regrouped in "lineages" of two hundred families that would be placed under the direction of a Christian chief with permanent control over them.[54] In this plan Moriscos could not possess weapons, nor could they marry without permission of the chief. They would have to pay a substantial contribution to the king each year, as well as one-fifth of their income, and they would have to bear identifying signs such as a letter branded on the face so they could not pretend they were Old Christians. In order to prevent excessive propagation in these lineages, Gutiérrez suggested castration of males, a proposal also favored by the bishop of Segorbe.[55]

But Don Manuel Ponce de León proposed greater moderation, declaring that "the cutting off of reproductive members is contrary to Catholic

[52] Pedro de Valencia, "Tratado," 103r–104: "Mui de extrañar es q sea España la que rodea el Mar y la Tierra, y llega hasta los fines de el Oriente, y de el occidente, a Chile, a la China, y al Japon, por convertir infieles . . . y que no cuide ni haga diligencia, para la conversion, o confirmacion en la fee de estos que tiene dentro de casas, que estan bautizados, y le corre obligación de enseñarlos, y confirmarlos."

[53] Pedro de Valencia, "Tratado," 84: "pero a Indias en ninguna manera conviene, porque harian daño en los Indios con la Doctrina y en la Paz de la tierra con la falta de lealdad."

[54] Don Alonso Gutiérrez, *Informe*, reprinted in Boronat y Barrachina, *Los moriscos españoles*, 1:634–638; and discussed in Domínguez Ortiz and Vincent, *Historia de los moriscos*, 69–70.

[55] Domínguez Ortiz and Vincent, *Historia de los moriscos*, 71.

zeal, inhumane, and barbarous."[56] Instead, he proposed that marriage be discouraged through the requirement of a large tribute from those wanting to marry. He urged that Moriscos be forbidden to move about freely, and that galley service be the punishment for those Moriscos who kept weapons. What is more, he declared, Moriscos should pay for the building of three strongholds on the Mediterranean to protect Spain from enemies, notably the Ottoman Turks and their allies.[57]

Fray Nicolás del Río argued for galley service for able-bodied Morisco males and perpetual prison for Morisco women and those who could not serve as galley slaves. In addition, Spain should make a concerted effort to rid itself of all Muslim teachers, whether male or female, and all midwives, "because these are the people who sustain all moorism."[58] Expressing the disgust of many clerics, Fray Nicolás wrote Philip III that despite their best efforts to Christianize them, Moriscos persisted in their "bad sect" publicly and shamelessly.[59] Those called in for questioning by the Inquisition "return to their homes more Moors than when they came," he complained, and those convicted are treated as heroic martyrs, their sanbenitos as a decoration of honor.[60]

By the end of January 1608, the Council of State had unanimously agreed to expel Moriscos. Some scholars argue that Philip III's closest adviser, the Duke of Lerma, led the change in opinion that favored expulsion.[61] Influenced by Archbishop Ribera of Valencia, Lerma could cite religious reasons for expelling Moriscos. Philip's wife, Margarita, also believed that Moriscos were defiling the "pure" Christian faith and may have influenced the king's decision. But Lerma undoubtedly found political reasons more convincing, because he saw Moriscos more as traitors than as apostates.[62]

Although Christians had many motives for opposing or supporting expulsion, political imperatives of the infant central state developing in Spain tipped the balance against the Moriscos. These people represented a common enemy or "counteridentity" that could serve to unite

[56] Letter of Don Manuel Ponce de León to the king, reprinted in García Arenal, *Los moriscos*, 239–245.

[57] Don Manuel Ponce de León, quoted in García Arenal, *Los moriscos*, 240.

[58] Nicolás del Río, quoted in Garcia Arenal, *Los moriscos*, 130–132; in fact, he asserted that there were more than six hundred alfaquines and alfaquinas who had been testified against in the Inquisition, but Moriscos protected them from imprisonment by the Holy Office.

[59] Memorial of Fray Nicolás del Río to Philip III, quoted in García Arenal, *Los moriscos*, 125–126.

[60] Nicolás del Río, quoted in Garcia Arenal, *Los moriscos*, 127.

[61] Domínguez Ortiz and Vincent, *Historia de los moriscos*, 171.

[62] Domínguez Ortiz and Vincent, *Historia de los moriscos*, 172–174.

all the different Christian people in this polyglot empire.[63] Along with Judeo-conversos and crypto-Jews, Moriscos had ostensibly chosen to convert to Christianity. Yet their difference served as a foil against which a national identity could be constructed. Moreover, this difference could be expressed through religion, which provided not only rituals and ideology, but also colorful metaphors and a language of resistance.[64] It is no accident that Christian authorities increasingly oppressed Judeo-conversos and Moriscos during the sixteenth century, or that they decided to expel Moriscos early in the seventeenth; for this was a critical time for the newly developing Spanish state in search of a unifying identity.

Yet the decision to expel Moriscos did not bring about complete and immediate Christian unity. In fact, some nobles acted as advocates for Moriscos. And many nobles continued to complain about the economic loss they would suffer with the expulsion of their Morisco vassals and farm laborers. As the Conde de Castellar wrote to the king in September 1609, the expulsion would mean not merely the reduction of nobles' income but "the universal ruin and desolation of this kingdom."[65] To quiet this criticism, the royal government promised nobles the property that Moriscos could not take with them, and agreed to exempt from the expulsion 6 percent of their vassals.[66]

On April 9, 1609, the very date that Spain signed a truce ending a disastrous war with the Dutch, Philip III issued the first decree to expel the Moriscos. Applying only to Moriscos in the Kingdom of Valencia, this order initiated a series of decrees that would subsequently expel Moriscos from all the Spanish kingdoms. In every case, the rhetoric of the decrees blamed Moriscos for harming good Christians. Because "the reason of good and Christian government" requires the expulsion from the kingdoms and republics of those things that "cause scandal and damage" to good subjects, danger for the state, and "offense and disservice to God our Lord": so the decree began. It proceeded to list all the rebellions, killings, murders, and robberies committed by Moriscos. Not content with this, the decree continued, these people have "conspired against my royal crown and these kingdoms," seeking aid and support from Turkey.[67]

[63] For more on this argument, see Anne Norton, *Reflections on Political Identity* (Baltimore: Johns Hopkins University Press, 1988); and my essay, "The Politics of Race, Ethnicity, and Gender in the Making of the Spanish State," in *Culture and the State in Spain 1550–1850*, ed. Tom Lewis and Francisco J. Sánchez (New York and London: Garland Publishing, 1999), 34–54.

[64] Sahlins, *Boundaries*, esp. 9, 107, and 123.

[65] Report quoted in García Arenal, *Los moriscos*, 247.

[66] Domínguez Ortiz and Vincent, *Historia de los moriscos*, 180.

[67] *Traslado de la cédula real.*

Many Christian leaders believed that expulsion was the only possible solution in the face of such Morisco treachery, but the prospect of expelling Morisco children raised a more difficult and emotional question. They were baptized, after all, and might be raised as good Christians. As Archbishop Ribera advised Philip III, children under a certain age should be kept in Spain and separated from their parents "so they do not fall into the same errors."[68] Yet others warned that Morisco parents would not willingly leave their youngest children behind, and they argued that to take Morisco children away from their parents would make the expulsion all the more difficult.[69] Morisco parents could be consoled, one opinion proposed, if they were told that taking into exile children of such "tender age" would subject them to great difficulties, and "they would die on the way, which would be a greater pity."[70] A less compassionate position declared that the parents had no grounds for complaint because they were traitors and "incorrigible apostates" whom the king had the right to execute if they resisted his orders.[71]

Yet to argue that younger Morisco children should be left in Spain to grow up as Christians raised a major problem of how to care for them. Considering a policy that Morisco children under five years of age could not go with their parents into exile, the Royal Council proposed that officials and ministers must procure enough Old Christian wet nurses or animals' milk for the babies because either "would be better than that the Morisca mothers and wet nurses remain."[72] However, if enough wet nurses and animals' milk could not be found, some argued, they should go with their parents, because to leave them "would be to kill innocents without necessity."[73] When they were weaned, Morisco children should be placed with good Christian masters who could teach them to be laborers, according to a report from the Royal Council. The children should work for their masters without any pay except clothing and food until they reached the age of twenty-five, as compensation for the cost of raising them.[74] A meeting between Jesuits and the bishop of Morocco proposed that Morisco children of

[68] Informe of August 27, 1609, from Don Juan de Ribera, quoted in Boronat y Barrachina, *Los moriscos españoles*, 2:523.

[69] The Marqués of Caraçena and Don Agustín Mexía, cited in a Royal Council report of September 15, 1609, quoted in Boronat y Barrachina, *Los moriscos españoles*, 2:548.

[70] Consulta from Segovia, September 1, 1609, quoted in Boronat y Barrachina, *Los moriscos españoles*, 2:525.

[71] Quoted in Boronat y Barrachina, *Los moriscos españoles*, 2:530.

[72] Report of the Royal Council, September 15, 1609, quoted in Boronat y Barrachina, *Los moriscos españoles*, 2:549.

[73] Boronat y Barrachina, *Los moriscos españoles*, 2:530.

[74] Royal Council, September 15, 1609, quoted in Boronat y Barrachina, *Los moriscos españoles*, 2:550.

seven years or younger should be kept in seminaries, but they should not be taught occupations such as making weapons or gunpowder.[75] Later, after the expulsion had begun, Philip III agreed in a general letter that children of Moriscos expelled from Valencia should not be enslaved but should live free.[76]

Assured that Old Christians could be found who would care for the children, and that their parents could be consoled by the knowledge that these children would be nothing but a burden to them on their journey—perhaps even dying on the way—Philip III ended the argument.[77] He decided that Moriscos going to Christian lands could keep their children of any age, but those embarking for "infidel lands" must leave behind their children under the age of seven.[78] Parents should turn the children over to prelates or devout persons, he declared, and a list of the children and those to whom they had been given must be sent to him. Although Christian leaders found many ways to justify the expulsion, this would be a time of great tragedy for Moriscos.

One Morisco response to the expulsion decree was to send a group of their wealthiest elders as ambassadors to ask that the king withdraw the order in exchange for payment of a large tribute. They offered to maintain four galleys to patrol the coastline of Spain, build defensive fortified towers along the coast, and accept other "extraordinary obligations." Perhaps suspecting that Moriscos made this offer merely as a delaying tactic while waiting for the Turkish fleet to attack, the noble whom they contacted simply answered that the expulsion was "the irrevocable will" of the king.[79]

Morisco Experiences of Banishment

We can only imagine the anguish of Morisco families preparing to leave their homes and their youngest children. The women in particular "made extraordinary demonstrations of emotion," a Christian observed, persuaded that Philip III meant not only to expel them from

[75] Consulta quoted in Boronat y Barrachina, *Los moriscos españoles*, 2:543.

[76] BN ms R 14165, J. Ripol, *Diálogo de consuelo por la expulsión de los moriscos de España* (Pamplona: Nicolas de Assiayn, 1613), 70.

[77] Suggestions for consoling Morisco parents are in the consulta from Segovia dated September 1, 1609, quoted in Boronat y Barrachina, *Los moriscos españoles*, 2:524–526. A report from the Royal Council dated September 15, 1609, suggests how Morisco children left by their parents can be raised, quoted in Boronat y Barrachina, *Los moriscos españoles*, 2:549–550.

[78] *Declaración del Bando*, n.p.

[79] Fonseca, *Justa expulsión*, 255–256.

his kingdoms but to kill them as well.[80] Figure 7 depicts some of this emotion in a drawing of the expulsion of the Moriscos. Old Christians acknowledged the difficulty Morisco parents would have in leaving their children of age seven or younger. As one adviser wrote, it was important "in the first place" to carry out the expulsion "without rebellion or scandal to the kingdom, quietly without bloodshed because the number of expelled ones is so great and their resistance" could cause "major inconveniences."[81] Citing an unnamed archbishop, the report asserted that it would be impossible for Moriscos to leave their homes and their own children "in the power of their enemies diverse in language and in religion."[82] Moreover, the archbishop had acknowledged that he believed it was impossible that the parents would want to leave Valencia if their children were taken from them, and that before they would leave them, they would "cut them in pieces."[83] In an attempt to avoid confrontations over this highly charged issue, not all of the edicts of expulsion required Moriscos to leave their youngest children when they left their communities; nor did all officials require Moriscos to give up their babies and young children at ports of embarkation.[84] Pedro de Gamboa, for example, reported that the first embarkation from Alicante in October 1609 carried Morisco "men, women, children, and nursing babies" to Oran in North Africa, where they disembarked six days later.[85] Relief is clearly evident in the report that the expulsion in Valencia was executed with prudence so that no nursing children had been left behind and the children who remained were left voluntarily by their parents. Neither the parents nor the children, the report concluded, could be considered a "danger for the kingdom."[86]

Yet it seemed that not all danger was past. Christians feared that Moriscos, now left with no hope of reversing the expulsion, would at-

[80] Fonseca, *Justa expulsión*, 255.

[81] AGS, Estado, legajo 213, "Consideración sobre los niños moriscos huerfanos y los que por salvarles las vidas, o por otros fines han quedado por voluntad de sus padres en Valencia," n.p.: "sin alvoroto ni escandalo del Reyno quietamente sin efusion de sangre por ser el número de los expulsos tan grande, y que de su resistancia se podian temer mayores ynconvenientes."

[82] AGS, Estado, legajo 213, "Consideración sobre los niños moriscos huerfanos," n.p.: "y aun alguna vez escrive el Arçobpo que tenia por ymposible que los padres saliendo contra su voluntad de sus casas y antigua naturaleza quisieren tambien salir de posados de sus hijos proprios y dexallos en poder del enemigos suyos diversos en lengua y en Religion."

[83] AGS, Estado, legajo 213, "Consideración sobre los niños moriscos huerfanos," n.p.: "hazer pedaços."

[84] Domínguez Ortiz and Vincent, *Historia de los moriscos*, 181.

[85] AGS, Estado, legajo 214: "hombres mugeres niños y niñas y criaturas de teta."

[86] AGS, Estado, legajo 213, "Consideraciones," n.p.

Fig. 7. Expulsion of the Moriscos. "Vision of the Fall of Castile," reprinted in David Kunzle, *The Early Comic Strip: Narrative Strips and Picture Stories in the European Broadsheet from c. 1450 to 1825* (Berkeley and Los Angeles: University of California Press, 1973), plate 2-22.

tack them. Rumors spread that Moriscos were recovering weapons they had hidden and buying others, especially flintlocks, from "Christians of bad soul."[87] Moriscos were moving into the mountains until spring, the rumors said, when help would come for them from Africa. A report to Philip III in October 1609 stated that "Moriscos have gone up to the mountains with some disorder, burning houses and desecrating Christian images."[88] Another rumor said a plot had been discovered in which Moriscos would pretend to gather at Easter to give presents of honey, wheat, hams, and other things to their noble lords, but at night they would set fires and kill many Christians in the uproar.[89] As such frightening rumors spread, some Old Christians reacted in panic, even in the midst of church services, crying, "Moros, moros." Others saw signs from heaven such as a cloud stained with blood. The Marqués de Carazena reported on the situation in Valencia where "within our houses [there are] fifty thousand declared enemies that can take up arms."[90] Fearing attacks by rebellious Moriscos, Christian officials made careful count of how many Old Christians could defend towns along the Moriscos' route to exile.

Rumors, of course, ran wild among Moriscos as well, for they heard of the impending expulsion even before it was announced. Some Morisco families left before 1608 for France and hoped to go from there to Tunisia, where the ruling Ottoman Turks welcomed immigration from Moriscos.[91] Months before the first expulsion decree, a ship bound for Italy set sail from Cartagena, carrying three men, their wives, and their children, all suspected of being Moriscos.[92] Clearly these Moriscos hoped to leave Spain on their own terms, carrying with them the precious metals, jewels, and letters of exchange forbidden by the terms of the expulsion.

However, most Moriscos had little choice as to when and how to leave the kingdoms of Spain. Because towns and cities did not all re-

[87] Fonseca, *Justa expulsión*, 257.

[88] AGS, Estado, legajo 214, letter for Don Agustín Mexía, dated October 27, 1609: "que algunos moriscos se avian subido a las sierras con alguna desorden quemando casas y haciendo desacato contra images de Christianos."

[89] Fonseca, *Justa expulsión*, 150.

[90] Fonseca, *Justa expulsión*, 269, for a panic during Mass, and 167 for sightings of a bloodstained cloud. For reports of how many Old Christians could be counted upon to defend towns along the route of exile from Valencia, see AGS, Estado, legajo 213; see the same legajo for lists of Old Christian households in Valencia, and the letter of August 19, 1609, from the Marqués de Carazena, for alarm about a Morisco threat: "dentro de nuestras casas cinquenta mil enemigos declarados que puedan tomar armas."

[91] Domínguez Ortiz and Vincent, *Historia de los moriscos*, 177–178.

[92] AGS, Estado, legajo 217, letter from the Marqués de Carazena, dated January 7, 1609.

ceive the expulsion order at the same time, many made the public announcements only a few days before Moriscos had to report for embarkation. In Valencia, for example, one announcement on August 22, 1609, directed all Moriscos to report at embarkation ports within three days. They could take only what they could carry.[93] Many quickly prepared for their journey into exile by trading for clothing whatever property they could not take out of Spain. They could wear layers of clothing, sew valuables into some of it, and later use the valuables and sell the extra clothing for food. Old Christians accused them of selling off even the seed needed for the next plantings. Moriscos paid off their debts with false money, they asserted, and they refused to do any more work for their lords. Knowing that they would soon leave Spain, they even "shamelessly" married within prohibited degrees of relatedness and circumcised their sons.[94]

Although Philip III asserted in the expulsion decree that he would shield the Moriscos "under my protection and shelter and royal security," they became fair prey for unscrupulous Christians hoping to profit from their misfortune.[95] The Marqués de Carazena wrote with some indignation to the king that "the disorders, robberies, and bad deeds of Old Christians" against the Moriscos of Valencia were growing. On their way to embarkation, he wrote, Moriscos perished from hunger. Those fleeing from the soldiers died at their hands, with some 1,000 found in the caves of the mountains where they had tried to hide.[96]

Perhaps stung by other reports of attacks on the Moriscos, the Duke of Lerma on behalf of the king wrote the patriarch president of Valencia that there should be "particular care to protect [the Moriscos] and punish those who did anything to the contrary."[97] Several towns wrote to the king that they had published his orders that no one "should mistreat by word or deed any Morisco or sing songs offensive to them." Anyone who disobeyed these orders would be punished with a fine of twenty thousand maravedís, or "for those of less quality public shame and two years in the galleys."[98] Yet none of this protected Moriscos in places such as the village of Ocaña, where a local official

[93] Lea, *The Moriscos of Spain*, 320.

[94] Fonseca, *Justa expulsión*, 262–264.

[95] *Traslado de la cédula real*, n.p.

[96] AGS, Estado, legajo 217: "Las desordens robos y maldadas de los Christianos Viejos que en este Reyno hazzen a los moriscos van creciendo."

[97] AGS, Estado, legajo 219, carpeta 109: "y que tengan particular cuydado de ampararles y castigar a los que hizieren lo contrario. . . . y a los de menos calidad verguenza publica y dos años de galeras."

[98] See the report from the town of Antequera "and other places," in AGS, Estado, legajo 213.

walked about showing a false letter which stated that Moriscos had poisoned some 90,000 gallons of oil in the town. Nor did these efforts prevent a youth gang from walking the streets of Pastrana one night, calling out, "Victory, victory to Santiago," to stir up feeling in the village against their Moriscos.[99] In areas where Moriscos resisted the order to report for embarkation, the royal government paid a bounty to Old Christians who hunted and killed them. Rather than killing many of the children, however, Old Christians captured and sold them into slavery for up to 15 ducats each.[100]

At ports of embarkation, many Moriscos lacked the fare required to board the ships that would take them into exile. An agreement had been reached in 1609 that ships would charge ten reales for each person, "a moderate price, although shipowners feel that it is very little." This same report from Denia noted that there were many poor Moriscos "and it is necessary that the rich ones pay for them."[101] Shipowners eager to make money on this enterprise undoubtedly put as many Moriscos on board as possible, provided they could pay the fare. Although the ships varied in size, most of them carried between 150 and 250 Moriscos each.[102]

Even when Moriscos reached the ships that were to take them into exile, they found no safety. Don Luis Faxardo wrote to Philip III from Cartagena of the arrest of four soldiers for attacking Moriscos on board a ship that they were supposed to be protecting. He requested criminal proceedings against them "for attacking, wounding, and robbing by night the Moriscos . . . under the royal standard of the royal captain of the said armada."[103] Moriscos suffered not only attacks by their guards on board the ships but also some periods of very bad weather and very little food. When strong winds hit ships that had set off for Berbery in October 1609, they returned to Cartagena, where they quickly exhausted the few provisions remaining in that port.[104] Repeatedly those

[99] AGS, Estado, legajo 219, carpeta 109. The notice reported 30,000 arrobas of oil, and an arroba is equivalent to between 2.6 and 3.6 fluid gallons. Note that Santiago, the patron saint of Spain, was known as "matamoros," or killer of Moors.

[100] Fonseca, *Justa expulsión*, 318–320.

[101] AGS, Estado, legajo 213, letter to king from Denia: "ay muchos pobres y es menester que los ricos paguen por ellos . . . es precio moderado aunque lo sienten los dueños de los navios que les parece poco."

[102] AGS, Contaduría Mayor de Cuentos, no. 60, segundo, legajo 415, contains many accounts of the numbers of passengers and expenses of the expulsion.

[103] AGS, Estado, legajo 214: "por aver salteado herido y robado de noche . . . a los moriscos que estan en la punta de poniente de estes puerto seguros por estar bajo el estandarte real de la capitana real de la dicha armada."

[104] AGS, Estado, legajo 213, esp. letters of Felipe Porres, the Marqués de Carazena, and Don Pedro de Toledo to Philip III.

responsible for the ships wrote to the royal government, requesting assistance in getting enough wheat, rice, garbanzo beans, codfish, and wine to feed the crew and passengers. Military concerns compounded all the uncertainties and hardships, for the Turkish fleet had left port in October 1609, just as the first Spanish ships were setting off to take Moriscos into exile.[105]

As they finally reached Oran, a major port of Berbery, most of the Moriscos found only more affliction. In October 1609 the Marqués of Santa Cruz had reassured Philip III from Denia that he was treating the Moriscos well and felt assured in "knowing that the Moors in Berbery had admitted them well."[106] However, in December the Conde de Aguilar wrote the king from Oran of his concerns about the 600 Moriscos he had brought there. "I know for certain that the Turks and Moors treat them badly," he wrote, and the Moriscos are "robbed and naked" on these beaches.[107] It is not surprising that another letter to Philip III told of four Moriscos who begged the captain to leave them and their families in Cartagena, where their ship had taken shelter from the bad weather. They said they were "good Christians," according to the captain, and "for the love of God . . . they want to live and die and keep the faith of God in the lands of Your Majesty."[108] The captain asked what the king wished to do about this request, but we have no record of his reply.

Although some Moriscos of Valencia had not yet left Spanish soil, the Crown issued the second decree of expulsion on December 9, 1609, for Moriscos of Castile. More than 18,000 gathered in Seville to leave on ships, many for France and Italy, destinations to which they were permitted to take their youngest children. Yet most Moriscos left for North Africa, and many had to leave their children. Some 300 small children were left in the warehouses of Seville, and people such as Ynés Rodríguez of Huelves received twenty reales to care for them and four reales more to buy them shoes and stockings.[109] In sending the

[105] AGS, Estado, legajo 214, "Aviso de la salida de la armada turquesca."

[106] AGS, Estado, legajo 213, letter from Marqués of Santa Cruz, dated October 22, 1609: "Tambien les ha asegurado mucho el saber que los moros en Berberia los an admitido bien."

[107] AGS, Estado, legajo 214, letter of Conde de Aguilar, dated December 17, 1609: "Tengo por cierto por los malos tratamientos que les hazan los turcos y moros a donde fuesen estos moriscos . . . que se an de benir muchos a anparar de estas playas y estorresa cuando se vean rovados y desnudos."

[108] AGS, Estado, legajo 214, letter of Don Pedro de Leyba, dated November 14, 1609: "y que por amor de dios so sillevan a tierra de moros sino que quieren vivir y morir y guardar la fee de dios en las tierras de V Md."

[109] AGS, Contaduría Mayor de Cuentas, legajo 415, no. 60, 2a, gives accounts for the cost of the embarkation and some of the costs of the care of the children. See also Domín-

king's decree to the city of Seville, Don Juan de Mendoça also instructed local officials in Andalucia to make an inventory of all real property of the departing Moriscos, which would go to the royal treasury.[110] Lists of these properties show that many of their former owners had been Morisco women in Seville and Ecija.[111]

As the decrees of expulsion followed for Aragon and Catalonia, some 25,000 Moriscos traveled overland across the Pyrenees into France. They found a cold welcome here, however, and many went on to North Africa and the eastern Mediterranean.[112] Other Moriscos left for Rome, Venice, Salonica, and Agde, which often served as temporary stopovers on the long trip to Turkey. Moriscos also settled in Egypt, Libya, and Constantinople, but the great majority went to Berbery despite reports that many Moriscos suffered bad treatment and died there.[113] Estimates vary for the number of Moriscos who left Spain during the expulsion, but it was probably around 300,000.[114]

Regardless of their destinations, or even whether they were among those allowed to stay in Spain, Moriscos who suffered through the expulsion may have found some consolation in the stories and legends of their culture. Aljamiado literature discovered three and four hundred years after it had been hidden in the sixteenth century includes many prophecies that foretell the restoration of Islam after a period of struggle.[115] Several Aljamiado stories from the Bible tell of people, such as Moses and Joseph, who survived exile. Moreover, the story of Carcayona shows how strong religious faith enables a Handless Maiden not only to survive two wilderness exiles but then to journey to a new land and build a city where all could worship Allah.[116]

The formal decrees expelling Moriscos from the Spanish kingdoms interrupted all exploration of a common ground between them and Old Christians. And they seemed to end Morisco attempts to accom-

---

guez Ortiz and Vincent, *Historia de los moriscos*, 186–190, for the embarkation and leaving of children in Seville.

110 AMS, Sección 4a, tomo 23, no. 35.

111 AGS, Contadurías Mayor de Cuentas, no. 60, 2, legajo 411, "Cuentas de moriscos de Sevilla y Ecija," 1610.

112 Lea, *The Moriscos of Spain*, 339–341. For more on the experience of Moriscos in France, see Domínguez Ortiz and Vincent, *Historia de los moriscos*, 226–228.

113 Domínguez Ortiz and Vincent, *Historia de los moriscos*, 230–231. For a report on the bad treatment of Moriscos in Berbery, see Cabrera de Córdoba, *Relaciones de las cosas*, 396.

114 Bunes Ibarra, *La imagen de los musulmanes*, discusses the estimates, 81–94.

115 López-Baralt, *Islam in Spanish Literature*, 198, suggests that these prophecies may be Morisco attempts to rewrite history.

116 "El rrecontamiento de la donzella Carcayona," in Guillén Robles, *Leyendas morisca*, 1:181–221. See also chapter 1, above.

modate the dominant Christian culture. The Christian account of the expulsion which alleged that Moriscos went to the points of embarkation happily and voluntarily also said that the women danced and sang, dressed in their best.[117] Perhaps some Moriscos had resolved that if they had to leave their homes in Spain, they would not leave as defeated victims; and the women wore jewelry and colorful clothing, in the words of one writer, to hide "something of the sorrow of their hearts."[118] Perhaps some seized the consolation of believing that, like Carcayona, they could survive their suffering and even build a new home where they could live in their own faith.

[117] Bleda, *Corónica de los moros*, 1001.

[118] Aznar Cardona, quoted in García Arenal, *Los moriscos*, 235.

7

WAREHOUSE CHILDREN, MIXED LEGACIES, AND CONTESTED IDENTITIES

SOLDIERS WATCHED over the expulsion of Moriscos from Seville in early 1610, some guarding the ships that took the Moriscos into exile and some posted at "the warehouses where the children were who had been taken" from them.[1] The 300 Morisco children left in these warehouses symbolize both mixed legacies and contested identities that followed the expulsion. Transformed instantly into orphans at the port of embarkation, these children would be obligated to work for Old Christians who took them in to raise them. A major legacy of pain resulted from the violence done to Moriscos not only in their expulsion and the requirement that they leave their youngest children, but also in the harsh rupture of bonds between the children and their parents.

Who would these children be as they became adults? Born as Moriscos and raised by Old Christians, they learned Christian doctrine and the shame of Morisco identity. Belonging both to troubling outsiders and hopeful insiders, these children would have to develop hybrid identities and cultures.[2] Most of them had to work for many years to repay Old Christian guardians for shelter and food.[3] Some, however, may have learned to love their guardians, especially when these adults followed the directive that they treat the children not as Moriscos "but as if they were their children."[4]

[1] AGS, Contaduría Mayor de Cuentas, no. 60, pt. 2, legajo 415: "los almaçenes donde estavan los niños que se quitaron." For more on Morisco children left in the warehouses, see Domínguez Ortiz and Vincent, *Historia de los moriscos*, 186–190; and chapter 6, above.

[2] James Clifford, *The Predicament of Culture: Twentieth-Century Ethnography, Literature, and Art* (Cambridge: Harvard University Press, 1988), discusses hybridity and cultural identities, esp. 4–7 and 338–339.

[3] For a discussion of how Morisco children should work to repay guardians, see Ripol, *Diálogo de consuelo*, 70; and Archbishop Juan de Ribera's letter to Philip III, of August 27, 1609, printed in Boronat y Barrachina, *Los moriscos españoles*, 2:523. According to Ripol, the king agreed that the children should be raised and taught until twelve years of age, and then they should work until they had compensated their guardians. Ribera suggested that the children should be required to work for their guardians until twenty-five or thirty years of age.

[4] Consulta from Segovia, September 1, 1609, printed in Boronat y Barachina, *Los moriscos españoles*, 2:525.

Not all Moriscos who escaped the order of expulsion were children, of course; yet exempted adults also faced issues of identity and contributed to often contradictory legacies. To placate nobles whose wealth depended on Morisco vassals, Philip III permitted some 6 percent of the Morisco population to remain in his kingdoms. He also exempted from the expulsion Moriscos who had taken religious orders and Morisco women who had married Old Christian men. Beatriz de Robles, for example, was a Morisca who did not have to leave during the expulsion, probably because she had married an Old Christian. Yet inquisitors prosecuted her later, not for following Islam, but for fashioning her own assimilated identity, which they viewed as a form of the Christian heresy of illuminism.[5] Although most Morisco slaves remained in Iberia under the control of Christian owners, many lived independently. Some became free through manumission or by saving wages to purchase freedom. Others simply fled and made their way to mountains and remote areas where they joined other Moriscos who had settled there, beyond the view of officials intent on expelling them. Some Moriscos left Spain but returned later, attempting to escape detection.

Morisco émigrés often established their own colonies, particularly in North Africa. Figure 8 depicts the geography of the Morisco expulsion and diaspora. Yet even where Muslims ruled, Moriscos found themselves perceived as too different to fit in, too "Christianized" to be accepted without suspicion. Their writings from exile suggest a people still attempting to negotiate their own identities and understand their unique experiences. Whether they departed or stayed in Spain, Moriscos left mixed legacies that become apparent as we explore their lives and writings in exile—documents that describe their attempts to survive in Spain and the impact of their expulsion on subsequent history. Their legacies include not only contested identities but also timeless legends and urgent lessons for our world in the twenty-first century.

Lives and Writings of Moriscos in Exile

"El Licenciado Molina," a Morisco relocated from Granada to Trujillo, wrote to an Old Christian friend, Don Jerónimo de Loaysa, after his expulsion from Spain.[6] Sending his letter from Algiers, he described

[5] This case is in AHN, Inquisición, libro 1259, 160; and legajo 2075, no. 31, "Relación de causas de fe," for 1624. See also my essay, "Contested Identities," 171–188.

[6] This letter is printed in both Ripol, *Diálogo de consuelo*, 75r–77r; and Janer, *Condición social de los moriscos*, app. 132, 350–351.

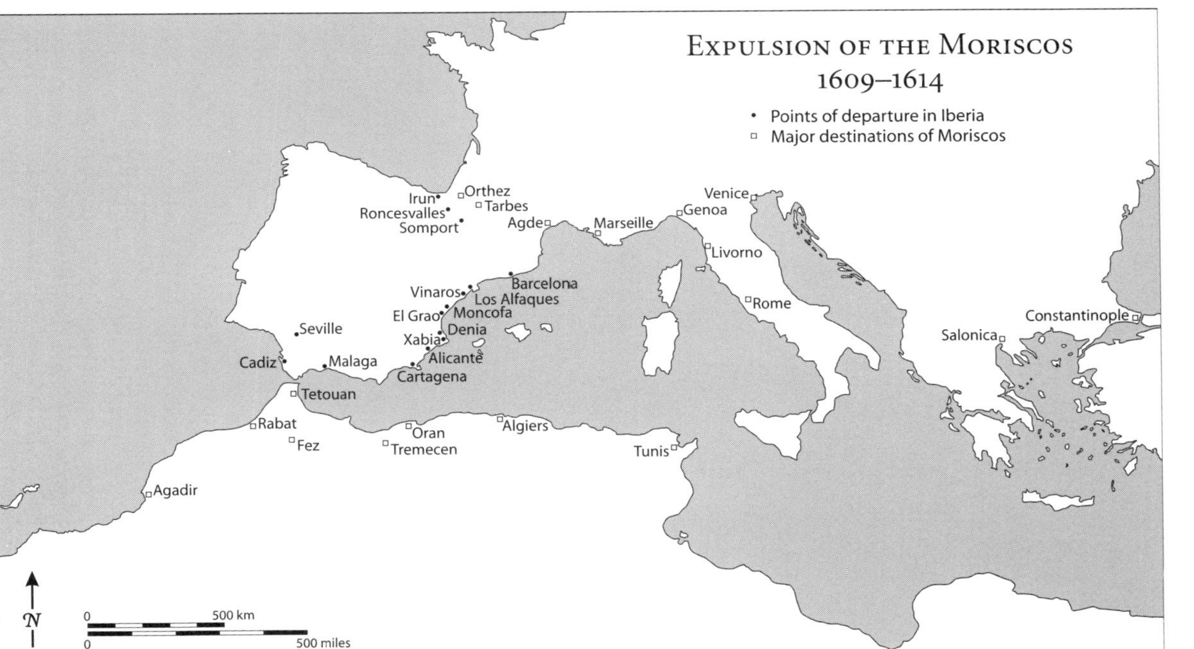

Fig. 8. Map prepared by Christopher Brest.

the journey of exile that he and other Moriscos from Trujillo had followed. They had gone first to Marseilles, "where we were well received, with great promises of support in everything." In just a few days, however, "everything turned around to the reverse," with the assassination of Henri IV. As royal policy suddenly no longer favored religious toleration, the French began to view Moriscos as spies for the king of Spain, apparently unaware of the irony.[7] Within fifteen days, most of the Moriscos' money had been taken and they were in danger of "losing themselves." Almost all of the 1,000 Moriscos in France decided to try to find a better place. They sailed for Italy, but the Italians "did not want us except to serve them, cultivate the fields, and other low occupations."[8] Since most of the Moriscos of Trujillo were merchants, they preferred to continue their search for a homeland and went on to Algiers, where Moriscos of Extremadura, La Mancha, and Aragon had settled. None of these Moriscos, Molina added, had escaped robbery by the sailors or rape of their wives and daughters.

Other reports from both Christians and Moriscos corroborate Molina's account of the misfortunes of Moriscos expelled from Spain. In October 1609 the Conde de Aguilar reported from Oran that he had disembarked 6,000 Moriscos and taken them "with security" to Tremecen, where they would "live as the rest of the Moors [as] vassals of the king." He noted, however, that Moriscos were as likely to be killed as to be warmly welcomed. In his words, "the Arabs are a people that will marry them and kill them."[9] A Christian report of 1610 in the municipal archive of Seville declared that "bad Christians" had tricked Moriscos into thinking that they would take them from Seville to France or to Berbery.[10] Instead, the Christians had robbed them and even killed some of them. When they finally arrived in Berbery, the account continues, Moors also robbed and killed some of the survivors.

[7] Undoubtedly, French feeling turned against Moriscos for more reasons than the sudden end of the tolerance supported by Henri IV. They arrived in large numbers, about 30,000, although fewer than 1,000 remained there; see Domínguez Ortiz and Vincent, *Historia de los moriscos*, esp. 228. Morisco emigrants also brought a foreign language and religion, as well as poor and ill people who would have to be supported. For more on Morisco emigration to France, see Louis Cardaillac, "Le passage des morisques en Languedoc," *Annales du midi* 83 (1970): 259–298; and Luis F. Bernabé Pons, *El Cántico islámico del morisco hispano tunecino Taybili* (Zaragoza: Institución Fernando el Católico, 1988), esp. 45–46.

[8] Janer, *Condición social de los moriscos*, app. 137, 350.

[9] AGS, Estado, legajo 214, Conde de Aguilar from Oran, October 7, 1609: "los Alarbes es gente que los desposaran y mataran . . . paraque bibiessen como los demas moros bassallos del Rey."

[10] AMS, *Efemérides*, "Noticias y casos," no. 1.

In North Africa, Moriscos established independent city-states, such as Salé, where former inhabitants of Hornachos founded a corsair republic.[11] Moriscos also settled in communities such as Tetouan, which became centers of *Andaluses,* as North Africans described immigrants from Iberia. Some became residents in old Moroccan cities, especially Fez. In Tunis an Ottoman ruler presided over the resettlement of Moriscos in agricultural communities, and the Ottoman bureaucracy helped Moriscos wherever they settled. Evidently favoring the immigration of Moriscos to counterbalance local Muslim resistance, Ottoman officials made special provision in Syria to distribute agricultural land to them.[12] However, Ottoman policy favoring Morisco immigration could not protect Moriscos from local opposition in places such as Oran and Algiers.[13]

Because of the strong and beneficent Ottoman presence in Tunisia, Moriscos who settled here were able to maintain their own identity as Hispano-Muslims even as they established new homes.[14] They had also suffered the hardships of travel and the depredations of thieves, but not the "systematic pillaging" of Algiers nor the rapid assimilation expected of immigrants in Morocco and some other places.[15] The Ottoman governor, Utman Dey, and a Tunisian religious leader, Abu al-Gayt al-Qassas, first welcomed Andalusian Moriscos for religious and humanitarian reasons. Seeking to protect the newcomers from xenophobia, these leaders made each family in Tunisia take in an Andalusian family. They also opened refuges for them in mosques and other sites of prayer.[16]

It seems likely that the Turkish governor had political as well as humanitarian motives, however. Undoubtedly aware of the larger Ottoman policy of strategically relocating ethnic minority populations, he could have seen the Morisco diaspora as an opportunity for creating a new community in Tunisia of culturally foreign immigrants dependent on their Turkish protectors. To Utman Dey, it must have seemed important that the newcomers preserve their culture and not assimilate completely with Tunisians, who did not like the Turks. He probably wanted to keep the Moriscos as an authentic ethnic group that could

[11] Vincent, *Minorías y marginados,* 215.

[12] Hess, *The Forgotten Frontier,* 121.

[13] Bernabé Pons, *El Cántico islámico,* 47.

[14] Miguel de Epalza, "Trabajos actuales sobre la comunidad de moriscos refugiados en Túnez, desde el siglo XVII a nuestros días," in *Actas del Coloquio Internacional sobre Literatura Aljamiada y Morisca,* ed. Alvaro Galmés de Fuentes (Madrid: Editorial Gredos, 1972), 436–437.

[15] Epalza, "Trabajos actuales," 430.

[16] Epalza, "Trabajos actuales," 430–431.

serve to offset local resistance to Turkish rule. Encouraging their elitist sense of being different as Andaluses, the Turkish governor favored their clear identity and reluctance to assimilate. Tunisians, on the other hand, saw the Morisco immigrants as "haughty, merry, and obstinate."[17]

The majority of Moriscos settling in Tunisia came from Aragon and places in Old Castile.[18] In their new homes, Moriscos carried out artisanal work in ceramics, soap, and silk making. They formed guilds and monopolies. With the encouragement of Utman Dey, they established agricultural colonies in the northern areas of Tunisia where political unrest had previously resulted in nomadism and unstable agriculture. Moriscos in Tunisia even used slaves in large-scale agricultural production, rather than in the domestic or public work so often performed by slaves.[19]

Regardless of where they had once lived in Iberia or where they had now settled in North Africa, Moriscos in exile lived openly as Muslims. Some had begun to practice polygamy even before they left Spain, perhaps more as a practical way to support unmarried and widowed Moriscas than as an expression of Islamic culture.[20] Unlike Madalena Morisca, whom we met in chapter 2 as inquisitors prosecuted her for bathing as a Muslim, Morisco exiles could freely practice their cultural traditions and faith.[21] Their writings indicate that these exiles looked zealously to the Qurʾan, pious traditions of Islam, and spiritual exercises that could reinforce their belief in the indivisible and divine source for both civil law and the just rule of conscience in all their acts.[22] Repeatedly they cited the same passages of the Qurʾan about communal prayer and *azala*, the ritual of praying five times a day while facing the East.[23] In Africa Moriscos wrote more often in Castilian than in Arabic. No longer subject to the hostility they had suffered in Spain, they did not have to preserve their literature clandestinely. Yet Africans noted their apparent ignorance of the Arabic language and some assumed it meant spiritual dissimulation.[24]

[17] Epalza, "Trabajos actuales," 433.

[18] Juan Penella, "El sentimento religioso de los moriscos españoles emigrados: Notas para una literatura morisca en Túnez," in *Actas del Coloquio Internacional sobre Literatura Aljamiada y Morisca*, ed. Alvaro Galmés de Fuentes (Madrid: Editorial Gredos, 1972), 451.

[19] Epalza, "Trabajos actuales," 433–434. For more on Morisco immigrants to Tunisia, see J. D. Latham, "Towards a Study of Andalusian Immigration and Its Place in Tunisian History," *Cahiers de Tunisie* 5 (1957): 203–252.

[20] Caro Baroja, *Los moriscos del Reino de Granada*, 252n.

[21] See chapter 2, above.

[22] Penella, "El sentimento religioso," 455.

[23] Penella, "El sentimento religioso," 455.

[24] Penella, "El sentimento religioso," 449.

Paradoxically, Africans saw these transplanted Morisco communities as vital and spiritual, but neither truly Muslim nor truly Christian.[25] Juan Rincón, a Morisco exiled from Huesca, acknowledged this ambiguous identity when he wrote: "Now I want to ask us what knowledge we can have of religion and of dogmas, what mode do we have to serve God, if we live continuously in perplexity and anguish? How can we be surprised that some of the sacred mysteries of our religion have come to be so strange and uncustomary?"[26] Ybrahin Taybili, who had lived as "Juan Pérez" in Toledo, wrote from Tunisia an eloquent *Cántico* that also presented an identity of ambiguity. Celebrating the strong Morisco faith in Islam, Taybili absolutely rejected the Christian beliefs of Spain, while also expressing Moriscos' love for the Iberian land and language in which they had been raised.[27] Not surprisingly, some Moriscos tried to return to Iberia. One report of 1613 asserted that more than 800 Moriscos had returned and the Count of Salazar had been commissioned to punish them.[28] In 1631 a group of Moriscos living in Rabat wrote to Philip IV to negotiate their return to Spain, offering to settle in Seville and give him cannons and boats if he would grant them twenty years' immunity from prosecution by the Inquisition.[29]

To resolve some of this ambiguity and acknowledge their own unique experience, Morisco writers retold the story of their expulsion. An anonymous Morisco in Tunisia wrote a sonnet in which he compared the Moriscos' journey with the Hebrews' miraculous escape from Egypt through the Red Sea. With courage they left Spain and its "pharaoh," he wrote.[30] They had to cross a sea, which became "a meadow of green flowers." In their "unique and pilgrim ingenuity," God's light had blessed them so that they became "not mortal, but divine."

El Licenciado Molina echoed this sense of the sacred in the Moriscos' journey of exile as he assured his Old Christian friend that he believed the expulsion was "divine inspiration."[31] He had seen prophecies more than a thousand years old, he wrote, which foretold these things that had happened to them. But these prophecies also declared that God

[25] Penella, "El sentimento religioso," 449.

[26] Juan Rincón, *Guía de Salvación*, quoted in Penella, "El sentimento religioso," 452.

[27] Mikel de Epalza, introduction to Bernabé Pons, *El Cántico islámico*, 5–26.

[28] Cabrera de Córdoba, *Relaciones de las cosas*, 522; and García Arenal, *Los moriscos*, 268. For Pedro de Arriola's 1610 report on expelled Moriscos attempting to return to Andalucia, see García Arenal, *Los moriscos*, 269–271.

[29] Domínguez Ortiz and Vincent, *Historia de los moriscos*, 235–236.

[30] This and subsequent quotations are in Bernabé Pons, *El Cántico islámico*, 130.

[31] For this and subsequent quotations on prophecies, see Janer, *Condición social de los moriscos*, app. 132, 351.

would send a king who would conquer all the world with only the word of God, against which neither siege nor artillery would prevail. "And I have seen another prophecy," he wrote, that had been recounted by an astrologer of Valencia, whence it had been brought this year. Describing the expulsion of the Moriscos as a "miracle," this prophecy told of "voracious, carnivorous, and treacherous wolves" who had banished "the most fruitful and unarmed gentle lambs."

"And believe me," wrote Molina, "I do not write this from passion or offense, but with the same intention as if I were in Spain." Evidently confident of their friendship and emboldened by the Muslim prophecies, he contrasted Spain with Algiers. "Here [in the Muslim world] they have not obliged us to any spiritual or corporal act which they make us say about what we have been." To this indirect criticism, he added some indirect and unsolicited advice: "I will be happy that you see the prophecies of Saint Isidro about this." Although we do not know the response of his friend, the seventeenth-century writer who included Molina's letter in his *Dialogue of Comfort for the Expulsion of the Moriscos of Spain* warned of the letter's "evils and poison." To him, the author of the letter implied that Muslims are people of God and Christians are their enemies—the reverse of the Christian viewpoint.[32]

The "prophecies of Saint Isidro" to which Molina referred also appear in the Morisco manuscript 774 in the Bibliothèque Nationale de Paris. Purporting to offer "the sketch of Spain, / which Saint Isidro presented," the poem asserts that it was from "a very old book called Secret / of the Secrets of Spain."[33] This prophecy addresses Spain as burning not only "in the passions / of your evils," but also in the hands of justice executed by Jews and a Church that has given its offices "in revilement" to the Marranos (converted Jews). "The blood of the small poor ones / will demand vengeance of you," the prophecy warns. "At that / time the Jews will be / Christians, and the knights hypocrites / and the clerics vainglorious." The warning that "a powerful serpent" will arise in the East near Constantinople undoubtedly referred to Christian fears of Ottoman Turks in the sixteenth and seventeenth centuries. "And so great will be the damage that the Moors will make, that within / Britain the new David will be reported," the prophesy continued, in clear reference to the challenge from tiny Britain to the mighty Goliath that Spain appeared to be in the early modern period.

[32] Ripol, *Diálogo de consuelo*, 77r.

[33] Mercedes Sánchez Alvarez, *El manuscrito misceláneo 774 de la Bibliothèque Nationale de Paris (Leyendas, itinerios de viajes, profecías sobre la destrucción de España y otros relatos moriscos)*, Edición, estudio y glosario por Mercedes Sánchez Alvarez (Madrid: Editorial Gredos, 1982), 246–249; this quotation is at 246.

More than a warning, Molina's letter evokes the pattern of many Moriscos who sought to explain their oppression and expulsion through Muslim prophecies about the suffering and ultimate redemption of the people of Islam. Religious fatalism appears as a theme in these prophecies and rewritings of history. One scholar has suggested that a double desire prompted Moriscos to join together their histories and invented legends in "historical accommodations."[34] On the one hand, a deep feeling of hope even in the midst of adversity appears in their legends, such as those of Carcayona and Job and his wife. On the other hand, their writings express a desire to comply with the ideas and the customs of the Christians, to mitigate the disharmony between Islam and Christianity, and to find ways to synthesize the two religions. They could draw upon their own traditional Muslim stories, such as those that express admiration for Jesus and his mother, Mary.[35] As counterpoint to these two desires runs a wish to express their hatred of the errors of Christianity and its abuse of them. Prophecies of the ruin of Spain, for example, describe Spanish Christians as "thieving wolves without kindness," infected with "arrogance and boasting and sodomy, and lust and blasphemy and vengeance and vainglory and tyranny and robbery and injustice."[36]

Compounding the sometimes conflicting desires of Moriscos, their centuries-long history of living as Muslims in Spain meant that literature from both the Islamic and Hispanic worlds directly affected Morisco writings and, in turn, was directly affected by it. Tirso de Molina's "Condenado por desconfiado" presents what some scholars believe is the theme of the Aljamiado legend of "Yusef el carnicero," for example. And others have found parallels between the mystical writings by Moriscos and those of Saint John of the Cross suggesting that each affected the other.[37] Far from being a "watertight compartment," Morisco literature sometimes used the Castilian language, rather than Arabic or Aljamía, especially in exile.[38]

[34] Penella, "El sentimento religioso," 455–456.

[35] Several of these stories are published in Guillén Robles, *Leyendas moriscas*, vol. 1; see also Vespertino Rodríguez, *Leyendas aljamiadas y moriscas*, 300–325.

[36] Bibliothèque Nationale de Paris, ms 290, 410–416, discussed in Penella, "El sentimento religioso," 462; and in Galmés de Fuentes, "El interés literario," 196.

[37] Alvaro Galmés de Fuentes, "La literatura española aljamiado-morisca," in *Grundriss der Romanischen Literaturen des Mittelalters*, vol. 9 of *La littérature dans la Péninsule Ibérique aux XIVe et XVe siècles*, ed. Walter Mettmann (Heidelberg: Carl Winter Universitätsverlag, n.d.), 130.

[38] The relationship of Aljamiado and Castilian literature is far more complex than this brief discussion can present. Excellent sources for further exploration include the many publications of Alvaro Galmés de Fuentes, esp. "La literatura española" at 130; and

The literature of Moriscos in North Africa reveals above all a deep and paradoxical complexity in their identities. It is not surprising, for example, that historical fatalism appears especially in the writings of Moriscos from Granada, who had experienced an earlier exile in the forced relocations of the 1570s and 1580s. Nor does it seem strange that writings of Moriscos from Granada, Andalusia, and Valencia included criticisms of Spanish Christian society, for these Moriscos remembered too well their recent suffering under oppression. In contrast, it seems understandable that writings from Aragonese Moriscos reflect more of the desire for religious syncretism; these people, after all, had experienced a longer and more complete assimilation into Christian society.[39]

No longer members of a Christian society, Moriscos in exile nevertheless expressed a parallelism between Christianity and Islam. They drew upon traditional Muslim stories of Muhammad that emphasized his miracles, his legitimate lineage, his roles as intercessor and agent for the divine. Some even transformed him into a hypostasis of the divinity, viewing him as an emanation from Allah, just as Christ was seen as an emanation from God the Father.[40] Using Muslim traditions already established, Moriscos in exile emphasized Muhammad's company of saints that they knew from Muslim stories of exemplary Muslims and martyrs. They even carried out certain practices that paralleled Christian rituals, such as the rosary. Using Muslim prayer beads, Moriscos recited the ninety-nine names of Allah, each of which implied that Allah was the essence and Muhammad his agent. Allah, for example, was named as pardon and Muhammad as pardoner.[41] Developed from their own Muslim traditions by Moriscos pressured to live as Christians in Spain before the expulsion, this parallelism continued even into exile and among many Moriscos who remained to live in Spain after the expulsion.

Morisco Attempts to Survive in Spain

Probably 10,000 to 15,000 Moriscos received exemption by royal dispensation and remained in Spain after the expulsion.[42] Exemption covered some Moriscos as members of a group, such as slaves or children under the age of seven. Others won exemption by individual petition,

Mikel de Epalza, especially his very helpful introduction to Bernarbé Pons, *El Cántico islámico*, 5–6.

[39] Penella, "El sentimento religioso," 462–463.

[40] Penella, "El sentimento religioso," 465–466.

[41] Penella, "El sentimento religioso," 467.

[42] Vincent, *Minorías y marginados*, 126–127.

such as the three grandsons of the Muslim who had surrendered to Ferdinand and Isabel the keys to the city of Ronda.[43] Exempted Moriscos also included artisans, if they were considered irreplaceable, and servants and others who carried out their responsibilities loyally and showed sincere conversion to Christianity. Female for the most part, this was a "fragmented society" that lived especially in urban areas.[44] Subject to continuing surveillance by clerics and inquisitors, these Moriscos had little opportunity to preserve their Muslim culture collectively. The fact that they had been granted exemptions from the expulsion suggests that they may already have been so well assimilated that they had no interest at all in practicing the rites and customs of their forebears.

However, Morisco and Muslim slaves remained in Spain not because they were so well assimilated, but because they belonged as property to Old Christians who profited from their labor. Nobles bought and sold slaves as a way to secure their future. In Cordova, for example, one noble widow bought a Morisco slave and then made a 25 percent profit when she sold him the next day.[45] Middle-class Christians invested in slaves as well, perhaps to emulate nobles, but also to profit from slaves' work and from speculation in the slave market. A combination of nobles, ecclesiastics, and merchants accounted for 60 percent of the buyers in the slave market of Cordova. They paid higher prices for female slaves because they had a longer life expectancy, reproduced more slaves for the owner, and provided domestic service that was usually in demand.[46]

The age of the slave affected the work that slaveowners could expect of them. From the age of eight, Morisco slaves were expected to bring in an income to the owner, usually by working for an artisan or doing domestic work. Bills of sale for young slaves often declared that they were old enough to have been legally enslaved, if they had not been born to slave women. Some owners resold very young slaves, inflating their ages by years from the time they had been bought months before.[47] Young Morisco slaves who sought their freedom by petitions

[43] Archivo Arzobispal de Sevilla (AAS), Colegio de Niñas del Espíritu Santo, legajo 10, contains Philip III's response of January 17, 1612, to a controversy over whether Francisco de Robles, Domingo de Velasco, and Francisco de Morales, Moriscos living in the village of Teba, could sell property belonging to them. "Por tanto mando a las justicias de la dicha villa de Teba y a las demas a quien esto tocare que no pongan impedimiento a los dichos Francisco de Robles, Domingo de Velasco y Francisco de Morales en la venta de sus bienes raices pues no ban de ser expelidos que tal es mi voluntad."

[44] Vincent, *Minorías y marginados*, 127.

[45] Aranda Doncel, *Los moriscos*, 142.

[46] Aranda Doncel, *Moriscos en tierras*, 142–151; Martín Casares, *La esclavitud*, 236–259.

[47] Aranda Doncel, *Moriscos en tierras*, 150–151.

stated that they had been captured when they were below the legal age for enslavement. Angela Fernández, slave of Lucas Hernández in Cordova, declared that her master had acquired her as a slave in the year 1583. However, she stated, "because I was a minor in age when they took me [captive] from Granada, I am free."[48]

Often living apart from their masters, Morisco slaves developed their own informal societies. Local groups of slaves who lived or met together in neighborhoods caught the eye of suspicious inquisitors. In Cordova, for example, the Inquisition punished a group of twenty-seven Morisco slaves, men and women, who were denounced for meeting together in a house in Porcuna to say Muslim prayers and to plan an escape to North Africa.[49] Other Morisco slaves joined together and went about as gangs by day and night free from any control by an owner. According to one complaint, these slaves lived in *corrales de vecindad* (buildings around a common courtyard), rather than with their owners. Moreover, they lived "in their own law, keeping their sect and performing its rites and ceremonies as they could in Berbery," free to do all this "because they cannot be expelled."[50] They sold produce and other food at low prices, cutting into the profits of poor Old Christians; and they committed robberies and murders against Old Christians. These Moorish slaves should be forbidden to live together in barrios or corrales, the complaint concluded, and they should not be allowed to carry arms.

No one complained, however, of those slaves and free blacks who belonged to a well-known confraternity in Seville. At the beginning of the fifteenth century, the archbishop of Seville had founded the Brotherhood of the Most Holy Christ of the Foundation to support and provide a hospital for blacks, "a class commonly poor and destitute."[51] Better known as the Brotherhood of the Little Blacks, the group became a true confraternity in the sixteenth century, with its own penitential rule. It was also at this time that blacks and slaves participated through their confraternity in observing Christian holy days. Their masques

[48] Aranda Doncel, *Moriscos en tierras*, 169: "porque hera menor de hedad quando me truxeron de Granada, estoy ya libre."

[49] Gracia Boix, *Autos de fe*, 163–166.

[50] BN ms 18.735, no. 53, *Papel de lo dañosso que es en los reynos de que aya moros y moriscos* (after 1619): "paraque no los puedan expelar . . . biven en corrales de vecindad en su misma ley guardando su secta y haciendo los ritos y ceremonias della como la pudieran hacer en berberia."

[51] José Bermejo y Carballo, *Glorias religiosas de Sevilla. Noticia histórica descriptiva de todas las cofradías de penitencia, sangre y luz, fundadas en esta ciudad* (Seville: Imprenta y Librería del Salvador, 1882), 7.

and other presentations won great admiration.[52] Although we cannot be certain that Morisco slaves belonged to this confraternity, this is clearly a possibility because it was said to be composed of dark-skinned slaves.[53]

Runaway slaves developed supporting networks that could help them escape to France or Muslim lands. They learned to copy "letters of emancipation" and forge legal forms that granted freedom to a former slave. They even included in their letters distinguishing physical characteristics of the person in question, such as moles, brands, and color of skin, hair, and eyes. As a remedy for the "many disorders" in early seventeenth-century Spain, officials were urged to prevent Moors, Turks, and Moriscos from "meeting together in streets or in houses or other parts, and particularly that they be prohibited from speaking Arabic, or another language of the Infidels because experience has shown that when they are speaking in it alone they do not deal with anything except to escape, and rob their masters or make some other curses in damage of the Republic." Moreover, authorities should order "that no slave sleep or spend the night in any house except that of his master, because all those who sleep away are fugitives, thieves, and evildoers."[54]

In an effort to impose some control over these slaves, as well as to find more men to row the royal galleys, Philip III ordered that all Moriscos brought as slaves from Berbery should be gathered up and handed over for galley service. In 1610 this order was announced publicly and printed for posting in towns and cities throughout his kingdoms.[55] When the king again tried to take slaves for galley service in

[52] A confraternity of slaves and free blacks was described by Don Antonio Espinosa y Carcel, in *Anales de la Ciudad de Sevilla*, reprinted in Joaquín Guichot y Parody, *Historia del Exmo. Ayuntamiento de la muy noble, muy leal, muy heróica é invicta ciudad de Sevilla*, 2 vols. (Seville: Tipografía de la Región, 1896), 2:293–294: "The Brotherhood of the Blacks, which has a chapel outside the walls of the city, and whose individuals are the most poor, prepared a masque as a sign of rejoicing."

[53] Bermejo y Carballo, *Glorias religiosas*, 382–387. Note that not all Moriscos were dark-skinned, but some were, and many who still lived in Spain following the expulsion were slaves.

[54] BN ms 1092, *Advertencias para el remedio de muchos desórdenes que hay en esta Corte* (early seventeenth century), 75–75r: "y que se preponase q los esclavos, moros, turcos, y moriscos no se junten en las calles ni en las casas ni otras partes unos con otos, y particularmente se las prohiba que no hablen en algaravia, ni otra lengua de Infieles porque se a visto por experiencia que quando estan hablando en ella a solas no tratan sino como sean de huyr, y robar a sus amos o hacer algunos otros maleficios en daño de la Repub[li]ca. . . . Y mandar que ningun esclavo duerma ni trasnoche en ninguna casa fuera de la de su amo, porque todos los q duermen fuera son fugitivos, ladrones y malhechores."

[55] An example of the posting made for Seville is *Don Luys Mendez de Haro y Sotomayor.*

1637, the inquisitor general from Seville wrote to the king of the "inhumanity" of taking slaves from masters "who have raised them at their tables as sons."[56] Most grievous was to take Christian slaves, "most of them born and raised in these kingdoms and that work to sustain their masters, who almost all are poor and widows and principal and honorable persons who do not have another way to live. . . . The slaves are imprisoned with much misery and need that they suffer in the prisons," the inquisitor general continued, and the owners give "pitiful demonstrations of desolation, weeping publicly through the streets carrying the sorrow of seeing themselves without their slaves."[57] Apparently unmoved, the royal order came again in 1639 to gather up slaves for galley service. This time owners protested and tried to hide their slaves or buy substitutes to send into galley service.[58] Evidently, they were not entirely successful, as a report from Seville in 1639 told of 102 slaves, blacks, mulattoes, and Berbers being taken "in collars" to galleys in nearby ports.[59] By the middle of the seventeenth century, Philip IV faced such a shortage of galley slaves that he dispatched ten thousand ducats to Seville for buying slaves to take the place of those who had completed their sentences of galley service.[60]

Some slaves saved enough money from their wages to purchase freedom from their masters, and others received freedom when their masters died. Unfortunately, some masters granted freedom to slaves when they ceased to be able to carry out useful work, through age or disability. In these cases, of course, the freed slaves could no longer depend on masters to provide them with food, shelter, or clothing.[61] Once freed, former slaves who had not been baptized could seek permission to leave Spain for Berbery. In Seville in 1626, former slaves requested this permission of Juan Tello, secretary of the Inquisition. The numbers of requests and lack of reports by Tello troubled a visitor sent by the Inquisition to review the tribunal in Seville.[62] His review showed that in April 1626 the following freed slaves had asked permission to leave Spain to go to North Africa after declaring that they

[56] AHN, Consejos, legajo 7155, no. 8, quoted in Domínguez Ortiz, "La esclavitud," 401.

[57] AHN, Consejos, legajo 7155, no. 8, quoted in Domínguez Ortiz, "La esclavitud," 402.

[58] Domínguez Ortiz, *Orto y ocaso*, 64.

[59] *Memorias sevillanas*, reported in Manuel Chaves, *Cosas nuevas y viejas (Apuntes sevillanos)* (Seville: Tipografía, 1904), 39–40.

[60] Domínguez Ortiz, "La esclavitud," 387n.

[61] Aranda Doncel, *Los moriscos*, 165.

[62] Testimony in this case is in AHN, Inquisición, legajo 2069, visitas, 1626, 692–746. Such review visits appear to have been a normal event for the various tribunals of the Holy Office.

had not been baptized and had paid the required money to the Conde de Castellar:

Two former slaves unnamed and unidentified
Ayamena, a female Moor, 31 years old, "scarred [or branded] on the forehead"; her 5-year-old son, Amete, "of white color"; Fatima, her 2-year-old daughter; and Maymona, her daughter of 4 months
Gaxa, a 45-year-old female Moor with two children
Merin, a male Moor, 43 years old
Mahoyuba, a female Moor of 76 years
Baca, a female Moor of 51 years from Berbery
Jamete, a male Moor, 41 years old
Sahara, a female Moor, 40 years old, "of medium body"
Boleas, 36 years old
Mayuda, a female of 32 years and her 3-year-old daughter Caltomilla, her 1½-year-old daughter Arbia, and Amar, a 7-year-old boy
Barco, a male Moor, 36 years old
Anfiesa, a female Moor, and 6-year-old daughter
Aly, a male Moor of 63 years, and his wife Fiesa, a Moor, 50 years old, "with a scar [or brand] between the eyebrows and another on the chin and another on the side of the nose"

Criticized for how he had handled these requests "without presenting any of the reports to the tribunal," Tello defended himself by declaring that he had given many years of good service for the Inquisition and was in poor health. We can only speculate on the difficulties that such delays caused the former slaves, now freed but still unable to go to North Africa. Morisco slaves could not request permission to go to North Africa because they had been baptized. Nevertheless, they also came before the Inquisition, accused of apostasy, continuing to follow the "sect of Muhammad," becoming renegades, and attempting to flee to Berbery where they would be free to live as Muslims.[63]

Children of slaves prompted special concern. Usually, children born to slave women assumed the slave status of their mothers and remained with their mothers, at least during infancy.[64] The bishop of Ori-

[63] BN ms 18.735, "Informe sobre los moros esclavos y libres de Sevilla," describes the many Moors, slave and free, who lived together in Seville and worked especially as retailers, but were also accused of stealing children and teaching Muslim doctrine; see also Domínguez Ortiz and Vincent, *Historia de los moriscos*, esp. 266.

[64] Juan Aranda Doncel, "Estructura de la población morisca en tres parroquias sevillanas: San Julian, San Román, y Santa Lucía," *Boletin de la Real Academia de Córdoba de Ciencias, Bellas Letras y Nobles Artes*, año 45, no. 96 (1976): 83. Cf. Domínguez Ortiz, "La esclavitud," 399, who notes that when a slave woman married a free man, the children assumed the free status of the father.

huela feared that slave mothers were raising another generation of infidels or false Christians. He wrote to Philip III in 1610 about the slaves in his district who did not want to be Christians and were an "impediment" to their own children's becoming Christians.[65] The women in particular present a problem "because they are used to being more effective in persuading the children to follow the said sect." He proposed that children of slaves should be sent elsewhere and dispersed so they would be separated from the ceremonies of the sect of Muhammad.

Morisco children left by their parents during the expulsion were not supposed to be enslaved; they were to be raised as good Christians by Old Christians in Spain.[66] Parents left some of these children voluntarily with Old Christian friends or in seminaries already established for Morisco children.[67] It may have been easier for parents to decide to leave their children who were blind, mute, crippled, incurably ill, or otherwise disabled, for the journey into exile would be full of hardship. However, parents were told to appear before commissions to register their children, reporting their ages, and in many cases those of seven years or younger were then taken from them. According to one report from Valencia, the Marquesa of Caracena "took [Morisco children] from the breasts of their mothers" as the parents were about to embark.[68] During the winter of 1609–1610, when thousands of Moriscos embarked on ships taking them into exile from Seville, officials took their youngest children from them and placed them in the warehouses of Martín de Verez, along with old and disabled Moriscos.[69] Soldiers guarded them night and day until Old Christians came to take them to homes where they would be raised.

Although most of these children went to private homes of Old Christians who had agreed to raise them, some went to schools where they boarded and learned Christian doctrine until they could be placed in Old Christian homes. In a sense these schools functioned as "bridges" between their former homes and those Old Christian homes where they were to grow into adults.[70] Called schools, seminaries, and houses of doctrine, the institutions had already been established in some cases

[65] Quoted in Boronat y Barrachina, *Los moriscos españoles*, 2:585.

[66] Don Juan de Mendoza, *Declaración del Bando que se a publicado de la expulsión de los moriscos* (Seville: Alonso Rodríguez Gamarra, 1610), n.p.

[67] See the very interesting study by François Martínez, "Les enfants morisques de l'expulsion (1610–1621)," in *Mélanges Louis Cardaillac*, ed. Abdeljelil Temini (Zaghouan: Fondation Temini Pour la Recherche Scientifique et l'Information, 1995), 499–539, esp. 518.

[68] Quoted in Martínez, "Les enfants," 524.

[69] AGS, Contaduría Mayor de Cuentas, no. 60, pt. 2, legajo 415; and Domínguez Ortiz and Vincent, *Historia de los moriscos*, 186–190.

[70] Martínez, "Les enfants," 523.

before the expulsion. In chapters 3 and 6 we considered the schools founded by Jesuits to educate Morisco children. La Casa de Niñas had been founded in 1606 in Valencia next to the Convent of Saint Ursula to educate and socialize Morisco girls. Following the expulsion, this institution offered refuge for Morisco girls who had been abused, transforming some of them from sexual prey into "definite Christians."[71] The school also received Morisco girls seeking spiritual comfort and, conversely, those whose masters decided that their spiritual and moral health required "correction." In 1615 the school placed thirty of the girls in Christian homes to create space to receive newcomers. Fourteen of the girls were not placed and remained in the school because they had serious maladies or disabilities and could not "serve anyone but God."[72]

Ideally, the Old Christians who agreed to raise Morisco children would treat them as their own sons and daughters, but such children usually came with a letter of *encomienda*. This document charged the family receiving them to teach them Christian doctrine and some occupation of service. The family would then place the children with masters who would turn their wages over to the sponsoring family. Generally, the girls worked as domestic servants, and the boys as agricultural laborers or for "mechanical officials" who did not deal in arms or in "things of letters," so that when they were grown they would not "aspire to more than what they had been taught."[73] Although Old Christian parents also sent their own offspring out to service, no document restricted the work that they could aspire to, nor did any document require all wages of their own biological children to be taken by the parents.[74]

The encomienda system for Morisco children set up a contradiction that imprinted their lives. On the one hand, they were restricted in what occupations they could learn, and these restrictions marked them as Moriscos. On the other hand, they were to be raised with good Christian teaching so they would "completely forget their origin and be taken for Old Christians."[75] The goal appeared to be complete assimilation, and yet both Church and State imposed controls on them that preserved their difference. Changing their surnames from those they had as Moriscos before the expulsion to the surnames of their Old

[71] Martínez, "Les enfants," 523.

[72] Quoted in Martínez, "Les enfants," 524.

[73] Quoted in Boronat y Barrachina, *Los moriscos españoles*, 2:525.

[74] See, for example, the interesting work of anthropologist Blanca Morell Peguero, *Mercaderes y artesanos en la Sevilla del descubrimiento* (Seville: Diputación Provincial de Sevilla, 1986), who describes families sending their own children out to service, 63–73.

[75] Martínez, "Les enfants," 518.

Christian masters after the expulsion answered a bureaucratic need for identifying them by which Old Christian was responsible for them. Yet this practice could not clarify their identity. Both Morisco and assimilated Christian, they were neither the one nor the other.[76]

The Inquisition played a major role in ritualizing the permanence of these children's Morisco identity. In Valencia, for example, tribunal records show that children as young as seven came before the Inquisition to confess past errors. Probably pressured by guardians and rectors, these Morisco children came in groups "voluntarily."[77] They confessed that they had kept some of the rites and ceremonies of Islam which they had learned from their Morisco parents. They knew that these were prohibited by Christian law, but they had lacked instruction in Christian faith, and now they wanted to save themselves from eternal damnation. They sought absolution of their sins and took the necessary steps of confession and repentance. For these sinners who "voluntarily" confessed, the Inquisition took a relatively benign approach of toleration and integration.[78] The Holy Office reconciled the Morisco children to the Church, giving hope for true integration; yet the entire process of appearing before the Inquisition emphasized the difference of these children from Old Christians.

Adult Moriscos exempted from the expulsion also developed mixed identities in postexpulsion Spain. Some assimilated so well that they seemed to "disappear" into Christian society. Their children married Old Christians and even became nuns and clerics. The Inquisition continued to prosecute Moriscos for holding on to Islam, but not to the same extent that it had in the years between the War of the Alpujarras and the expulsion. Some Moriscos returned clandestinely from exile and were able to establish new identities. However, an unfortunate few had to appear before inquisitors, denounced as Muslims living illegally in Spain.

Inquisitors heard of Beatriz de Robles, a Morisca, who had not left during the expulsion, probably because she had married an Old Christian.[79] They did not prosecute her for being "of the sect of Muhammad," however; instead, they accused and convicted her in 1624 of illuminism, a Christian heresy which asserted that the faithful could find God through their own internal experiences rather than through sermons and rites of priests. Unwisely, Beatriz de Robles had told neigh-

[76] Martínez, "Les enfants," 526. Note that Moriscos had to accept Christian names at baptism, and many chose as their surname their place of residence or origin. Following the expulsion, these children had to accept yet another name—that of their Old Christian master.

[77] Martínez, "Les enfants," 527.

[78] Martínez, "Les enfants," 528.

[79] AHN, Inquisición, legajo 2075, no. 31; and Perry, "Contested Identities," 171–188.

bors about her visions in which God paid her "a thousand tender compliments" and let her know that she was "very beloved and favored."[80] Moreover, her raptures during communion greatly impressed the women with her, who showed signs of sharing her illuminist heresy. From Inquisition records, we cannot determine her motives or those of the people who denounced her to inquisitors.

Both Morisca and Christian visionary, this middle-aged woman who lived in a small village near Seville reveals the complexities of identities for Moriscos who did not leave Spain with the expulsion. She had to accept the identity imposed on her by Church and State, but she may also have attempted to shape her own identity. Her inner religious experiences resonate with certain Muslim traditions, such as those of Sufi mystics and visionaries like Rabiʿa of Basra, who had provided a model for individual mystical experiences that had flourished in Islamic Iberia.[81] Moreover, it is possible that Beatriz turned to enthusiastic Christian piety in an effort to disarm Christian critics and to fill a spiritual need when she could no longer call on Islam. Her internal visionary experiences may have subverted the attempts of clerics to control and monitor her religious life; perhaps they also exemplified syncretic attempts to bridge the chasm between Islam and Christianity.

Inquisitors imposed a comparatively light sentence on Beatriz de Robles, but not all Moriscos were so fortunate. Sentenced not for apostasy but for illuminism, Beatriz was required to appear in an auto de fe and then to work as a servant in a hospital for women under the direction of an assigned confessor. Most Moriscos penanced by the Inquisition following the expulsion had been accused of apostasy, becoming a renegade, or attempting to enter or to leave Spain illegally. They received harsher sentences of perpetual prison, galley service, and exile. One woman, an "apostate Berber," received the most severe sentence when she was handed over to secular authorities to be burned in 1648.[82]

[80] AHN, Inquisición, legajo 2075, no. 31: "muy querida y favoresida de Dios y le decia mill requiebros." AHN, Inquisición, libro 1299, contains the illuminist heresies identified in 1525 that became the basis for prosecuting illuminists, or *alumbrados*, as they were called in early modern Spain. Spanish clerics were especially concerned with the alumbrados' "doctrine of pure love," which to them seemed too close to the heresy of the Free Spirit, discussed in Norman Cohn, *The Pursuit of the Millennium: Revolutionary Messianism in Medieval and Reformation Europe and Its Bearing on Modern Totalitarian Movements* (New York: Harper Torchbooks, 1961), 170, 186–187.

[81] For more on Sufism, see Lammens, *Islam*, 117; Ibn Khaldun, *The Muqaddimah*, 3:76 and 100; López-Baralt, *Islam in Spanish Literature*, 42–43. For Rabiʿa of Basra, see Margaret Smith, *Rabiʿa the Mystic and Her Fellow-Saints in Islam: Being the Life and Teachings of Rabiʿa al-ʿAdawiyya Al-Quaysiyya of Basra Together with Some Account of the Place of Women Saints in Islam* (1928) (Cambridge: Cambridge University Press, 1984).

[82] Antonio Domínguez Ortiz, *Autos de la Inquisición de Sevilla (siglo XVII)* (Seville: Servicio de Publicaciones del Ayuntamiento de Sevilla, 1981), 84.

Impact of the Expulsion on Subsequent History

Attempts to solve "the Morisco problem" neither ended difference nor brought it under control. Only months after the expulsion began, witnesses denounced to the Inquisition many Moriscos who had received exemption by swearing to the regent of the royal tribunal of Aragon that they had lived as "good Christians." María Mocandali, for example, was denounced to inquisitors after she had received exemption by swearing such an oath.[83] In her case, a witness testified that she lived as a Moor and that he had seen her meet with other Moriscos to celebrate the birth of a baby girl with the Muslim ceremony of "las fadas." She was imprisoned on January 31, 1611. Because this was her first offense, she received a relatively moderate penalty. On May 30, inquisitors condemned her to reconciliation in a public auto de fe, confiscated her goods, and ordered her to wear the penitential habit, live in prison for one year, and pay a fine of ten ducats.

In another case, the suspect did not fare so well. María Taraiona, Morisco widow and resident of Zaragoza, had received exemption from the royal regent, although later authorities discovered that she had been reconciled in a public auto de fe in 1583 for "having lived as a Moor."[84] Following the expulsion, five witnesses came forward to testify that they had seen her meet and talk with other Moriscos and carry out the prayers of Islam in her own home early in the morning. She was arrested on February 4, 1611, and appeared in audiences on February 7, 10, and 12. On March 9 she confessed that she had been reconciled earlier for having lived as a Moor. Naming people with whom she had carried out the rites and ceremonies of Islam, she asked for absolution and offered to live and die as a good and Catholic Christian. She was not able to challenge the testimony against her, however, and on June 3 inquisitors condemned her to be "relaxed" to secular authorities, who would burn her following an auto de fe. In these and many similar cases, inquisitors found that the expulsion had not rid Spain of all its false converts.

Many other Inquisition cases against Moriscos showed that the expulsion had failed to seal Spanish frontiers against the illegal passage of "infidels." That Morisco slaves attempted to leave for Berbery is not so surprising, nor that some Moriscos returned to Spain after leaving during the expulsion.[85] More disturbing were the cases of free Moriscos

[83] AHN, Inquisición, libro 991, 168.

[84] AHN, Inquisición, libro 991, 162–163: "por haver vivido como mora."

[85] Examples of Moriscos, slave and free, attempting to escape are in AHN, Inquisición, legajo 2049, expediente 7, and legajo 2071, no. 4. For expelled Moriscos attempting to

who sought to leave Spain after the expulsion began. Their attempts called into question assumptions that officials knew which Moriscos were "good Christians" and ought to be exempt from the expulsion. Moreover, their movements across the boundaries of Spain raised more questions about identity and the difficulties of protecting "good" Christians from the dangerous impurity of "bad" Christians.

Consider, for example, the case of María de Aguilar and her husband, Alonso López Vegarra, which came before the Inquisition in 1635.[86] A resident and merchant in San Lucar de Barrameda, Alonso made many trips to Berbery and the city of Tetouan. There he communicated with Moors and observed with them the sect of Muhammad. María had been born in Berbery, but her father had raised her and taught her the Catholic Christian religion. Baptizing her "with his own hand," her father had raised her in the Catholic faith and in abhorrence of Islam. From Berbery she came to Spain to "keep herself, live, and die as a Christian." However, her husband decided to move his house and wealth to Berbery, and his wife, as well. He told María that he was taking her to Portugal, but she knew that he intended to take her to Berbery.

Now, "moved by zeal for the same faith and for her salvation," she left the house of her husband and went to accuse him before the Inquisition. She found refuge in the house of a widow who was sister to a familiar of the Holy Office. But the commissioner of the Inquisition not only did not proceed on the part of María de Aguilar; he even sought to make her return to her husband's home. She turned for help to her confessor and to her uncle, Joan de Tapia, a Morisco who had lived in France following the expulsion of the Moriscos and then returned to Spain. Apparently hearing that Joan de Tapia had come to San Lucar, Alonso demanded that the secular justice arrest Joan and keep him in prison until he revealed where María, his niece and Alonso's wife, was living. Unfortunately, she had boarded a boat from Seville to return to San Lucar and evidently died in a shipwreck. Now the Inquisition was asked to ascertain the "truth" not only in the accusation against Alonso, "but of the many other Moors who are in San Lucar." Clearly, the expulsion had neither rid Spain of Moriscos nor prevented their movement in and out of Iberia.

Inquisition cases involving Moriscos continued throughout the seventeenth century, although in smaller numbers after the expulsion. As late as 1693, Sebastiana María del Castillo, a Morisca who attempted

return, see the letter of Pedro de Arriola to Philip III, printed in García Arenal, *Los moriscos*, 269–271; and Cabrera de Córdoba, *Relaciones de las cosas*, 522.

[86] AHN, Inquisición, legajo 2059, expediente 7.

to go to Berbery with a Moor, was exiled from four cities, forbidden to be near seaports, and given one hundred lashes while riding a donkey.[87] Many of the Inquisition cases raised questions of what was to be done with property left by Moriscos as they fled illegally to Berbery.[88] Others disputed property inherited by Morisco children and challenged their relatives' taking them to Berbery.[89] Far from solving problems, the expulsion and its enforcement by the Inquisition seem to have merely produced additional difficulties.

In fact, Spain suffered continuing disadvantages from the expulsion of the Moriscos. To be sure, scholars of the nineteenth century tended to overstate the grave consequences of the expulsion for Spain. Nevertheless, it is difficult to agree with a twentieth-century scholar who has argued that the expulsion neither depopulated Spain nor led to a loss of skilled citizens.[90] Effects of the expulsion varied widely from region to region, with Valencia losing nearly one-third of its population and the richest agricultural areas of Aragon left nearly deserted and in ruins.[91] Nobles continued to lament the serious economic effects of the expulsion, urging the Crown to repopulate the lands of Granada and Valencia, which had depended especially on the labor of Moriscos. A letter to Philip III told him that the expulsion had left unoccupied more than a thousand houses in the Kingdom of Valencia, so that an advertisement had been made in the Azores seeking islanders willing to be shipped to Iberia to repopulate that kingdom.[92]

Even apologists for the expulsion acknowledged that it was a mixed blessing. It caused certain disadvantages for Christians, such as loss of population, vassals, and wealth, Damián Fonseca wrote. Moriscos had taken gold and silver with them, he asserted, but he added that their "miserable end" provided an appropriate punishment for them.[93] Jaime Bleda compared the expulsion of the Moriscos with that of

[87] The case of Sebastiana María del Castillo is in AHN, Inquisición, legajo 3014, and is discussed in Domínguez Ortiz, *Autos*, 118, who found seventy-seven cases in the tribunal of Seville between 1614 and 1700, at 34, esp.

[88] For example, AHN, Inquisición, legajo 2070, expediente 14, contains "Autos en razón de los bienes que quedaron en San Lucar de Barrameda pertenezientes a unos moriscos que pasaron fugitivos a Berbería," dated 1643.

[89] Examples are in AHN, Inquisición, legajo 2059, expediente 7 (1635), and legajo 2070, expediente 14, fols. 5–14 (1643).

[90] López Martínez, *Mudejares y moriscos*, 68–69.

[91] Domínguez Ortiz and Vincent, *Historia de los moriscos*, discuss the very grave consequences of the loss of Moriscos, 201–223.

[92] AGS, Estado, legajo 213, contains letters from the Marqués de los Vélez to Philip III asking his help in repopulating his lands; the notice for advertising in the Azores is in AGS, Estado, legajo 218.

[93] Fonseca, *Justa expulsión*, 322, 334–348.

Hagar and Ishmael, which saddened Abraham, but "was confirmed with the decree of God."[94]

With or without divine approval, the expulsion did not eliminate Moriscos from Spain, or from many other regions of the world. Moriscos added to the numbers and diversity of population in several areas under Ottoman rule and enlarged the already existing settlements of the hybrid Andaluses in North Africa. Clearly, their presence outside Spain continued to aggravate a "threat" that deeply concerned Spanish Christians in the sixteenth and seventeenth centuries. Moriscos even found ways to come to the Western Hemisphere, although royal decrees prohibited from entering these areas "Moors, Jews, heretics, those reconciled [by the Inquisition] or newly converted to our holy faith."[95] Usually lacking the wealth to buy a forged genealogy showing their purity of blood, some Moriscos came as slaves who became free in the realms of New Spain or Peru. Even far from Iberia, however, Moriscos could not easily escape the Inquisition, for that institution in the Western Hemisphere reflected the same consciousness of Islam as a menacing difference.[96]

Although Christian attitudes toward Moriscos reflected much diversity and ambiguity, one of the continuing legacies of imperial Spain would be a historical memory that seemed to retain only one part of the Morisco experience: an ideology that transformed difference into deviance, beliefs into threats. Spain had no monopoly on this ideology, of course, but Spaniards were able to extend it to the most distant corners of the far-flung Spanish Empire. We might ask a question about how historical memory becomes selective. Why, for example, did this country remember from its history the violence rather than the times of relatively peaceful coexistence among its different religious groups? One answer may be that violence generates a more persistent memory. It evokes horror, a strong protective reaction, a determination to never again suffer victimization. Once a violent act is committed, it seems to demand reprisal again and again. Tragically, the memory of violence and the determination to protect oneself from further victimization lead to yet more victims and a vicious cycle of violence and reprisal.

A second answer is the political value of historical memory. In early modern Spain, the political imperatives of the state that was forming among the several Iberian kingdoms required a common enemy more

[94] Bleda, *Corónica de los moros*, 906.

[95] Quoted in Peter Dressendörfer, "Crypto-musulmanes en la Inquisición de la Nueva España," in *Actas del Coloquio Internacional sobre Literatura Aljamiada y Morisca*, ed. Alvaro Galmés de Fuentes (Madrid: Editorial Gredos, 1972), 477.

[96] See, for example, the inquisitorial edict from Mexico City in 1584, quoted in Dressendörfer, "Crypto-musulmanes," 481.

than they needed a tradition of peaceful coexistence. To unify all the many regions of Spain, secular and ecclesiastical leaders encouraged a Christian identity formed in reaction against Morisco difference. The Reconquest would become a far more powerful historical memory as the newly developing state combined it with the "Morisco problem" of the sixteenth and early seventeenth centuries. This problem did not end with the expulsion, and in many ways it continues in our own world. It raises the universal question of how people can best deal with difference. If they see it as a threat, they will make it into deviance that must be oppressed.

Even in the more secular modern world, human beings use divine providence to explain and legitimize their uses of power. What is striking is that cruelties inflicted in the name of a divinity do not vanish from memory. Instead, they become a part of the collective consciousness that seeks revenge in a spiral of violence from generation to generation.[97] Unfortunately, we more easily forget the messages of hope and comfort in our legends and beliefs. Where are Rahma and Carcayona to balance the example of sword-wielding Zarçamodonia and the women who fought with stones and roasting spits?

We began this study with the arrival in the port of Seville of nearly 5,000 Moriscos who had been uprooted from their homes in Granada to be forcibly relocated elsewhere. Historical records tell us that some observers at that time felt compassion for their misfortunes. Is it too much to hope that others felt compassion some forty years later in this same port when Moriscos obeying the expulsion order had to leave 300 of their children in warehouses near the waterfront? Capable of both shocking cruelty and generous compassion, we human beings must take responsibility for our acts. Yet we can also learn from the past. How we decide to use our historical memory directly affects how we live in the present and shape the future. We can attempt to abolish differences, or we can try to live with them and learn to value them in our own time.

[97] Fields, "What One Cannot," points out that the isolated individual cannot grasp fundamental features of memory, which relies on socialization to provide a context, 159. For more on the problems and possibilities of "collective memory," see Bogumil Jewsiewicki, "Collective Memory and the Stakes of Power: Reading of Popular Zairian Historical Discourses," *History in Africa* 13 (1986): 195–223.

BIBLIOGRAPHY

ARCHIVAL AND PRIMARY SOURCES

AAS. Colegio de Niñas del Espíritu Santo. Legajo 10.

AGS. Cámara de Castilla. Legajos 2157, 2158, 2161, 2163, 2164, 2166, 2169, 2170, 2171, 2172, 2180, 2183, 2186, 2187, 2188, 2189, 2190, 2196, 2811.

AGS. Consejo de Cámara. Legajo 2052.

AGS. Contaduría Mayor de Cuentas. No. 60, segunda. Legajos 411, 415.

AGS. *Catálogo XIX del Archivo de Simancas: papeles de estado, Sicilia, virreinato Español*. Valladolid: El Archivo, 1951.

AGS. Estado. Legajos 213, 214, 217, 218, 219.

AGS. *Mapas, planos y dibujos: (años 1503–1805)*. Madrid, 1980.

AHN. *Bibliografía de archivos españoles y de archivística*. Madrid, 1963.

AHN. Inquisición. Legajos 107, 2022, 2049, 2057, 2059, 2068, 2069, 2070, 2071, 2072, 2075, 2962, 3014.

AHN. Inquisición. Libros 991, 1244, 1254, 1259, 1263, 1299.

AHN. *Inventorio de los libros 1225 a 1281: con índices de personas, materias y lugares*. Madrid: Archivo Histórico Nacional, 1979.

AMS. Colección del Conde de Aguila. Tomo 7, letra A, no. 73.

AMS. *Efemérides*. "Noticias y casos." No. 1.

AMS. Sección Especial. Papeles del Señor Conde de Aguila. Libros en folio. Tomo 27, no. 3.

AMS. Sección 4. Siglo XVII. Escribanías de Cabildo. Tomos 11, 22, 23, 29.

BN. *Advertencias para el remedio de muchos desórdenes que hay en esta corte*. Madrid, [early seventeenth century]. Ms 18.735, no. 53; and ms 1092.

BN. Arzobispo Martín de Ayala. "Doctrina Christiana, en lengua araviga y castellana." Valencia: Joan Mey, 1566. Ms R 8782.

BN. Aznar Cardona, Pedro. *Expulsión justificada de los moriscos españoles*. Huesca: Pedro Cabarte, 1612. Ms R 2856.

BN. *Batallas de los primeros tiempos del islamismo*. Ms 5337.

BN. Bleda, Jaime. *Corónica de los moros de España*. Valencia: Felipe Mey, 1618. Ms R 15.119.

BN. *Cédula real sobre los moriscos*. Ms VED 195-19.

BN. Fonseca, Damián. *Justa expulsión de los moriscos de España: con la instrvccion, apostasia, y traycion dellos: y respuesta á las dudas que se ofrecieron acerca desta materia*. Rome: Iacomo Mascardo, 1612. Ms R 11918.

BN. Francisco de Sarria. *Alegación porque se justifica el cautiverio de los hijos de los Moriscos, no siendo de legítimo matrimonio travada, y contrahido con Christianos Viejos*. Ms 721.

BN. *La historia de la doncella Carcayona, hija del rey Nachrab con la paloma*. Ms 5313.

BN. "Informe sobre los moros esclavos y libres de Sevilla." Ms 18.735.

BN. María de San José. "Carta que escribe una pobre, y presa descalça consolándose a sus Hermanas, y hijas que por berla así estaban afligidas, del año 1593." Ms 3537.

BN. Nuñez Muley, Francisco. "Memoria al presidente." Ms 6176.

BN. *Papel de lo dañosso que es en los reynos de que aya moros y moriscos.* [After 1619]. Ms 18.735, no. 53.

BN. Pedro de Valencia. *Obras varias.* Zafra, 1606. Ms 8888.

BN. *Pragmática y declaración sobre los moriscos del Reyno de Granada.* Madrid: Alonso Gómez, 1572. Ms VE 26-1.

BN. *Provisión real de su Magestad, sobre la orden que se ha de tener en los negocios tocantes a los moriscos del Reyno de Granada, que pretendieren ser Christianos viejos.* Madrid: Guillermo Droy, 1585. Ms R 7.673.

BN. *Relación muy verdadera sacada de una carta que vino al Illustre Cabildo y regimiento desta ciudad.* Seville: Alonso de la Barrera, 1569. Ms R 31.736.

BN. Ricoldo de Montecrucio. *Reprobación del Alcoran.* Ms R 4.037.

BN. Ripol, J. *Diálogo de consuelo por la expulsión de los moriscos de España.* Pamplona: Nicolas de Assiayn, 1613. Ms R 14165.

BN. Sandoval, Juan de, S.J. *De Instauranda Æthiopium Salute.* Cartagena, [ca. 1642]. Ms R 12.179.

BN. *Traslado de la cédula real que se publicó en la ciudad de Córdova a diez y siete días del mes de enero.* Cordova: n.p., 1610. Ms VE 36-4.

BN. *Tratado jurídico.* Ms 4987.

PUBLISHED WRITINGS OF THE PERIOD

Cabrera de Córdoba, Luis. *Relaciones de las cosas sucedidas en la corte de España, desde 1599 hasta 1614.* Madrid: J. Martín Alegria, 1857.

Calderón de la Barca, Pedro. "Amar después de la muerte." In *Teatro Selecto,* 2:451–569. 2 vols. Madrid: Librería de Perlado, Páez y Compañía, 1910.

Centurion, Adam. *Información para la historia del Sacromonte, llamado de Valparaiso y antiguamente Illipulitano junto a Granada.* Pt. 1. 1632.

Cerda, Juan de la. *Vida política de todos los estados de mugeres: en el qual se dan muy provechosos y Christianos documentos y avisos, para criarse y conservarse devidamente las mugeres en sus etados.* Alcalá de Henares: Juan Gracian, 1599.

Constituciones del Arçobispado de Sevilla. Hechas i ordenadas por el ilustríssimo i reveredíssimo Señor, Don Fernando Niño, de Guevara, Cardenal i Arçobispo de la S. Iglesia de Sevilla, en el synodo, que celebro en su cathedral año 1604. Seville: Alonso Rodríguez Gamarra. 1609.

Declaración del Bando que se a publicado de la expulsión de los moriscos. Seville: Alonso Rodríguez Gamarra, 1610.

Espinosa, Juan de. *Diálogo en laude de las mujeres.* 1580. Ed. Angela González Simón. Madrid: Consejo Superior de Investigaciones Científicas, 1946.

Hurtado de Mendoza, Diego. *La guerra de Granada.* Vol. 21 of *Biblioteca de Autores Españoles.* Madrid: Atlas, 1946.

Leyes de moros del siglo XIV. Memorial Historico Español. Madrid: Real Academia de la Historia, 1853. 5:11–246.

Luis de León, Fray. *La perfecta casada.* 1583. Vol. 37 of *Biblioteca de Autores Españoles.* Madrid: M. Rivadeneyra, 1855. 211–246.

Mármol Carvajal, Luis del. *Historia del rebelión y castigo de los moriscos del reino de Granada.* 1600. Vol. 21 of *Biblioteca de Autores Españoles.* Madrid: Atlas, 1946.

Don Luys Mendez de Haro y Sotomayor, Marqués del Carpio . . . Asistente deste ciudad de Seville y su tierra, y Capitan general de la gente de guerra della, por el Rey nro Señor, etc. Seville: Bartolomé Gómez, 1610. In Ignacio Bauer Landauer, *Papeles en mi archivo: Relaciones y manuscritos (moriscos),* 165–166. Madrid: Editorial Ibero-Africano-Americana, [19??].

Mendoza, Don Juan de. *Declaración del Bando que se a publicado de la expulsión de los moriscos.* Seville: Alonso Rodríguez Gamarra, 1610.

Ocaña, Antonio de. *Carta que Antonio de Ocaña, morisco de los desterrados de España, natural de la villa de Madrid, embió desde Argel a un su amigo a la dicha villa.* Seville: Juan Serrano de Vargas, 1618.

Pérez de Hita, Ginés. *Guerras civiles de Granada.* 1595–1597. Ed. Paula Blanchard-Demouge. 2 vols. Madrid: E. Bailly-Bailliére, 1913–1915.

Weiditz, Christoph. *Das Trachtenbuch des Christoph Weiditz.* 1531–1532. Berlin and Leipzig: Von Walter de Gruyter and Company, 1927.

SECONDARY SOURCES

Aarne, Antti. *The Types of the Folktale: A Classification and Bibliography.* Trans. and enl. Stith Thompson. Folklore Fellows Communications, vol. 75, no. 184. Helsinski: Helsingin Liikekirjapaino Oy, 1961.

Abu-Lughod, Lila. *Veiled Sentiments: Honor and Poetry in a Bedouin Society.* Berkeley and Los Angeles: University of California Press, 1986.

Adelson, Leslie A. *Making Bodies, Making History: Feminism and German Identity.* Lincoln: University of Nebraska Press, 1993.

Ahmed, Leila. *Women and Gender in Islam: Historical Roots of a Modern Debate.* New Haven: Yale University Press, 1992.

Aranda Doncel, Juan. "Estructura de la población morisca en tres parroquias sevillanas: San Julian, San Román, y Santa Lucía." *Boletín de la Real Academia de Córdoba de Ciencias, Bellas Letras y Nobles Artes,* año 45, no. 96 (1976): 77–84.

———. *Los moriscos en tierras de Córdoba.* Cordova: Monte de Piedad y Caja de Ahorros de Córdoba, 1984.

———. "Las prácticas musulmanas de los moriscos andaluces a través de las relaciones de causas del tribunal de la inquisición de Córdoba." In *Las prácticas musulmanas de los moriscos andaluces (1492–1609),* ed. Abdeljelil Temini, 11–26. Zaghouan: Centre d'Etudes et de Recherches Ottomanes, Morisques, de Documentation et d'Information, 1989.

Bahl, Vinay. "Cultural Imperialism and Women's Movements." *Gender and History* 9:1 (April 1997): 1–14.

Barkai, Ron. *Cristianos y musulmanes en la España medieval (El enemigo en el espejo).* Madrid: Ediciones Rialp, 1984.

Bauer Landauer, Ignacio. *Papeles de mi archivo. Relaciones y manuscritos (moriscos)*. Madrid: Editorial Ibero-Africano-Americana, n.d.

Beezley, William H., and Linda A. Curcio-Nagy. Introduction. In *Latin American Popular Culture: An Introduction*, Ed. William H. Beezley and Linda A. Curcio-Nagy, xi–xxiii. Wilmington, DE: Scholarly Resources, 2000.

Benitez Sánchez-Blanco, Rafael. "Guerra y sociedad: Málaga y los niños cautivos, 1569." *Estudis: Revista de Historia Moderna* 3 (1974): 31–54.

Bennett, Judith. "Feminism and History." *Gender and History* 1:3 (1989):251–272

Bermejo y Carballo, José. *Glorias religiosas de Sevilla. Noticia histórica descriptiva de todas las cofradías de penitencia, sangre y luz, fundadas en esta ciudad*. Seville: Imprenta y Librería del Salvador, 1882.

Bernabé Pons, Luis F. *El Cántico islámico del morisco hispano tunecino Taybili*. Zaragoza: Institución Fernando el Católico, 1988.

Birriel Salcedo, Margarita María. "La experiencia silenciada, las mujeres en la historia de Andalucía. Andalucía moderna." In *Las mujeres en la historia de Andalucía*. Actas del II Congreso de Historia de Andalucía. Cordova: Junta de Andalucía, 1994.

———. "Las instituciones de la repoblación del Reino de Granada (1570–1592)." In *Hombre y Territorio en el Reino de Granada (1570–1630). Estudios sobre repoblación*, ed. Manuel Barrios Aguilera and Francisco Andújar Castillo, 89–132. Almería: Instituto de Estudios Almerienses, Universidad de Granada, 1995.

———. "Mujeres y familia, fuentes y metodología." In *Conceptos y metodología en los estudios sobre la mujer*, ed. Barbara Ozieblo, 43–69. Málaga: Universidad de Málaga, 1993.

———. "Notas sobre el matrimonio de los moriscos granadinos." In *Mélanges Louis Cardaillac*, ed. Abdeljelil Temini, 1:97–107. Zaghouan: Fondation Temini Pour la Recherche Scientifique et l'Information, 1995.

Borja de Medina, S.I., Francisco. "La Compañía de Jesús y la minoría morisca (1545–1614)." *Archivum Historicum Societatis Iesu* 57 (1998): 3–136.

Boronat y Barrachina, Pascual. *Los moriscos españoles y su expulsión: Estudio histórico-crítico*. 2 vols. Valencia: Francisco Vives y Mora, 1901.

Borrero Fernández, Mercedes. "El trabajo de la mujer en el mundo rural sevillano durante la baja edad media." In *Las mujeres medievales y su ámbito jurídico*, ed. María Angeles Durán and Cristina Segura Graiño, 191–199. Madrid: Técnicas Gráficas, 1983.

Bosch Vilá, Jacinto. *La Sevilla islámica, 712–1248*. No. 92 of *Historia de Sevilla*, ed. Francisco Morales Padrón. Seville: Universidad de Sevilla, 1984.

Bouhdiba, Abdelwahab. *Sexuality in Islam*. Trans. Alan Sheridan. London: Routledge & Kegan Paul, 1985.

Bramon, Dolors. "El rito de las fadas, pervivencia de la ceremonia preislámica de la ʿAqiqa." In *Las prácticas musulmanas de los moriscos andaluces (1492–1609)*, ed. Abdeljelil Temini, 33–42. Zaghouan: Centre d'Etudes et de Recherches Ottomanes, Morisques, de Documentation et d'Information, 1989.

Braudel, Fernand. *The Mediterranean and the Mediterranean World in the Age of Philip II*. Trans. Sian Reynolds. 2 vols. New York: Harper Torchbooks, 1976.

Bravo Villasante, Carmen. *La mujer vestida de hombre en el teatro español: Siglos XVI–XVII.* Madrid: Sociedad General Española de Librería, 1976.

Bridenthal, Renate, and Claudia Koonz, eds. *Becoming Visible: Women in European History.* Boston: Houghton Mifflin, 1977.

Bullough, Vern and Bonnie. *Cross-Dressing, Sex, and Gender.* Philadelphia: University of Pennsylvania Press, 1993.

Bunes Ibarra, Miguel Angel de. *La imagen de los musulmanes y del norte de Africa en la España de los siglos XVI y XVII: Los charácteres de una hostilidad.* Madrid: Consejo Superior de Investigaciones Científicas, 1989.

Burns, Robert Ignatius, and Paul Edward Chevedden. *Negotiating Cultures: Bilingual Surrender Treaties in Muslim-Crusader Spain under James the Conqueror.* Leiden: Brill, 1999.

Burshatin, Israel. "Written on the Body: Slave or Hermaphrodite in Sixteenth-Century Spain." In *Queer Iberia: Sexualities, Cultures, and Crossings from the Middle Ages to the Renaissance*, ed. Josiah Blackmore and Gregory S. Hutcheson, 420–456. Durham: Duke University Press, 1999.

Butler, Judith. *Bodies That Matter: On the Discursive Limits of "Sex."* New York: Routledge, 1993.

Butler, Judith, and Joan W. Scott, eds. *Feminists Theorize the Political.* New York and London: Routledge, 1992.

Bynum, Caroline Walker. *Fragmentation and Redemption: Essays on Gender and the Female Body in Medieval Religion.* New York: Zone Books, 1992.

Cáceres Enríquez, Jaime. "La mujer morisca o esclava blanca en el Perú del siglo XVI." *Sharq al-Andalus* 12 (1995): 565–574.

Canning, Kathleen. "The Body as Method? Reflections on the Place of the Body in Gender History." *Gender and History* 11:3 (November 1999): 499–513.

Cano, A., M. Lillo, E. Molina, A. Ramos, and C. Ruíz. "La mujer andalusi, elementos para su historia." In *Las mujeres medievales y su ámbito jurídico*, eds. María Angeles Durán and Cristina Segura Graiño, 183–189. Madrid: Técnicas Gráficas, 1983.

Capdevila Orozco, José. *Errantes y expulsados. Normativas jurídicas contra gitanos, judíos, y moriscos.* Cordova: F. Baena, 1991.

Carande, Ramón. *Sevilla, tortaleza y mercado: Las tierras, las gentes y la administración de la ciudad en el siglo XIV.* 3rd ed. Seville: Diputación Provincial de Sevilla, 1982.

Cardaillac, Louis. "Un aspecto de las relaciones entre moriscos y cristianos: polémica y taqiyya." In *Actas del coloquio internacional sobre literatura aljamiada y morisca*, 3:107–122. Madrid: CLEAM, 1978.

———. "Le passage des morisques en Languedoc." *Annales du midi* 83 (1970): 259–298.

Cardaillac-Hermosilla, Yvette. "Quand les morisques se mariaint . . ." *Sharq al-Andalus* 12 (1995): 477–505.

Carmen Carlé, María del. *La sociedad hispano medieval. Grupos períficos: Las mujeres y los pobres.* Barcelona: Editorial Gedisa, 1988.

Caro Baroja, Julio. *Los moriscos del Reino de Granada (Ensayo de Historia Social).* Madrid: Artes Gráficas, 1957.

Carrasco, Rafael. *Historia de los sodomitas. Inquisición y represión sexual en Valencia*. Barcelona: Laertes Editorial, 1986.

Casey, James, and Bernard Vincent. "Casa y familia en Granada." In *La familia en la España mediterránea (siglos XV–XIX)*, ed. Francisco Chacón, 172–211. Barcelona: Crítica, 1987.

Castro, Américo. *The Spaniards: An Introduction to Their History.* Trans. Willard F. King and Selma Margaretten. Berkeley and Los Angeles: University of California Press, 1971.

Chaves, Manuel. *Cosas nuevas y viejas (Apuntes sevillanos)*. Seville: Tipografía, 1904.

Chejne, Anwar G. *Islam and the West: The Moriscos*. Albany: SUNY Press, 1983.

Clifford, James. *The Predicament of Culture: Twentieth-Century Ethnography, Literature, and Art*. Cambridge: Harvard University Press, 1988.

Cohn, Norman. *The Pursuit of the Millennium: Revolutionary Messianism in Medieval and Reformation Europe and Its Bearing on Modern Totalitarian Movements.* New York: Harper Torchbooks, 1961.

Collantes de Terán Sánchez, Antonio. *Sevilla en la baja edad media: La ciudad y sus hombres*. Seville: Ayuntamiento, 1977.

Corteguera, Luis R. *For the Common Good: Popular Politics in Barcelona, 1580–1640*. Ithaca: Cornell University Press, 2002.

Davis, Natalie Zemon. *Society and Culture in Early Modern France*. Stanford: Stanford University Press, 1975.

Dekker, Rudolf M., and Lotte C. van de Pol. *The Tradition of Female Transvestism in Early Modern Europe*. New York: St. Martin's Press, 1989.

Delgado Gallego, José María. "Maurofilia y maurofobia, dos caras de la misma moneda?" In *Narraciones moriscas*, 22–30. Seville: Editoriales Andaluzas Unidas, 1986.

De Pauw, Linda Grant. *Battle Cries and Lullabies: Women in War from Prehistory to the Present*. Norman: University of Oklahoma Press, 1998.

Díaz, Ada María. "Toward an Understanding of *Feminismo Hispánico* in the U.S.A." In *Women's Consciousness, Women's Conscience*, ed. Barbara Hilkert Andolsen, Christine E. Gudorf, and Mary D. Pellauer, 51–61. San Francisco: Harper & Row, 1987.

Domínguez Ortiz, Antonio. *Autos de la Inquisición de Sevilla (siglo XVII)*. Seville: Servicio de Publicaciones del Ayuntamiento de Sevilla, 1981.

———. "La esclavitud en Castilla durante la edad moderna." *Estudios de Historia Social de España* 2 (1952): 369–428.

———. *Orto y ocaso de Sevilla. Estudio sobre la prosperidad y decadencia de la ciudad durante los siglos XVI y XVII*. Seville: Diputación Provincial de Sevilla, 1946.

Domínguez Ortiz, Antonio, and Bernard Vincent. *Historia de los moriscos: Vida y tragedia de una minoría*. Madrid: Revista de Occidente, 1978.

Doubleday, Simon R. "On the Age of Spanish Ghosts." Unpublished paper presented to the Society for Spanish and Portuguese Historical Studies, Madrid, July 2003.

———. *The Wandering Ghosts of Spanish History.* Cambridge: Harvard University Press, forthcoming.

Douglas, Mary. *Purity and Danger: An Analysis of Concepts of Pollution and Taboo.* New York and Washington: Frederick A. Praeger, 1966.

Dressendörfer, Peter. "Crypto-musulmanes en la Inquisición de la Nueva España." In *Actas del Coloquio Internacional sobre Literatura Aljamiada y Morisca,* ed. Alvaro Galmés de Fuentes, 475–494. Madrid: Editorial Gredos, 1972.

Edelman, Lee. *Homographesis: Essays in Gay Literary and Cultural Theory.* New York and London: Routledge, 1994.

Elliott, J. H. *Imperial Spain 1469–1716.* London: Penguin, 1990.

Ellis, Deborah S. "Domesticating the Spanish Inquisition." In *Violence against Women in Medieval Texts,* ed. Anna Roberts, 195–209. Gainsville: University Press of Florida, 1998.

Epalza, Mikel de. *Los moriscos antes y después de la expulsión.* Madrid: Editorial Mapfre, 1992.

———. "Trabajos actuales sobre la comunidad de moriscos refugiados en Túnez, desde el siglo XVII a nuestros días." In *Actas del Coloquio Internacional sobre Literatura Aljamiada y Morisca,* ed. Alvaro Galmés de Fuentes, 427–445. Madrid: Editorial Gredos, 1972.

———. "La voz oficial de los musulmanes hispanos, mudéjares y moriscos, a sus autoridades cristianas. Cuatro textos en árabe, en castellano y en catalán-valenciano." *Sharq al-Andalus* 12 (1995): 279–297.

Erikson, Kai T. *Wayward Puritans: A Study in the Sociology of Deviance.* New York: John Wiley and Sons, 1966.

Estés, Clarissa Pinkola. *Women Who Run with the Wolves.* New York: Ballantine, 1995.

Fields, Karen. "What One Cannot Remember Mistakenly." In *History and Memory in African-American Culture,* ed. Genevieve Fabre and Robert O'Meally, 150–163. New York: Oxford University Press, 1994.

Foucault, Michel. *Discipline and Punish: The Birth of the Prison.* New York: Random House, 1995.

Fournel-Guérin, Jacqueline. "La femme morisque en Aragon." In *Les Morisques et leur temps,* 525–538. Paris: Centre National de la Recherche Scientifique, 1983.

Franz, Marie-Louise von. *The Feminine in Fairy Tales.* Dallas: Spring Publications, 1972.

Fuerch, Michelle Ann. "Tratado jurídico: Edición Crítica del manuscrito Aljamiado-Morisco Inédito 4987 de la Biblioteca Nacional de Madrid." Ph.D. diss., Wayne State University, Detroit, MI, 1982.

Galmés de Fuentes, Alvaro. "El interés literario en los escritos aljamiado-moriscos." In *Actas del Coloquio Internacional sobre Literatura Aljamiada y Morisca,* ed. Alvaro Galmés de Fuentes, 189–209. Madrid: Editorial Gredos, 1972.

———. *El libro de las batallas. Narraciones é épico-caballerescas. Estudio literario y edición del texto por A. Galmés de Fuentes.* Madrid: Editorial Gredos, 1975.

———. "La literatura española aljamiado-morisca." In *Grundriss der Romanischen Literaturen des Mittelalters,* vol. 9 of *La littérature dans la Péninsule Ibérique aux XIVe et XVe siècles,* ed. Walter Mettmann, 117–132. Heidelberg: Carl Winter Universitätsverlag, n.d.

Galmés de Fuentes, Alvaro. "Lle-yeísmo y otras cuestiones lingüisticas en un relato morisco del siglo XVII." In *Estudios dedicados a don Ramón Menéndez Pidal*, 7:273–307. Madrid: Consejo Superior de Investigaciones Científicas, 1957.

———. *Los moriscos (desde su misma orilla)*. Madrid: Instituto Egipcio de Estudios Islámicos, 1993.

Garber, Marjorie. *Vested Interests: Cross-dressing and Cultural Anxiety.* New York and London: Routledge, 1992.

García Arenal, Mercedes. *Inquisición y moriscos. Los procesos del Tribunal de Cuenca.* Madrid: Siglo Veintiuno, 1983.

———. *Los moriscos.* Madrid: Editora Nacional, 1975.

———. "El problema morisco: propuesta de discusión." *Al-Qantara* 13 (1992): 499–503.

García Ballester, Luis. *Los moriscos y la medicina: Un capítulo de la medicina y la ciencia marginadas en la España del siglo XVI.* Barcelona: Editorial Labor, 1984.

García Cárcel, Ricardo. *Herejía y sociedad en el siglo XVI: La inquisición en Valencia 1530–1609.* Barcelona: Ediciones Península, 1980.

———. "Las mujeres conversas en el siglo XVI." In *Historia de las mujeres en occidente*, ed. Georges Duby and Michelle Perrot, trans. Marco Aurelio Galmari, 3:597–615. Madrid: Taurus, 1992.

Gaya Nuño, J. A. *Historia del arte español.* Madrid: Editorial Plus Ultra, n.d.

Gestoso y Pérez, José. *Sevilla monumental y artística.* 3 vols. Seville: Andalucia Moderna, 1892.

Gibb, H.A.R., and J. H. Kramers, eds. *The Shorter Encyclopaedia of Islam.* Ithaca: Cornell University Press, 1961.

Glick, Thomas F. *Islamic and Christian Spain in the Early Middle Ages: Comparative Perspectives on Social and Cultural Formation.* Princeton: Princeton University Press, 1979.

———. "On Converso and Marrano Ethnicity." In *Crisis and Creativity in the Sephardic World, 1391–1648*, ed. Bernard R. Gampel, 59–76. New York: Columbia University Press, 1997.

González Moreno, Joaquín. *Aportación a la historia de Sevilla.* Seville: Editorial Castillejo, 1991.

Grabar, Oleg. *The Alhambra.* Cambridge: Harvard University Press, 1978.

Gracia Boix, Rafael. *Autos de fe y causas de la Inquisición de Córdoba.* Cordova: Diputación Provincial, 1983.

Gramsci, Antonio. *Selections from the Prison Notebooks of Antonio Gramsci.* Ed. and trans. Quintin Hoare and Geoffrey Nowell Smith. New York: International Publishers, 1972.

Grayzel, Susan R. *Women and the First World War.* New York and London: Longman, 2002.

Greene, Molly. *A Shared World: Christians and Muslims in the Early Modern Mediterranean.* Princeton: Princeton University Press, 2002.

Guichard, Pierre. *Al-Andalus: Estructura antropológica de una sociedad islámica en occidente.* Barcelona: Barral Editores, 1976.

Guichot y Parody, Joaquín. *Historia del Exmo. Ayuntamiento de la muy noble, muy leal, muy heróica é invicta ciudad de Sevilla*. 2 vols. Seville: Tipografía de la Región, 1896.

Guillén Robles, Francisco. *Leyendas moriscas sacadas de varios manuscritos existentes en las Bibliotecas Nacional, Real, y de D. P. de Gayangos*. 3 vols. Madrid: M. Tello, 1885.

Halavais, Mary. *Like Wheat to the Miller: Community, Convivencia, and the Construction of Morisco Identity in Sixteenth-Century Aragon*. New York: Columbia University Press, 2002.

Hall, Catherine. *White, Male and Middle-Class*. New York: Routledge, 1992.

Harris, A. K. "Forging History: The Plomos of the Sacromonte of Granada in Francisco Bermúdez de Pedraza's *Historia eclesiástica*." *Sixteenth Century Journal* 30:4 (1999): 945–966.

Harvey, L. P. *Islamic Spain 1250 to 1500*. Chicago: University of Chicago Press, 1990.

———. "El Mancebo de Arévalo y la literatura aljamiada." In *Actas del Coloquia Internacional sobre Literatura Aljamiada y Morisca*, ed. Alvaro Galmés de Fuentes, 21–41. Madrid: Editorial Gredos, 1972.

———. "Una referencia explícita a la legalidad de la práctica de la taqiya por los moriscos." *Sharq al-Andalus* 12 (1995): 561–563.

Hasenfeld, Galia. "Women between Islam and Christianity: The Moriscos according to Inquisition Trial Records from Cuenca." Ph.D. diss., Tel-Aviv University, 2002.

Hegyi, Ottmar. *Cinco leyendas y otros relatos moriscos (ms 4953 de la Biblioteca Nacional, Madrid)*. Madrid: Editorial Gregos, 1981.

Henderson, Mae Gwendolyn. "Speaking in Tongues: Dialogics, Dialectics, and the Black Woman Writer's Literary Tradition." In *Feminists Theorize the Political*, ed. Judith Butler and Joan W. Scott, 144–166. New York and London: Routledge, 1992.

Hepworth, Mike, and Bryan S. Turner. *Confession: Studies in Deviance and Religion*. London: Routledge & Kegan Paul, 1982.

Hess, Andrew C. *The Forgotten Frontier: A History of the Sixteenth-Century Ibero-African Frontier*. Chicago and London: University of Chicago Press, 1978.

Hill, Jonathan D. Introduction. In *Rethinking History and Myth: Indigenous South American Perspectives on the Past*, ed. Jonathan D. Hill. Urbana and Chicago: University of Illinois Press, 1988.

The Holy Qur'an: Text, Translation and Commentary. Trans. and comm. Abdullah Yusuf Ali. 2 vols. Cambridge, MA: Hafner Publishing Co., 1946.

hooks, bell. *Yearning: Race, Gender, and Cultural Politics*. Boston: South End Press, 1990.

Hufton, Olwen. "Women and Revolution." *Past and Present* 53 (1971): 90–108.

Ibn ʿAbdun. *Sevilla a comienzos del siglo XII. El Tratado de Ibn ʿAbdun*. Ed. and trans. Emilio Gracía Gómez and E. Levi-Provençal. Seville: Servicio Municipal de Publicaciones, 1981.

Ibn Khaldun. *The Muqaddimah: An Introduction to History*. Trans. Franz Rosenthal. 3 vols. New York: Pantheon, 1958.

Janer, Florencio. *Condición social de los moriscos de España. Causas de su expulsión, y consecuencias que ésta produjo en el órden económico y político*. Madrid: Real Academia de la Historia, 1857.

Jewsiewicki, Bogumil. "Collective Memory and the Stakes of Power: Reading of Popular Zairian Historical Discourses." *History in Africa* 13 (1986): 195–223.

Jiménez Lozano, José. *Judíos, moriscos y conversos*. Valladolid: Ambito, 1982.

Kamen, Henry. *Inquisition and Society in Spain in the Sixteenth and Seventeenth Centuries*. Bloomington: Indiana University Press, 1985.

Keegan, John. *A History of Warfare*. New York: Knopf, 1993.

Kubler, George, and Martin Soria. *Art and Architecture in Spain and Portugal and Their American Dominions 1500 to 1800*. Middlesex, UK: Penguin Books, 1959.

Kunzle, David. *The Early Comic Strip: Narrative Strips and Picture Stories in the European Broadsheet from c. 1450 to 1825*. Berkeley and Los Angeles: University of California Press, 1973.

Labarta, Ana. "Contratos matrimoniales entre moriscos valencianos." *Al-Qantara* 4 (1983): 57–87.

Lammens, H. *Islam, Beliefs and Institutions*. Trans. Sir E. Denison Ross. London: Methuen & Co., 1968.

Lapeyre, Henri. *Geografía de la España morisca*. Trans. Luis C. Rodríguez García. Valencia: Diputación Provincial de Valencia, 1986.

Lapidus, Ira M. *A History of Islamic Societies*. Cambridge: Cambridge University Press, 1988.

Latham, J. D. "Towards a Study of Andalusian Immigration and Its Place in Tunisian History." *Cahiers de Tunisie* 5 (1957): 203–252.

Lea, Henry Charles. *The Moriscos of Spain: Their Conversion and Expulsion*. New York: Burt Franklin, 1968.

Lehfeldt, Elizabeth. "Ruling Sexuality: The Political Legitimacy of Isabel of Castile." *Renaissance Quarterly* 53 (2000): 31–56.

Leyes de moros del siglo XIV. In *Memorial Histórico Español*, 5:11–246. Madrid: Real Academia de la Historia, 1853.

Longás, Pedro. *Vida religiosa de los moriscos*. Madrid: Ibérica, 1915.

López-Baralt, Luce. *Islam in Spanish Literature: From the Middle Ages to the Present*. Trans. Andrew Hurley. Leiden: E. J. Brill, 1992.

———. "Noticia de un nuevo hallazgo. Un códice adicional del Kama Sutra español en la Biblioteca de Palacio de Madrid (ms. 1767)." *Sharq al-Andalus* 12 (1995): 549–559.

López Martínez, Celestino. *Mudéjares y moriscos sevillanos*. Seville: Rodríguez, Giménez y Compañía, 1935.

Lozoya, Marqués de. *Historia del Arte Hispánico*. Tomo 1. Barcelona: Salvat Editores, 1931.

Márquez Villanueva, Francisco. *El problema morisco (desde otras laderas)*. Madrid: Prodhufi, 1991.

Martín Casares, Aurelia. *La esclavitud en la Granada del siglo XVI. Género, raza y religión*. Granada: Universidad de Granada and Diputación Provincial de Granada, 2000.

Martínez, François. "Les enfants morisques de l'expulsion (1610–1621)." In *Mélanges Louis Cardaillac*, ed. Abdeljelil Temini, 499–539. Zaghouan: Fondation Temini Pour la Recherche Scientifique et l'Information, 1995.

Martz, Linda. "Pure Blood Statutes in Sixteenth-Century Toledo: Implementation as Opposed to Adoption." *Sefarad* 54 (1994): 83–107.

McKendrick, Melveena. *Women and Society in the Spanish Drama of the Golden Age: A Study of the Mujer Varonil*. London: Cambridge University Press, 1974.

Melammed, Renée Levine. *Heretics or Daughters of Israel? The Crypto-Jewish Women of Castile*. Oxford and New York: Oxford University Press, 1999.

———. "Sephardi Women in the Medieval and Early Modern Periods." In *Jewish Women in Historical Perspective*, ed. Judith R. Baskin, 115–134. Detroit: Wayne State University Press, 1991.

———. "Sixteenth-Century Justice in Action: The Case of Isabel López." *Revue des études juives* 145:1–2 (1986): 51–73.

———. "Women in (Post-1492) Spanish Crypto-Jewish Society." *Judaism* 41:2 (Spring 1992): 156–168.

Meyerson, Mark D. Introduction. In *Christians, Muslims, and Jews in Medieval and Early Modern Spain: Interaction and Cultural Change*, ed. Mark D. Meyerson and Edward D. English. Notre Dame, IN: University of Notre Dame Press, 1999.

———. *The Muslims of Valencia in the Age of Fernando and Isabel: Between Coexistence and Crusade*. Berkeley and Los Angeles: University of California Press, 1991.

Mirrer, Louise. *Women, Jews, and Muslims in the Texts of Reconquest Castile*. Ann Arbor: University of Michigan Press, 1996.

Moi, Toril. *Sexual/Textual Politics: Feminist Literary Theory*. London and New York: Methuen, 1985.

Monter, E. William. *Frontiers of Heresy: The Spanish Inquisition from the Basque Lands to Sicily*. Cambridge: Cambridge University Press, 1990.

Moore, R. I. *The Formation of a Persecuting Society: Power and Deviance in Western Europe, 950–1250*. Oxford: Basil Blackwell, 1987.

Morales Padrón, Francisco. *Sevilla: La ciudad de los cinco nombres*. Madrid: Turner, 1987.

Morcillo, Aurora. *True Catholic Womanhood: Gender Ideology in Franco's Spain*. DeKalb: Northern Illinois University Press, 2000.

Morell Peguero, Blanca. *Mercaderes y artesanos en la Sevilla del descubrimiento*. Seville: Diputación Provincial de Sevilla, 1986.

Nader, Helen. *The Mendoza Family in the Spanish Renaissance 1350 to 1550*. New Brunswick: Rutgers University Press, 1979.

Nash, Manning. *The Cauldron of Ethnicity in the Modern World*. Chicago: University of Chicago Press, 1989.

Nicolás Cabrillana, Ciezar. *Almería morisca*. Granada: Universidad de Granada, 1982.

Nirenberg, David. *Communities of Violence: Persecution of Minorities in the Middle Ages*. Princeton: Princeton University Press, 1996.

———. "Conversion, Sex, and Segregation: Jews and Christians in Medieval Spain." *American Historical Review* 107:4 (2002): 1065–1093.

Norton, Anne. *Reflections on Political Identity.* Baltimore: Johns Hopkins University Press, 1988.

Nykel, A. R. *A Compendium of Aljamiado Literature.* New York and Paris: Macon, Protat Frères, 1929.

Ojeda Rentas, Miriam. "Literatura de ficción como arma política de resistencia para los moriscos españoles del siglo XVI." In *Las prácticas musulmanas de los moriscos andaluces (1492–1609)*, ed. Abdeljelil Temini, 151–159. Zaghouan: Centre d'Etudes et de Recherches Ottomanes, Morisques, de Documentation et d'Information, 1989.

Paz Torres, Maria. "Estudio preliminar." In Francisco Guillén Robles, *Leyendas moriscas. Sacadas de varios manuscritos existentes en las bibliotecas Nacional, Real y de P. de Gayangos*, 1:lxxxii–cxvii. 2 vols. Granada: Universidad de Granada. 1994.

Penella, Juan. "El sentimento religioso de los moriscos españoles emigrados: Notas para una literatura morisca en Túnez." In *Actas del Coloquio Internacional sobre Literatura Aljamiada y Morisca*, ed. Alvaro Galmés de Fuentes, 447–473. Madrid: Editorial Gredos, 1972.

Perry, Mary Elizabeth. "Beyond the Veil: Moriscas and the Politics of Resistance and Survival." In *Spanish Women in the Golden Age: Images and Realities*, ed. Magdalena S. Sánchez and Alain Saint-Saëns, 37–53. Westport and London: Greenwood Press, 1996.

———. "Contested Identities: The Morisca Visionary, Beatriz de Robles." In *Women and the Inquisition*, ed. Mary E. Giles, 171–188. Baltimore: Johns Hopkins University Press, 1998.

———. "Las mujeres y su trabajo curativo en Sevilla, siglos XVI y XVII." In *El trabajo de las mujeres: siglos XVI–XX*, ed. María Jesús Matilla and Margarita Ortega, 40–50. Madrid: Universidad Autónoma de Madrid, 1987.

———. "The 'Nefarious Sin' in Early Modern Seville." *Journal of Homosexuality* 15:3–4 (Spring 1988): 63–84. Reprinted in *The Pursuit of Sodomy: Male Homosexuality in Renaissance and Enlightenment Europe*, ed. Kent Gerard and Gert Hekma, 67–89. New York and London: Harrington Park Press, 1989.

———. "Patience and Pluck: Job's Wife, Conflict and Resistance in Morisco Manuscripts Hidden in the Sixteenth Century." In *Women, Texts and Authority in Early Modern Spain*, ed. Marta Vicente and Luis R. Corteguera, 91–106. New York and London: Ashgate, 2003.

———. "The Politics of Race, Ethnicity, and Gender in the Making of the Spanish State." In *Culture and the State in Spain 1550–1850*, ed. Tom Lewis and Francisco J. Sánchez, 34–54. New York and London: Garland Publishing, 1999.

Peters, Edward. *Inquisition*. New York: The Free Press, 1988.

Phillips, Carla Rahn. "Morisco Household and Family Structure in the Late Sixteenth Century." In *Estudios en homenaje a don Claudio Sánchez-Albórnoz en sus 90 años*, 373–388. Anexos de Cuadernos de Historia de España. Avila: Seimagen, 1990.

———. "The Moriscos of La Mancha." *Journal of Modern History* 50:2 (1978): D1067–D1095.

Pitt-Rivers, Julian. *The Fate of Shechem, or the Politics of Sex: Essays in the Anthropology of the Mediterranean*. Cambridge: Harvard University Press, 1971.

Propp, Vladimir. *Morphology of the Folktale*. Trans. Laurence Scott. Austin and London: University of Texas Press, 1979.

Ribera, Julián. *Historia de la música árabe medieval y su influencia en la española*. Madrid: Editorial Voluntad, 1927.

Ribera, Julián, and Miguel Asín. *Manuscritos árabes y aljamiados de la biblioteca de la junta*. Madrid: Junta para Amplicación de Estudios é Investigaciones Científicas, 1912.

Ribera y Tarragó, Julián. *La enseñanza entre los musulmanes españoles: Bibliófilos y bibliotecas en la España musulmana*. Cordova: Real Academia de Córdoba, 1925.

Rowbotham, Sheila. *Women, Resistance and Revolution: A History of Women and Revolution in the Modern World*. New York: Vintage, 1974.

Ruiz, Teófilo F. *Spanish Society, 1400–1600*. Harlow, UK, and New York: Longman, 2001.

Sahlins, Peter. *Boundaries: The Making of France and Spain in the Pyrenees*. Berkeley and Los Angeles: University of California Press, 1989.

Said, Edward W. *Orientalism*. New York: Pantheon, 1978.

Sánchez Alvarez, Mercedes. *El manuscrito misceláneo 774 de la Bibliothèque Nationale de Paris (Leyendas, itinerios de viajes, profecías sobre la destrucción de España y otros relatos moriscos)*. Edición, estudio y glosario por Mercedes Sánchez Alvarez. Madrid: Editorial Gredos, 1982.

Sánchez Blanco, Rafael Benitez. "Guerra y sociedad: Málaga y los niños cautivos." *Estudis: Revista de Historia Moderna* 3 (1974): 31–54.

Sánchez Ortega, María Helena. *La mujer y la sexualidad en el antiguo régimen: La perspectiva inquisitorial*. Madrid: Ediciones Akal, 1992.

———. "Sorcery and Eroticism in Love Magic." In *Cultural Encounters: The Impact of the Inquisition in Spain and the New World*, ed. Mary Elizabeth Perry and Anne J. Cruz, 58–92. Berkeley and Los Angeles: University of California Press, 1991.

———. "Woman as Source of 'Evil.' " In *Culture and Control in Counter-Reformation Spain*, ed. Anne J. Cruz and Mary Elizabeth Perry, 196–215. Minneapolis: University of Minnesota Press, 1992.

Scott, James C. *Domination and the Arts of Resistance: Hidden Transcripts*. New Haven and London: Yale University Press, 1990.

———. *Weapons of the Weak: Everyday Forms of Peasant Resistance*. New Haven and London: Yale University Press, 1985.

Scott, Joan Wallach. "Experience." In *Feminists Theorize the Political*, ed. Judith Butler and Joan W. Scott, 22–40. New York and London: Routledge, 1992.

———. *Gender and the Politics of History*. New York: Columbia University Press, 1988.

Scott, Joan Wallach, and Louise Tilly. *Women, Work and Family*. New York: Holt, Rinehart and Winston, 1978.

Shatzmiller, Maya. *The Berbers and the Islamic State*. Princeton: Markus Wiener Publishers, 2000.

Shepherd, Simon. *Amazons and Warrior Women: Varieties of Feminism in Seventeenth-Century Drama*. Brighton, UK: Harvester, 1981.

Sibley, David. *Outsiders in Urban Societies*. New York: St. Martin's Press, 1981.

Sicroff, Albert A. *Los estatutos de limpieza de sangre. Controversias entre los siglos XV y XVII*. Trans. Mauro Armiño. Madrid: Taurus, 1985.

Silverblatt, Irene. "Political Memories and Colonizing Symbols: Santiago and the Mountain Gods of Colonial Peru." In *Rethinking History and Myth*, ed. Jonathan D. Hill, 174–194. Urbana and Chicago: University of Illinois Press, 1988.

Smith, Margaret. *Rabiʿa the Mystic and Her Fellow-Saints in Islam: Being the Life and Teachings of Rabiʿa al-ʿAdawiyya Al-Quaysiyya of Basra Together with Some Account of the Place of Women Saints in Islam*. Cambridge: Cambridge University Press, 1984.

Smith, Paul Julian. *Representing the Other: 'Race,' Text, and Gender in Spanish and Spanish American Narrative*. Oxford: Clarendon Press, 1992.

Smith, Sidonie. "Who's Talking / Who's Talking Back? The Subject of Personal Narrative." *Signs* 18:2 (Winter 1993): 392–407.

Spivak, Gayatri Chakravorty. *In Other Worlds*. London and New York: Methuen, 1987.

Starr-LeBeau, Gretchen. *In the Shadow of the Virgin: Inquisitors, Friars, and "Conversos" in Guadalupe, Spain*. Princeton: Princeton University Press, 2003.

Surtz, Ronald E. "Morisco Women, Written Texts, and the Valencia Inquisition." *Sixteenth Century Journal* 32:2 (2001): 421–433.

Tapia Sánchez, Serafín de. *La comunidad morisca de Avila*. Salamanca: Gráficas Varona, 1990.

Temini, Abdeljelil, ed. *Las prácticas musulmanas de los moriscos andaluces (1492–1609)*. Actas del III Simposio Internacional de Estudios Moriscos. Zaghouan: Centre d'Etudes et de Recherches Ottomanes, Morisques, de Docmentation et d'Information, 1989.

Thompson, E. P. "The Moral Economy of the English Crowd in the Eighteenth Century." *Past and Present* 50 (1971): 76–136.

Trinh Minh-ha. *When the Moon Waxes Red: Representation, Gender and Cultural Politics*. New York and London: Routledge, 1991.

———. *Woman, Native, Other: Writing Postcoloniality and Feminism*. Bloomington: Indiana University Press, 1989.

Tueller, James. "The Assimilating Morisco: Four Families in Valladolid prior to the Expulsion of 1610." *Mediterranean Studies* 7 (1997): 167–177.

———. *Good and Faithful Christians: Moriscos and Catholicism in Early Modern Spain*. New Orleans: University Press of the South, 2002.

Valero Cuadra, Pino. "La leyenda de la doncella Carcayona." *Sharq al-Andalus* 12 (1995): 349–366.

Vespertino Rodríguez, Antonio, ed. *Leyendas aljamiadas y moriscas sobre personajes bíblicos*. Madrid: Editorial Gredos, 1983.

Vincent, Bernard. "50,000 moriscos almerienses." In *Almería entre culturas siglos XIII al XVI*. Coloquio Almería Entre Culturas. Almería: Instituto de Estudios Almerienses, 1990.

———. "Les Jesuites chroniqueurs récits de la guerre des Alpujarras." *Chronica Nueva* 22 (1995): 429–466.

———. *Minorías y marginados en la España del siglo XVI*. Granada: Diputación Provincial de Granada, 1987.

———. "The Moriscos and Circumcision." In *Culture and Control in Counter-Reformation Spain*, ed. Anne J. Cruz and Mary Elizabeth Perry, 78–92. Minneapolis: University of Minnesota Press, 1992.

———. "Las mujeres moriscas." In *Historia de las mujeres en occidente*, ed. Georges Duby and Michelle Perrot, trans. Marco Aurelio Galmari, 3:585–595. Madrid: Taurus, 1992.

von Franz, Marie-Louise. *The Feminine in Fairy Tales*. Dallas: Spring Publications, 1972.

Wagner, Klaus. "Un padrón desconocido de los mudéjares de Sevilla y la expulsión de 1502." *Al-Andalus* 36 (1971): 373–382.

———. *Regesto de documentos del Archivo de Protocolos de Sevilla referentes a judíos y moros*. Seville: Universidad, 1978.

Weiditz, Christoph. *Authentic Everyday Dress of the Renaissance: All 154 Plates from the "Trachtenbuch."* New York: Dover Publications, 1994.

———. *Das Trachtenbuch des Christoph Weiditz*. The Netherlands, 1531–1532. Berlin and Leipzig: Von Walter de Gruyter and Company, 1927.

Wheelwright, Julie. *Amazons and Military Maids: Women Who Cross-dressed in the Pursuit of Life, Liberty and Happiness*. London: Pandora Press, 1989.

Wiegers, Gerard. *Islamic Literature in Spanish and Aljamiado*. Leiden and New York: E. J. Brill, 1994.

Woodhouse, Annie. *Fantastic Women: Sex, Gender and Transvestism*. New Brunswick: Rutgers University Press, 1989.

INDEX

Page numbers in italic refer to the illustrations.